100 THINGS CELTICS FANS
SHOULD KNOW & DO
BEFORE THEY DIE

Donald Hubbard

TRIUMPH
BOOKS

Triumph Books and colophon are registered trademarks of Random House, Inc.

Library of Congress Cataloging-in-Publication Data

Hubbard, Donald, 1959–
    100 things Celtics fans should know & do before they die / Donald Hubbard.
    p. cm.
    ISBN 978-1-60078-411-8
    1. Boston Celtics (Basketball team)—History—Miscellanea. I. Title. II. Title: One hundred things Celtics fans should know and do before they die.
    GV885.52.B67H83 2010
    796.323'640974461—dc22

                                                            2010018372

This book is available in quantity at special discounts for your group or organization. For further information, contact:

Triumph Books
542 South Dearborn Street
Suite 750
Chicago, Illinois 60605
(312) 939-3330 | Fax (312) 663-3557
www.triumphbooks.com

Printed in U.S.A.
ISBN: 978-1-60078-411-8
Design by Patricia Frey
Editorial and page production by Prologue Publishing Services, LLC
All photos courtesy of the New England Sports Museum unless otherwise specified

To Nancy

Contents

Foreword

When the Boston Celtics selected me in the first round of the 1969 draft, the team had just won its 11th title in 13 years, led by four future Hall of Famers and ably supported by such wonderful players as Satch Sanders, Emmette Bryant, Don Nelson, Larry Siegfried, and Mal Graham. The team was aging, though, and before my rookie year, Bill Russell and Sam Jones retired, leaving a massive void in the roster. But general manager Red Auerbach had always rejuvenated his lineup, and he had no intention of resting on his laurels.

I had encountered success at the University of Kansas and as part of the gold medal Olympic basketball team in Mexico City in 1968, but I received no special treatment upon my arrival in Boston. We rookies were herded into a summer camp on the South Shore of Boston called Camp Milbrook, where we ate camp food, played basketball in the gym and under the sun, and had a blast.

The ensuing 1969–1970 season was not so enjoyable, as the club missed the playoffs for the first time in 20 years. But then, in the next year's draft, Auerbach chose a red-haired, undersized center from Florida State named Dave Cowens. By 1974, with the help of the extraordinary John Havlicek and welcome additions like Paul Silas and Don Chaney, the Celtics began winning championships again.

One of the most beautiful things about being a Celtics player or a fan is that the team constantly reinvents itself, winning championships in different eras but with the same philosophy espoused by Red Auerbach: having great, smart players dedicated to the team concept and tenacious defense results in titles. Call it the Celtic mystique or, for those doubters, something less mysterious, but the basic formula has always worked. After I left the Celtics, Larry Bird, Robert Parish, Dennis Johnson, Kevin McHale, Cedric Maxwell,

Danny Ainge, and Bill Walton took up the challenge and brought three more titles to Boston.

And you are seeing it now with Paul Pierce, Kevin Garnett, Ray Allen, Rajon Rondo, and Kendrick Perkins, winning it all in 2008 and reaching the Finals again in 2010. Great players, but smart ones, too. Defense and the subordination of individual statistics to the team's ultimate goal equaled titles in the late 1950s, as they do again under coach Doc Rivers.

This book's author, Donald Hubbard, has been given the unenviable task of compressing the history and the fan experience of the team down to only 100 items, but I believe he has captured the essence of the Celtic mystique. He insisted on compiling a work that does not read like an Internet article, but rather restores some lost treasures for current readers, whether it be about the failed Boston basketball franchises before Walter Brown founded the Celtics, or calling up Gene Guarilia, the Nate Robinson of his day.

Don has transmitted his love of basketball, and the Celtics in particular, to his readers, so new fans as well as old can enjoy the lore of this great franchise. He has assured me that when I played for the Celtics, he always cheered me and never booed me, and I think I believe him. No matter, he has remained a steadfast fan, passing on his love for the team to his son with a 12-pack ticket package during the 2003–2004 season, a 36-win campaign for the Celtics. I know that is what he is doing with this book—passing on his love of the Celtics—so enjoy it from cover to cover, and if you choose to boo the team in the future, never forget to cheer us when we deserve praise. We hear your cheers, and you too are a large part of the Celtic mystique and their phenomenal success.

—Jo Jo White

1 Red

Without Arnold "Red" Auerbach, the Boston Celtics may have folded as many of the other original NBA franchises did. Certainly, team owner Walter Brown had lost money and borrowed significant sums to keep the club alive, but in the first four years of the franchise, the Celtics never won and elicited very little enthusiasm in the local sports populace.

In contrast, Auerbach had coached successfully with the Washington Capitols for three years, starting in 1946–1947, compiling winning records each year. But philosophical and perhaps personal issues developed between him and the team owner, so Red resigned and accepted an offer by Ben Kerner to coach the Tri-Cities Blackhawks. If Red had issues before, they increased exponentially in his experiences with Kerner, a man he despised. Even though the Blackhawks achieved a mediocre 28–29 record, Kerner interfered one time (literally once) too many with player personnel decisions for Red's tastes, so he resigned after one year.

An inauspicious history with two previous professional club owners behind him, Auerbach accepted the offer of a now desperate Walter Brown to coach Boston. The two bonded, as Brown only concerned himself with performance and results, allowing Red to direct his faculties toward winning. The two got along fine. Soon Red rooted into team culture the need for each player to appreciate his role and to subordinate personal honors to team titles. An aficionado of fast-paced action, Red instituted the fast break into the Celtics' offense, as guards whisked downcourt to score before the opposition set up defensively.

Red Auerbach did not live in Boston, not full-time, anyway. He always considered the Washington, D.C., area his primary residence and spent his off-season time there with his wife and two daughters. He visited Washington as schedules and time permitted during the season and returned to his family once the playoffs ended, but he ensconced himself in Boston the remainder of the year.

He maintained an apartment in the Hotel Lenox in Boston's Back Bay for several years and probably enjoyed the relative anonymity of this lifestyle, as most of his neighbors were visitors from out of town or from outside of Massachusetts, and probably had no inkling of the identity of the balding chap clutching cartons of Chinese food in the elevator up to his room.

With NBA franchises crashing all over the place, Auerbach persevered, picking up center "Easy" Ed Macauley and, whether he wanted to or not, a flashy dribbler named Bob Cousy. Adding a sharpshooter named Bill Sharman, he molded his men into a playoff team, but they never won the last game of the Finals. He needed a big man, and through considerable finagling, he landed Bill Russell on his team, thus creating the most dominant club in league history.

Detractors assert that Auerbach did not know how to coach until Bill Russell joined the team, and anyone could have won from that point forward. Disliking the man is one thing, failing to understand him is quite another. For instance, the Red Sox's general manager starting in the mid-1960s, Dick O'Connell, considered hiring Auerbach as the major league team's manager, due to Red's unique ability to maximize the potential of each player he coached. A star player under Auerbach backed up this analysis, confirming that Red knew how to form a team around the right blend of players and then get each player to excel. He could press the right buttons as easily as lighting a cigar, even if he stayed with the Celtics and did not take the helm of the Red Sox.

Give this man a cigar! With his other famous prop, a rolled-up program, Red Auerbach exhorts his players toward greatness.

He made friends and enemies all over the place, lacing into officials and alienating opposing coaches and players. Lakers coach Fred Schaus once said, "I respect Auerbach as a coach. But I don't like him. I just plain don't like him. And he knows it." Often, even some Celtics did not get along with him, as he bargained very hard at times with stars and subs alike for their contracts. The smart ones circumvented Red and negotiated directly with team owner Walter Brown, until Brown died in 1964. Thereafter, serving most years as general manager, he drove some very good players out of town over relative chump change, often letting the valuable player walk or endure a trade out of town. On occasion, he replaced the departing player with a chump.

He coached the team through the end of the 1966 season, retiring a champion, never to return to coaching due to self-admitted burnout. Sagely, he chose Bill Russell as the next head coach and continued to light up cigars at the end of games his team had all but sewn up. It irritated opposing players, coaches, and fans, and once he discovered the effect this had on others, he lit them up with more gusto than ever. It was infinitely more satisfying to light up a good cigar than to flip someone the middle finger, though the malice attached to each gesture did not differ.

Red got on the nerves of others but was not a simple Dickensian figure, lacking in dimension. He felt deeply for his fellow man but had a difficult time expressing his feelings in conventional ways, so oftentimes he showed his concern by talking to someone at length about an issue. He also offered people rides to the airport as a gesture of empathy. For instance, when Bill Russell and some African American teammates refused to play an exhibition in an area that promoted separate but unequal treatment, Red gave them a ride to the airport. He did this also for a player he cut and then asked back the next year to try out, only to cut this same player a second time. Off to Logan Airport went the heartbroken player, escorted by Red, naturally.

Red's Black Shoes

Under Auerbach, the Celtics wore black basketball shoes, a nod to economy as they did not have to be cleaned as often and thus lasted longer than their white counterparts. Supposedly, Auerbach favored them for another reason, believing visually that someone running with black shoes appeared to be running slower than someone wearing white shoes. Auerbach reasoned that this created a false sense of security in the opponents as the Celts ran their fast break down the court.

By way of further illustration of Red's somewhat stealthy humanity, in the 1982 NBA Draft, Red chose a player named Landon Turner in the 10th round, the two-round draft still years away. Turner had starred on Indiana University's 1981 national champions but subsequently became paralyzed from the waist down after a car accident. A wonderful gesture from a man who never stopped having a heart.

Red left as a coach at the end of 1966 and then later resigned as GM to become club president, a role he had to relinquish when Rick Pitino came to town. Bad karmic move, yet Red outlived this period and continued to serve the Celtics until his death in 2006. Long before then, he witnessed his fictional No. 2 retired and raised to the rafters of the Boston Garden.

2 Russ

To begin to understand Bill Russell, every basketball fan needs to know a bit about Neil Johnston, a Hall of Fame center for the Philadelphia Warriors in the 1950s. For the three seasons from 1953 to 1955, he led the NBA in scoring and participated in six straight All-Star Games, none of which meant a thing once Russell completed playing for the U.S. Olympic basketball team and began his professional career in 1956. After Russell joined the Celtics, he owned Neil Johnston, rendering the Warriors' center and many players like him obsolete, swatting away their shots.

Once Bill Russell's revolutionary impact on the NBA is appreciated, then credit must be extended to other franchises that saw the change in the game and no longer brought in dinosaurs, but fought fire with fire. So the Neil Johnstons disappeared or never got past being backups, while exciting and talented players like Wilt

Bill Russell exhibits the form for an open shot he almost never had the chance to take during a game. The Celtics center thrived in crowds, hounding opposing shooters and grabbing rebounds in traffic. As long as he suited up, he was the finest basketball player in the universe.

Chamberlain came to oppose Russell, and this is where Russell's greatness can be most appreciated. Even after other teams caught up, Russell continued to dominate, the best player in the league, who led the Celtics to 11 titles in 13 years.

In the 1950s and 1960s every sports hero had a biography out in paperback, with the sport that athlete played essentially irrelevant, as the formula of those publications dictated that the star come off as purebred, happy with everything, and more than pleased to recount his exploits and participation in All-Star Games and championships.

As he did in so many instances, Bill Russell broke the mold with the publication of *Go Up for Glory* in 1966. Rather than sitting back with an ice-cold glass of milk and telling America that everything was just swell, Russell related the struggles he and others endured in mid-century America as African Americans. The misinformed took the book as an insult; after all, how could Russell, a financially comfortable and revered athlete act like such an ingrate? By confronting racism, *Go Up for Glory* made itself about so much more than sports.

Since then, Bill Russell has collaborated on a number of books, the literary Russell coming off as a much more likable person than the real-life version. For decades he did not sign autographs and often extended rudeness, not courtesy, to well-wishers and fans. As an African American playing in Boston during its worst days of segregation, and just before busing blew the top off of everything, he had it tough, but he always seemed to find ways to make matters worse for himself.

So, early on, the dichotomy of Bill Russell unfolded, a popular and outgoing teammate, but too often a tactless and ungracious personality to the public. At this critical juncture in Boston's history (before court-mandated busing), Russell became a lightning rod not only to the bigots in the city neighborhoods and the hypocrites in the suburbs, but also to the vast majority of fans who otherwise were favorably disposed to him and his struggles.

At least he got off to a good start, coming off his senior year with the University of San Francisco earning another national championship and leading the U.S. basketball team to a gold medal in the Melbourne Olympics. The good karma continued as he arrived to the Celts late in the 1956–1957 season (due to his Olympics' obligation) and gradually worked his way into the lineup, starring in the NBA Finals that year as his team beat the St. Louis Hawks. His injury early in the third game of the Finals the next year helped the Hawks avenge themselves, but he shut the door on that nonsense almost entirely for the rest of his career, leading his team to 10 of the next 11 titles.

Many excellent players suited up for the Celitcs during their dynasty, but Russell was the constant. He started his career with established stars such as Cousy and Sharman and fellow rookie Tommy Heinsohn, and outlasted all of his original teammates. In his final season he coached John Havlicek, Sam Jones, and Don Nelson, just missing playing with Jo Jo White.

He earned five MVP trophies and, except for his rookie season when the Olympics occupied part of the year, always made an All-Star squad and always finished in the top 10 in minutes played during a season. Even that last statistic partially misleads, as he often paced the league in total minutes played and ended in the top five in that category each year after his rookie year and before his final one. He led the league four times in rebounds and remains the second-leading rebounder in history.

Because Russell was such a team-oriented player, contrasted with his contemporary, Wilt Chamberlain, the risk exists to view him solely as some amorphously gifted athlete who made his team better, always great, but no one quite knows why. While it is accurate that Russell primarily chased titles and not individual goals, his greatness is quantifiable. After all, this is the player who always ended each season in the top three in rebounds per game and is second all-time in rebounds per game with 22.5. The man averaged over 22 rebounds per game and is also second all-time in minutes per game.

Incorrectly, due to his brilliance on defense, slapping back opponents' shots and igniting fast breaks, he is not remembered as an offensive force. This despite contributing an average of over 15 points a game to his team and carving himself into the top five in field-goal percentage the first four years of his career. He not only sparked a fast break with his work on the defensive boards and his passing, but he always hustled down the court to become a factor on the offensive end.

He did many things well, but perhaps best, he did not treat his talented teammates as sidemen, puffing up his own numbers and squandering their potential. After Lakers coach Fred Schaus saw his very strong team dismantled in the 1962 Finals, he remarked, "There is still no one on the horizon who can counteract the things Bill Russell can do to you." Routinely in this era, *Sports Illustrated* led with headlines or teasers that "this year" some team might catch the Celtics, and yet in their preseason prognostications, the editors always conceded that if Bill Russell stayed healthy, the Celtics would repeat as champions, and they almost always did.

A lot of credit belongs to Red Auerbach, who understood Russell's prickly personality and catered to him at times, knowing Russell hated losing, and as long as he had that trait, the social graces mattered little. Plus, Russell got along with his teammates off the court, and in games he ceaselessly tried to make them better. Since Russell played nearly entire games during the regular season, Auerbach largely let Russell sit during practices, drinking tea, knowing that satisfaction came in winning wars, not prevailing in battles.

Along the way, Auerbach and Russell became friends, and Red probably took advantage of the friendship he had developed with his star to ensure the Celtics kept winning titles. Russell might not sign autographs for strangers, but he would never let down a friend.

The first African American head coach in NBA history, he led the Celtics to two championships in three years, before he retired both as a player and coach after the 1969 playoffs. After leaving the Celtics, his ventures have met with mixed results, with coaching stints in Seattle and Sacramento not proving as gratifying as his time in Boston. A popular basketball commentator, he found little satisfaction in that capacity and voluntarily left it. Although he deliberately kept the retirement of his Celtics' number private, he did return to Boston decades after leaving to have a more public honor accorded to him, and only then did he seem to make peace with the city in which he enjoyed his greatest professional triumphs.

3 Larry Legend

Since Red Auerbach shrewdly drafted him as a junior, Larry Bird's potential to come to Boston was debated and anticipated, with the cynics worrying that he might pass on the Celtics and enter the draft after his senior year. And what a senior year! Taking previously unheralded Indiana State to the NCAA Championship Game, only to finally lose to Magic Johnson and Michigan State, his value continued to ascend. Shrewdly, Bird picked a local agent, Bob Woolf, who tantalizingly took Bird to a Celtics game during the "will he or won't he?" phase, which only made him more desirable in the eyes of the local fandom.

Red Auerbach probably did not want to spend as much as he did to bring Bird aboard (a then very high $650,000), but he had been outmaneuvered. In the end, the Celtics got the bargain, as Larry Bird not only had the skills and dedication to make it as a

Even without his glasses, retired Celtics superstar John Havlicek would have no trouble discerning the greatness of No. 33, Larry Bird. Neither Havlicek nor Bird ever left any unexpended effort on the court during their careers.

professional, but he helped bring titles back to the franchise and, with Magic, made professional basketball in general a much more appealing and lucrative sport.

Bird came to Boston at the dusk of a very ugly and thankfully brief era in team history. Selfish players like Sidney Wicks and Curtis Rowe had created a disruptive atmosphere and coaches got dismissed until Bill Fitch took over operations. If Fitch left any doubt concerning proper deportment at team practices and during games, Bird erased them, backing up the newfound commitment that characterized the team.

Remarkably, in Bird's first season, the Celtics went 61–21, this after having compiled a 29–53 record the previous year. Fitch and Bird cannot take all of the credit for the surge. After all, the team did pick up M.L. Carr and Gerald Henderson in that interim, but Bird can claim most of the plaudits. On the court, Bird averaged 21.3 points a game and placed third in three-point field-goal percentage, en route to Rookie of the Year honors.

The next year, the Celtics only improved their regular-season record by one game but added Kevin McHale and Robert Parish, thus forming the nucleus of the excellent Celtics squads through the remainder of the decade. At the conclusion of their first year together as the Big Three, Bird, McHale, and Parish led the team to a title. And Bird famously got to tell the world what he truly thought of Moses Malone's game when, at the team's victory parade, he noticed one fan's sign and shouted out that, yes, "Moses Malone does eat shit!"

Fitch's act curdled after the '81 season and by the end of the Eastern Conference Semifinals two years later, when the Bucks swept the Celts, he was gone, with K.C. Jones replacing him as head coach. While Bird openly professed his respect for Fitch, the Legend also played very well under Jones, as the club won the 1984 and 1986 championships.

By this time, Bird had appeared on the cover of *Time* magazine, and many fans and scribes alike began to anoint him as the greatest basketball player of all time. Old-timers and boosters of Magic Johnson and the young Michael Jordan might object, but Bird sailed to the MVP award at the end of the 1984, 1985, and 1986 seasons and won Finals MVP awards in '84 and '86. During the 1986 All-Star festivities, Bird surveyed his competition for the three-point shooting contest and informed his peers, "I want all of you to know I am winning this thing. I'm just looking around to see who's gonna finish up second." He won, of course, and it looked like the good times would continue to roll.

Of course they did not, a point punctuated by the sudden death of draft choice Len Bias in the off-season coupled with a return of the ailments that had marred Bill Walton's professional career. Although few predicted it at the time, the Celtics would not win another title until 2008. Bird continued to perform at a phenomenal level, averaging 28.1 and 29.9 points per game in '87 and '88, achieving first-team All-NBA each season. But other teams had ascended too quickly for the Celtics to prevail.

Except for six games, he missed all of the 1988–1989 season to have bone spurs removed from the heels of both feet, returning to play 75 games the next year and average 24.3 points a game. But now he found himself on the wrong side of 30 with a chronic back problem, an issue that predated his professional career in some form or other, and he only played 60 and then 45 games the next two seasons. While his teammates sat on the bench during games, it became an increasingly familiar sight for fans to see Bird lying on the hardwood floor of the court to reduce his back pain.

He never stopped playing great, he just no longer always played healthy, a point brought home to the parquet in the fifth game against the Pacers in the opening round of the 1991 playoffs. Bird hit the floor hard in the second quarter, leaving the game. Everyone naturally assumed his cranky back had given out at the worst moment, with his team leading by two in the deciding game.

Yet in the third quarter he emerged, trotting from the runway onto the floor, to rejoin his team. He hurt like hell, but he got back in the game, not simply to provide moral support or some type of spark, but to score enough points to help his team win, which they did that day by three points to advance to the next round. Even though he had been out much of the game and played in agony for the last quarter and a half, he scored 32 points with nine boards and seven assists.

Though Bird's Celtics never played in the Finals again after 1987, Bird earned a spot on the 1992 U.S. Olympic basketball team. As part of the Dream Team, he helped to continue the rise of international basketball and punctuated his career with a gold medal—not an NBA title, but otherwise close to a perfect ending.

One of the most grounded superstars of his era, he lived in a very modest home in one of Boston's nicer suburbs, and then went back home to see his friends and family in French Lick, Indiana. When he first visited Boston, like Dave Cowens, he engaged autograph seekers in conversation, instantly creating equality between superstar and fan. It changed over time due to an unfortunate incident and overzealous fans, an occupational hazard of playing basketball in Boston, making it nearly impossible to excel on the court and maintain an otherwise mundane existence off of it.

Statistically, he flew off the charts, perennially a top 10 free-throw-percentage shooter and seven times a top 10 entrant as a three-point shooter. He rebounded well, most notably on the defensive end, stole balls, and fed the ball to his teammates unselfishly. Twelve times he played in the All-Star Game and on three occasions was selected as the Most Valuable Player in the league. Entirely overlooked, on four other occasions he placed as runner-up in the MVP voting.

The only thing Bird did not do particularly well was dribble the ball—it sometimes appeared that he was trying to dribble a super ball. But he knew his limitations and did not let himself lose the ball, often capitalizing on his skill as one of the greatest passers in NBA history. For much of his career he had Dennis Johnson to drive the ball for him. In other words, he dished it out before he could get in trouble, and almost always created opportunities for his teammates to score.

A self-proclaimed Hick from French Lick, he invited others to underestimate him, making it that much easier to burn the pompous opponent. This extended off the court, where he impressed few as an intelligent man, which he decidedly was and is. One telling story illustrates the folly of this perception. During a flight delay, his teammates scattered, generally looking for a place to get a drink or watch a game. Larry Bird sat back in the terminal, his legs stretched out, reading Arthur Schlesinger's biography of Robert F. Kennedy.

Since he only played 13 years in the NBA (with the 1988–1989 campaign almost completely washed out due to injuries), there is a tendency to believe he retired as a young player, but he actually left the game as a 35-year-old with a chronic back problem. Although he had earned a reputation as a person who saved every nickel he ever made, he retired rather than formally checking in for the 1992–1993 season, feeling he did not want to cheat his employer out of money if he no longer could perform. Larry Bird left the Celtics with honor.

After retiring as a player, he worked for the Celtics' front office for a number of years, stepping aside when Rick Pitino became the head coach and took over much of the operations of the franchise. Had Bird stayed on and handled the player personnel decisions while Pitino coached, the Celtics may have experienced success, but this what-if apparently never came close to happening, causing Bird to completely pull up stakes and move back to Indiana, where he now oversees the operations of the Pacers.

Larry Bird has achieved much in life, his dedication to the game of basketball providing many opportunities he used to his advantage. Obscured in the trajectory of his career on the court is his success overcoming poverty and a difficult home life. His mother had to work all the time to support a large family, and while his father worked hard when he worked, Larry's father had to battle a number of personal issues that probably sprung in large part from his exposure to combat in the service of his country in two wars.

Most informed basketball fans and commentators agree that Larry Bird was one of the greatest basketball players, but more attention needs to be focused on what obstacles he overcame to become such an accomplished athlete and successful executive.

Kevin McHale

It was unfair really, trying to defend against Kevin McHale, particularly in the low post. Seemingly, God had already created the perfect forward for the paint and then at the last moment decided to pull his arms out, giving him a wing span not seen on any player since Naismith nailed up the peach baskets in the Springfield YMCA. Bill Walton once said of him, "He was the second-best low-post player of all time, after Jabbar. In his strategy against bigger guys, he was brilliant—subtle finesse, deft fakes, and all." Opinions differ, because some players and fans considered McHale the greatest of all low-post men.

Born in Hibbing, Minnesota, in 1957, just about the time another famous native son named Bob Dylan was leaving it, McHale starred at the University of Minnesota, where he was later voted their greatest basketball player ever. Then, as part of one of the greatest swindles in NBA history, he came to Boston at the same time as Robert Parish before the 1980–1981 season. From the outset, he gave Auerbach headaches, proving a much harder signing than Larry Bird, and while Red notoriously dealt players in this time period if they gave him a hard time, he caved for McHale.

He entered the game as the club's sixth man, spelling Cedric Maxwell, as coach Bill Fitch began to work him into the lineup. In fact, he won the NBA's Sixth Man Award twice, and as he progressed, he became a starter as he made Maxwell expendable. Titles came to Boston in 1981, 1984, and 1986, as he formed, along with Larry Bird and Robert Parish, perhaps the greatest frontcourt trio in the history of the league.

It almost did not come to this. In 1983 he signed an offer sheet with the New York Knicks, a move designed to force the Celtics to either pay the young forward more than the team management wanted to at this stage or let him leave for New York. It is unclear who exactly should receive credit for this move, Red Auerbach or the team owner at the time, but in a master stroke, the Celtics then presented offer sheets to three Knicks players—Marvin Webster, Sly Williams, and Rory Sparrow. The Knicks lost their nerve and chose to retain their own players and dropped their bid for McHale, having lost their opportunity to obtain a superstar at the expense of three average players.

McHale rewarded his bosses by continuing to improve, and during the 1983–1984 season he participated in his first All-Star Game, playing in seven of them in his career. By 1985–1986 he was averaging over 20 points a game. One of the keys to his scoring prowess was the combination of moves he possessed, a dizzying delight of moves plucked from his repertoire for the right situation.

The Celtics did not win another title after 1986 until 22 years passed, but no one can blame Kevin McHale for contributing to this downward trend. In 1986–1987 he achieved a feat no one in NBA history had previously accomplished, shooting field goals at more than a 60 percent clip (.604) and also bettering 80 percent for free throws (.836) for a full season. Chosen for the first-team All-NBA for the only time in his career, he matched his field-goal shooting percentage in 1987–1988 (having led the league in that category for the second consecutive year) and ranks 13th all-time in

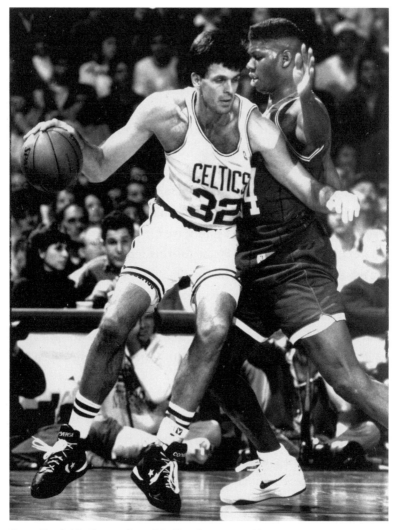

Is it a Bird? No. Is it a plane? No. Is it Superman? Now you are getting warmer. Here Kevin McHale is figuring out which of his moves will drive him past his opponent, inexorably for another score.

the NBA for field-goal percentage. He held the team record for points scored in a game (56) all too briefly, as Larry Bird broke it a mere nine days later.

As late as 1989–1990 he finished seventh in the league in field-goal percentage and eighth in free-throw percentage, a remarkable feat as he had in 1987 sustained his first serious injury, a broken bone in his right foot. (He still knowingly played with this condition through the 1987 playoffs.)

Defensively, he excelled also, earning either first or second All-Defensive Team recognition on six occasions in his career. He rebounded and blocked shots well and kept his dribbling and left-handed shooting to a minimum, although when challenged by a teammate to shoot from the left more, he made all three left-handed hook shots he attempted in one game. The only serious criticism of his game lay in his hesitancy to pass, particularly when he had the ball in the low post. Never a threat to ring up triple-doubles, he only had 10 assists in a game once, but for such a staunch presence under the basket, the criticism resembles more of the nit-picking variety than a gaping hole in his game.

By the early 1990s, injuries began to impede his effectiveness, in particular, chronic problems with his legs, back, and ankle that marred his efforts. By 1992–1993, his final year, even fans winced at the obvious agony he forced himself to compete with; truthfully, it was like watching a horse suffer.

And yet McHale had one great burst of excellence left in him. In the playoffs that final year against Charlotte, Reggie Lewis of course fell on the court, leading to his being restricted from playing the remainder of the series, foreshadowing his untimely death. McHale rose to the occasion, averaging 19 points per game in that series, the last games he ever played as a Celtic. He retired that year and was inducted into the Hall of Fame in 1999.

Much more accessible to the fans than Larry Bird or Robert Parish, McHale spoke at church breakfasts and even appeared on the hit television show *Cheers*, a brilliant move that instantly made him a TV friend to millions of Celtics fans along with the fictional

Sam Malone, Carla, Norm, Cliff, and Frasier. He made his team-mates laugh.

Ironically, McHale earned some of his greatest praise from sources outside of the Celtics organization, with Charles Barkley one his many vocal admirers. Part of his problem is that he played in the shadow of Bird and also endured verbal slaps from his team-mate, with Bird once rather incredibly maintaining that Dennis Johnson was his greatest teammate. At this time, anything Larry Bird said went down with the same force and effect as gospel in Boston, but to his credit, McHale did not engage in a war of public opinion, choosing to let Larry be Larry.

After his career ended, Kevin McHale largely spent his time as an executive with the Minnesota Timberwolves, even head-coaching them on occasion, but his ease with the public, knowledge of the game, and innate wit suggested his talents lay in a more fruitful area. After the Timberwolves relieved him of his duties, he landed on his feet as a television analyst, probably a better fit than an office type, given his personality and quick wit. As anyone who ever played against him will attest, in Kevin McHale, you cannot keep a great man down.

5 The Old Boston Garden

Built in 1928, the Boston Madison Square Garden housed the Boston Bruins and later the Celtics, in addition to the Beatles, the Rolling Stones, rodeos, circuses, and boxing and wrestling matches. It was so booked that when the Boston Celtics scheduled their first home game, it had to take place in the Boston Arena.

Oft romanticized, both before and after its razing, the old Boston Garden, by and large, was not really a good place to watch

Celtics Home Games Weren't Always at Home

It seems like it happened so long ago, but as recently as 1995, the Celtics played an exhibition game at the Hartford Civic Center, part of a 21-year tradition in which the team came down for one exhibition and three regulation games a season, conceived in large part to keep the Knicks from poaching Connecticut fans and to get a higher gate from the larger, more modern Civic Center.

The games were inconvenient for Celtics players, who enjoyed driving in from their suburban Boston homes to the Garden, and in many ways the Hartford games became away games, or at best, ones played at a neutral site. And say what you will about the Garden, its roof never caved in as it did at the Civic Center.

The Celtics have not entirely abandoned Connecticut, having scheduled some exhibitions at the Mohegan Sun in the new millennium and even playing one in Hartford in October 2009. While it is a treat for the team's considerable fan base in the Nutmeg State, there is little chance they will ever play regulation games in the state again, with the new Garden more than capable of providing the seating and accommodation for packed houses of fans.

Less fortunate are those fans in small-town New England who used to see the Celtics, particularly during Red Auerbach's coaching reign, come to their local armories or school gymnasiums. It is debatable which team was the "home" or "away" team, but if the players did not cotton to Hartford, they absolutely hated these junkets.

The accommodations were terrible, and some local school star, semi-pro player, lobster fisherman, or lumberjack always seemed to want to make a name for himself by going after a Celtic, so after a while the team brought in referees with the express purpose of protecting its franchise players. The exhibitions did little for anybody, as the Celtics would have gotten a better tune-up by playing the Washington Generals or a less menacing opposition, like Bill Laimbeer and the Pistons. Fortunately for all concerned, these games mercifully ended.

a basketball game. In contrast to Fenway Park, it had no odd angles or giant Green Monster to distinguish it from any other old and outmoded venue across America. For hockey fans, it possessed a measure of grace since it had the smallest rink in the NHL, but even that quirk disappeared when the ice melted and the parquet came out. Other great basketball cities demolished their dinosaurs, often without much comment or accompanying sadness, but in

Boston, the thought of tearing down the Garden for all too many equated with taking the wrecking ball to the Old State House, Faneuil Hall, or Paul Revere's house.

Its major issues did not spring from age so much as from short-sighted engineering. Like the famous John Hancock Tower, where the windows began blowing out of the building soon after installation, the Garden suffered from poor planning and construction. It may have mattered little during much of the Celtics' history, when the joint often did not sell out during the Russell years, but with the coming of Bird and Company, the place almost always sold out, leaving too many fans with obstructed seats.

Again, friendly Fenway has obstructed seats, too, but generally a fan only loses a relatively small fraction of the action. In the Garden, an obstructed seat often left one unable to see a net on one side of the floor or to see anything but the ankles and sneakers of the ball players running up and down the court. Some seats were situated directly behind a steel girder, meaning the patron could not see a thing.

The fact that fans resorted to obstructed seats during this era begged the question why, even during a playoff game, only approximately 15,000 fans could be admitted. And as the NBA seasons stretched further into the early summer, the absence of air-conditioning dampened the experience for all concerned. For instance, in the fifth game of the 1984 Finals against L.A., the Garden reached a stifling 97 degrees.

Traditionally, opposing coaches and fans accused Auerbach and the Garden staff with altering the temperature of the venue, either transforming it into a sauna or a giant meat locker. Leaving aside the point that neither side got an advantage this way—since each team toiled under identical and objectionable conditions—the environmental impediments made the fans suffer, too. Again, not a great place to watch a game. For the record, Eddie Lee always believed that the parquet, like an old pool table, had several dead spots, accounting for some strange bounces of the basketball.

When asked about wildlife that passed into the venerable arena, superintendent Eddie Lee used to deadpan that of course some animals got in, like the elephants and giraffes when the circus visited. Then he winked and confessed that, every now and then, a rat or two might have made the Garden his home.

And yet this was the same place where Havlicek stole the ball and Russell made Wilt quake and Cowens jumped after balls and Bird passed to DJ and where thousands of fans saw their first game with Dad and Mom or their friends or their first date. The dear old building held too many memories to ever come down, some fans maintained, better leave it as a museum to one's own fond past.

This sentimentality sunk the old Garden ultimately, as the team faded into mediocrity after Larry, Kevin, and Robert stopped coming through the doors. The memories waned after every front-office misstep brought the fans further away from any realistic chance of seeing the Celts compete with the finest teams in the league. Like Puff the Magic Dragon, the old Garden became a useless relic, particularly when the argument began to gain ground that the failure to have a state-of-the-art facility deterred the Celtics in their efforts to land top-level talent. Why live in a cold, snowy New England climate and play in an old bandbox when sunny weather, modern locker rooms, and lasers awaited a prospective player?

It was nonsense, of course, but it struck a chord with many fans who now looked at the venerable old barn as a liability. Folks got tired of living off of ancient memories, they now wanted a return to glory, and in any event the Garden was a terrible place to watch a game. Greed ultimately provided the death knell as new owners calculated increased revenues with more seating and the insertion of gobs of corporate luxury-box seating.

Own a Piece of the Old Garden

The old Garden bricks and seats have been sold, but diehard fans need not despair as the opportunity to buy one still exists on the Internet, with all caveats concerning authenticity accompanying any proposed purchase of memorabilia. The giant clock/scoreboard is currently hanging in the food court of the Arsenal Mall in Watertown, Massachusetts. That's about it, although the site of the old Garden itself, now a parking lot, reputedly has fewer dead spots in it than the parquet that once sat above this hallowed ground.

And so in 1993 construction began on a new sports arena behind the old Garden. For a brief period of time, after the new venue opened, the two arenas coexisted uncomfortably. A high school game might be played in the old Garden occasionally, but eventually it became unsafe to do anything in it, what with bricks falling down and a lack of maintenance. So in 1997 the wreckers began tearing the place down, and for a while the old trolleys of the green line gave passengers a view of the seats in certain sections, before all went to dust. Years later even the green line tracks came down, removing the darkness that embraced Causeway Street even on a sunny day.

And then once the old Garden became a vacant area, people mourned its passing. They paved the parquet and put up a parking lot, and many fans began to hate the new Fleet Center (now renamed the TD Banknorth Garden), with its stupid lasers and overpriced concessions, even though the highest seats in the nose-bleed section provided its patrons with better views than some of the premium seats in the old Garden. The teams still mostly struggled until Kevin Garnett and Ray Allen joined Paul Pierce to bring a 17th banner to Boston. Then and only then did the romanticism taper away, as a new generation followed the team and created dreams of their own.

6 Cooz

Watching old footage of Bob Cousy dribbling the ball down the court (and there are plenty of opportunities to do so even without surfing the Net), it is impossible to not come away with the sense that one has witnessed an anachronism. People could do that back then? It is somewhat like watching an old Roman gladiator movie to see one of the combatants wearing a watch, and yet with the Cooz you always got the genuine article.

Originally from the Yorkville neighborhood in New York, Cousy played college ball at Holy Cross College in Worcester, Massachusetts, under Hall of Fame coach Doggie Julian. Soon, Bob Cousy owned New England, having starred for the powerhouse Holy Cross teams of the late 1940s, the winner of the 1947 NCAA tournament. Undoubtedly Cousy practiced and perfected moves, but improvisation also characterized his game; after one game, during which he had completely faked out an opponent, he was asked about it and had to admit he created the move on the spot.

His greatest talent initially almost proved to be his largest handicap in landing a professional job in Boston. Red Auerbach famously did not want Cousy to play on his team, passing up a territorial pick for him and then hoping to obtain another player when surviving NBA franchises gobbled up stars from defunct ones. Auerbach's problem with Cousy is that he saw more sizzle than steak in his game, and when pressed by the Boston media about his feelings on the nearby college star, he bluntly replied that he did not want a "local yokel."

Auerbach happily ate his words once he had to take Cousy and saw his talent first-hand, and he and the Cooz became very close friends thereafter. Cousy in fact was one of only a handful of people who called Auerbach by his first name, Arnold. The Celtics had never had a star player until Cousy and Easy Ed Macauley joined the club in the fall of 1950, and with a skilled coach, the foundation for the later dynasty was installed. Once Red became a fan, he had to admit, "All the other players just want to stand still and watch [Cousy]."

Although the Celtics made the playoffs after the 1950–1951 season, they did not advance far. Fortunately, the club picked up some backcourt help with the recruitment of Bill Sharman. Now, instead of only two scoring threats, the team had another guard who could shoot, but although the team made the playoffs the next four years, they never returned to Boston with a championship. It took Bill Russell to finally get the team into position to compete for championships, at which point Cousy played on six championship teams in his final seven years in Boston.

Statistics are generally dull and frequently misleading, but in Cousy's case they justifiably show his dominance at point guard: chosen as an All-Star in all 13 years he played (mercifully leaving aside his brief comeback as player/coach with the Royals in 1969), while being elected league MVP once and All-Star MVP twice. He led the league in assists eight years in a row, and even though he served as a point guard (before anyone called them that) and generally let Bill Sharman take the choicest shots, the Cooz also made the top 10 in total points scored in a season and free-throw percentage eight times in his career.

Two other features of his personality proved vitally important to his teammates during his tenure in Boston. At the same point Cousy came aboard in Boston, the team had drafted the first African American player in team history, Chuck Cooper, and he and Cooz became fast friends. Cousy not only extended his friendship but also stood by his teammate at some critical junctures as the league adjusted to changes in American society.

His scruples also shone when he contributed to the formation of the NBA's players' union in the mid-1950s. It took another decade for the union to fully flex its muscles, but the initial formative work had been done by Cousy.

For those Celtics fans not old enough to see him play, he earned a place in their consciousness broadcasting for the team for several years, scarcely giving his audience a hint of the very competitive nature that characterized his play. In December 1950, for instance, he was thrown out of a game against Syracuse for fighting (soon followed by teammate Chuck Cooper), after "flatten[ing] Whitey Macknowski of the Nationals with the prettiest punch the Garden has seen in many a night." In all during that game, the referees tossed four players for fighting, and seven others fouled out. "Gentleman" Bob Cousy led the charge, while also leading his team to a victory that evening.

After his career he also coached successfully at Boston College and much less notably with the Cincinnati Royals. With Cincy he not only attempted a comeback as a player/coach at 41 years of age but also did not get along at all with resident superstar Oscar Robertson. No, Bob Cousy did not belong there; Worcester and Boston beckoned him, at which time he fully dedicated himself to his broadcasting career.

His No. 14 was retired by the Celtics in 1963, and he was inducted into the Basketball Hall of Fame in 1971, one of the most popular players in team history.

7 The First Championship

Before the 1956–1957 season began, the Celtics and Hawks executed their blockbuster deal, which culminated in Bill Russell joining Boston and Easy Ed Macauley and Cliff Hagan going to St. Louis, the Hawks' original home. Russell did not join his new team too soon, as he spent the first part of the campaign on the U.S. Olympic team. This development gave another rookie, Tommy Heinsohn, hailing from Holy Cross, the opportunity to play all year as a pro, thus qualifying him for the Rookie of the Year award, which he duly won, lighting up the scoreboards all year by dint of his shooting skills.

The still wobbly new league at that time only contained two divisions with four teams in each. Despite lacking the services of Russell for much of the year, the team still won the Eastern Division handily over the Syracuse Nationals both in the regular season and thereafter, sweeping them in the playoffs.

While the Celtics clearly posted the finest regular-season record in the NBA by far (44–28), the Hawks struggled, tying two other teams in the Western Division, the Minneapolis Lakers and Fort Wayne Pistons, with a 34–38 mark. By the time the Hawks emerged from their playoffs, victory seemed predestined for Boston.

The Hawks refused to participate in any coronation. Having stocked up their team with future Hall of Famers Cliff Hagan at guard and Ed Macauley at center, the team already boasted a third immortal, forward Bob Pettit, subsequently rated as one of the 50 greatest players in NBA history. They quickly asserted themselves in the first game of the Finals by defeating Boston at home in double overtime, 125–123. Boston won the next game by a 119–99 score, and the next four games followed a similar pattern, with the Celtics alternating between dominating in victory or losing by a very narrow margin.

The seventh and deciding game fortunately took place in Boston Garden.

Surprisingly, Celtics sharpshooters Bob Cousy and Bill Sharman brought cold hands to the game, with Cooz shooting 2-of-20 and Sharman gunning away at a meek 3-of-20. Enter

Give this man a Tommy Point! Here Celtics rookie forward Tommy Heinsohn covers his face in the seventh game of the 1957 Finals against the St. Louis Hawks. But in a few moments he'll celebrate his club's first NBA title.

Tommy Heinsohn, gunner supreme, a man about whom it was often said that he only shot the ball when he had it. Heinsohn scored 37 points, only two behind the Hawks' great Pettit.

Asked whether he felt pressure, Heinsohn warmed up, replying, "Pressure?…'Course I feel pressure, like no one else. But if the shot's there, take 'em. So I took 'em. What the deuce is a guy supposed to do with that ball? Eat it?"

Bill Russell saved the team with a key shot late in the game that propelled him out of bounds. The Hawks' Jack Coleman then drove the ball down the court, at which point Russ got up and ran coast-to-coast until he caught up and blocked an otherwise easy layup. The game went into overtime.

Like many games of the era, things got rough, with Heinsohn and Arnie Risen of the Celtics fouling out, along with visitors Jack Coleman, Jack McMahon, Macauley, and Hagan following suit. In the end, the fouls hurt the Hawks the most, for midway through the second overtime with the score tied at 121, Frank Ramsey drew a foul from Macauley that sent Easy Ed out of the game to be replaced by very rusty player/coach Alex Hannum. Ramsey made a foul shot, and then Bill Russell skyed to block the Hawks' ensuing shot from Med Park at the other end of the floor, setting up a successful field-goal try by Ramsey for a three-point lead. At that point the Garden was rocking, "resounding with cheers."

The Hawks bled two foul shots to bring them within 124–123, but then referee Mendy Rudolph called the Hawks' Alex Hannum for traveling. After the Celtics inbounded the ball, Hannum mugged Jim Loscutoff, who went to the free-throw line to sink one shot, missing the second. With one second left, Hannum inbounded, but the Hawks' last shot missed, giving the Celtics their first championship.

Bill Russell leapt onto the court, and the fans came onto the parquet to lift their favorite players up and into the dressing room. The team threw Red Auerbach into the shower, but Red retaliated by cutting off Russ' goatee. While some Celts had experienced a bad game, Bill Russell did not, bringing down 32 rebounds, and the team's depth provided the difference, with Arnie Risen, Jack Nichols, and Andy Phillip joining Loscy to provide valuable minutes and points that the Hawks could not duplicate.

Postgame, Russell admitted he was "[n]ever so scared in my life…. Man, I was shaking all over my body. See me leap out there when it was over? Felt like jumping all night long, I was so happy." Even with a poor shooting night from the guards, the Celtics had enough other players contribute to prevail. The best team had won.

One out of Five, Not Too Shabby

While Bob Pettit earned selection as one of the NBA's 50 greatest players at the 1997 All-Star Game, 10 players who suited up for the Celtics for either a significant part of their career, if not their entire career, also made the cut. Joining Pettit and the other luminaries were Nate Archibald, Kevin McHale, Larry Bird, Robert Parish, Sam Jones, Bob Cousy, Dave Cowens, Bill Russell, Bill Sharman, and John Havlicek. A few other men, each with brief stops in Boston, made the team: Bill Walton, Dave Bing, and Pete Maravich.

Banner 17

Finally, after two decades of futility, the Boston Celtics' fortunes promised to change, as its NBA-second-worst record of 24–58 in 2006–2007 gave them a great chance of winning that spring's draft lottery and the No. 1 overall pick. Ten years earlier, M.L. Carr had guided the team to an awful record in hopes of securing a lottery selection—actually, *the* lottery pick in the person of Wake Forest's Tim Duncan. The club did not win the "Duncan rights" and endured another decade of frustration.

The spring of '07 promised a far different result because, unlike 10 years ago, there was not just one difference-maker, but two: center Greg Oden of Ohio State and forward Kevin Durant of Texas. Celts general manager Danny Ainge had been spotted seated next to Durant's mother at a college game, and while this drew criticism, it seemed destined that this time the Celtics would get their man. In a classy move, the Celtics sent M.L. Carr as their representative at the lottery to see how the rights sorted out, hopefully with smiling faces all around for Celtic Nation to see and take sustenance from.

It all went bad early. The Portland Trail Blazers got the first pick, which they promptly used to lock up Oden. Then the Seattle Supersonics, a team on the verge of extinction (or for romantics, a new life as the Oklahoma City Thunder) won the rights to the second choice, which their management reflexively and wisely used for Durant. The Celtics plunged all the way to the fifth spot in the draft.

Unlike 10 years ago, the Celtics had a Plan B. Danny Ainge, himself a former Celtics star guard, subsequently crafted a draft-night deal with Seattle, whereby the Supersonics got the Celtics' first pick (Jeff Green of Georgetown University), forward Wally Szczerbiak, guard Delonte West, and a second-round choice in exchange for shooting guard Ray Allen and the eventual rights to Glen "Big Baby" Davis.

Allen, a star hailing originally from the University of Connecticut, had already scored nearly 17,000 points in his NBA career and played on seven All-Star teams. But many Celtics fans came away from the draft disappointed, as the Celtics seemingly passed on youth for an aging star who may have seen his best games already. At the Celtics' sponsored draft party at the TD Banknorth Garden, many guests came to the event excited and left puzzled and in a decidedly non-festive mood. Even worse, the legendary Bob Cousy surveyed this development and any future such moves in a most discouraging manner, opining, "I didn't have that kind of confidence in aging free agents, especially guys...who haven't won anything."

But Ainge disagreed and had one more shoe to drop. Back in Minnesota, general manager Kevin McHale, himself a former Celtics superstar, had a very unhappy power forward in Kevin Garnett on his squad, made all the more isolated after the forward had a talk with team owner Glen Taylor, who had already begun taking steps to paint an exit for veteran players out of town. Garnett started placing phone calls to friends around the league to scout out

Boston as his next possible destination, alleviating some of his initial concerns. McHale knew what he had to do, and talks accelerated concerning moving Garnett to Boston.

On July 31, 2007, that is exactly what happened in a blockbuster, seven-players-for-one deal between the Celtics and the Timberwolves. In exchange for Garnett, Minnesota obtained a very talented Al Jefferson, Gerald Green, Sebastian Telfair, Ryan Gomes, Theo Ratliff (most valuable as someone possessing an expiring contract), two draft choices, and cash. Suddenly, Ainge's draft-day trade for Ray Allen made sense, as he now had the Celtics' first big three with Garnett, Allen, and long-suffering Celt Paul Pierce, since Larry Bird, Kevin McHale, and Robert Parish once walked through the team dressing-room doors.

Garnett took a flight into town, was introduced at a press conference with Ray Allen and Paul Pierce, and won the town over immediately. A tired Garnett said all the right things and then sought out a dinner in the North End of town.

The Celtics had just acquired two of the hardest working players in NBA history to complement the Truth, and while the two acquisitions had largely wiped out their bench, players now wanted to come to Boston, and Ainge replenished the reserves. Meanwhile, young players like point guard Rajon Rondo and center Kendrick Perkins stood on the verge of quantum leaps in the quality of their own play, assisted by the hard-working stars in their midst.

The team chemistry only solidified as the club flew over to Italy in early October to train and play against the Toronto Raptors. A fun preseason meant little if the karma did not extend through to the new campaign; laden with emotion, Paul Pierce lauded the team's fans, stating, "You've stuck with us through the good times and bad times. It's time to turn these times around."

The club opened at home against the Washington Wizards, and they waxed their opponents as Garnett scored 22 points, grabbed

Ubuntu

Leading into the 2007–2008 season, Celtics coach Doc Rivers preached the southern African concept of "ubuntu" to his team, a philosophy that mandates the attainment of the greater good, even at the expense of individual rewards. Big three stars Paul Pierce, Kevin Garnett, and Ray Allen quickly embraced ubuntu, as they sacrificed individual plaudits for the team's 17th title. Too bad that Red Auerbach had not lived to witness the team's success; still, one can almost hear him growling, "Ubuntu? Never heard of it! It's nothing more than what we preached when I coached. Let Wilt get all of the scoring titles, we want the only title that counts!"

20 rebounds, and made five assists. Pierce added 28, and Allen contributed 17 as the Garden rocked for the first time in several years with "Let's go, Celtics!" chants from the fans. The bench augmented the effort by going on an 11–2 run with Allen and Garnett taking a breather for most of that time. An appreciative Ray Allen observed, "The people were rocking."

The Garden kept rolling in late November when the Lakers came to town, led by Kobe Bryant, who had never played against a great Celtics team. Although L.A. usually turned out the movie stars at their home games, Boston had in their seats that evening Arnold Schwarzenegger, Maria Shriver, and Ellen Pompeo, causing Paul Pierce to deadpan, "We're starting to bring celebrities out. That's what I like." The real celebrities were on the parquet, as center Perkins scored 21 points and had nine boards, with Rajon Rondo adding 10 assists. Ray Allen schooled Kobe Bryant on defense as Boston cruised 107–94. When the team defeated Toronto a little over a week before Christmas, their record stood at 20–2, the best franchise start since the 1963–1964 Bill Russell–led team.

Their most challenging stretch during the regular season occurred in mid-March when they had to endure the dreaded "Texas Triangle," scheduled to play back-to-back-to-back away games against San Antonio, Houston, and Dallas.

On St. Patrick's Day, newly acquired Celt Sam Cassell dropped a huge three-pointer with less than a minute in the game to put his team ahead 89–87, as the team overcame a 22-point deficit at one point to defeat the defending-champion Spurs. Modestly, Cassell added, "You know me, I'm going to make some shots." Rondo, Garnett, and Pierce each added 20 or more points in the tough victory.

Next the Houston Rockets, riding a 22-game winning streak (the second longest in NBA history at that time), hosted the Celtics. Controversy circled Kevin Garnett, recently accused by the Timberwolves' owner Glen Taylor of having tanked the last handful of games the previous year—an absurd charge since the commendably intense Garnett could not tank brushing his teeth in the morning. Joked Sam Cassell, "I wish he did tank a couple of practices."

Like the previous game, the Celtics played without Ray Allen, leaving the heroics to teammate Tony Allen, who after being fouled hard by a Rockets player, calmly made both free throws before having to leave the game. The remaining Boston players had little difficulty ending the Rockets' streak, prevailing by a 94–74 margin. Afterward, Houston's Tracy McGrady asserted, "I've never seen a defense like that…that was defense at its best."

Lastly, Doc Rivers had to focus his players on the Dallas Mavericks, led by Dirk Nowitzki, Josh Howard, and Jason Kidd. Garnett starred with 20 points and 13 rebounds, but Ray Allen, back from his injury, saved the day with a three-point shot that put his team in the lead, 90–88, with 33 seconds left. Allen credited his coach, saying, "The play Doc drew up brought me to the ball, and the shot fell." Allen had had a tough day, arriving at the arena with three assistant coaches to practice his shooting, only to be denied entrance by a security guard. Allen eventually got in and perfected his touch as Boston cleared the last hurdle by defeating Dallas, having won all three games of the Texas Triangle for the first time since 1986–1987.

Shortly after, the Celtics concluded the season and faced their first playoff foe, the Atlanta Hawks. Led by former Celt Joe Johnson, the much younger Hawks team took the Celtics to a seventh game in the first round of the playoffs before they were vanquished. It should not have come down to a seventh game, as the Celtics dominated the Hawks during the season and had won 29 more regular-season games.

A couple ominous developments appeared during this series, as Ray Allen seemingly lost his scoring touch and Boston only won at home. Paul Pierce participated in a couple unfortunate incidents, the first occurring in the third game when the league fined him $25,000 for allegedly taunting the opposing bench with a "Bloods" gang sign. He also fouled out and threw his headband on the floor, an act that incurred an additional technical foul in a tough, three-point Game 6 loss. But Pierce also was probably most responsible for advancing his team to the next round.

It did not get any easier in the conference semis against LeBron James and the Cleveland Cavaliers. A runner-up in the 2007 Finals (swept by the Spurs), Cleveland had rebuilt their team considerably since then, even adding a couple former Celts, Delonte West and Wally Szczerbiak. Again, the Celtics won every game at home and lost away, with Pierce and Garnett keeping the team alive on defense with point guard Rajon Rondo showing increasing poise leading his team down the court. Ray Allen continued to puzzle everyone with a cold hand.

In the seventh and deciding game at home, the Celtics narrowly won the game by a 97–92 score, James accounting for 45 points, almost half his team's tally. Unfortunately for Cleveland, Paul Pierce nearly matched their star basket for basket with his own 41 points, a feat made more remarkable because the Celts' captain made a greater percentage of his shots than LeBron.

After the game, a disappointed James did display a firm grasp of NBA history by linking this game to another notable Celts' victory: "We both tried to will our team to victory, and just like Dominique Wilkins, I ended up on the short end and the Celtics won again....I think the second round of the postseason, Game 7, these fans will finally have an opportunity to forget a little bit about what Larry Bird and Dominique Wilkins did and remember what Paul and LeBron did. This will go down in history." The Celtics moved on to the Eastern Conference Finals against the Detroit Pistons.

All of the players who made the Celtics-Pistons games so special in the past had long since retired, and the series had lost much of

Ray Allen, Kevin Garnett, James Posey, and Paul Pierce look on during a break in Game 4 of the NBA Finals against the Lakers on June 12, 2008, in L.A. Led by the big three of Garnett, Pierce, and Allen, the Celtics went on to win the series 4–2 and take home their league-best 17th title. Photo courtesy of AP Images its cachet due to the Celts' long malaise. But the Pistons fielded much of the team that had surprisingly won the 2004 championship. The Celtics did not have the luxury of keying on one star, as they had in the previous series with LeBron, but had to contend with Tayshaun Prince, Rasheed Wallace, Rip Hamilton, Antonio McDyess, and Rick Pitino's old castoff, star point guard Chauncey Billups.

The Boston talk show hosts and their listeners rightly began worrying about this match-up almost the moment their team barely made it past the last round. In essence, if the Celtics scraped by a young one-man team, what chance did they have against a veteran club in Detroit, which had won its last title due to the sum of its parts prevailing over more esteemed playoff opponents? Rhetorical fretting aside, Boston defeated the Pistons, in six games no less, because they too played team ball and Kevin Garnett and Paul Pierce, in particular, each alternated having big games. Early on, Allen commented on his cold hand, stating, "They're wondering why it's not going in—just like I am." It did not stay that way, as Allen regained his touch, scoring 29 points in the fifth game.

In drill-press fashion, the Celtics wore down and defeated the Pistons, even winning two games at the Palace of Auburn Hills, their first road victories in almost a month and a half. Both teams played together well as units, but the more talented team won, a fact displayed by the contributions of Celtics bench players such as James Posey, P.J. Brown, Leon Powe, and Eddie House. Paul Pierce started shouting out, "Beat L.A.! Beat L.A.!"

John Lennon once sang about "the karmic wheel," and it looked as if all of the Celtics' luck had run out before or during their games with Los Angeles. Critics accused Kevin Garnett of wearing out, Ray Allen just received a diagnosis of diabetes for his young son, and in the first game of the Finals, Paul Pierce grabbed his right knee in agony. For Pierce, it was no joke, he had to be carried off the floor in a wheelchair, admitting, "I just couldn't

Duck Boat Ride of Champions

Unbeknownst to the public, coach Doc Rivers took Paul Pierce, Kevin Garnett, and Ray Allen on a private ride on one of the city's major attractions, the "Duck Tours." The tours have caught on in other locales, but for the uninitiated, old WWII landing craft have been converted so tourists can jump on and ride through the streets of Boston, learning about historical sites and events. At the end, the craft enters the Charles River for a boat ride. But Rivers did not have a fun little sightseeing trip in mind—the Duck boats double as the vehicles for transporting championship Red Sox and Patriots teams through the city. Doc wanted them to get used to the Duck craft, so they could ride them the next time as champions.

move." Soon after, center Kendrick Perkins left the game with an injury, not to return that afternoon.

The Celtics had struggled all the way in their first three series and now potentially had to face the team of the millennium without the Truth. Unfortunately for L.A., Shaquille O'Neal had left the building, and Paul Pierce made a dramatic appearance (again a memory of Bird, circa Game 5 of the first round of the 1991 playoffs) later in the game and actually outscored Kobe Bryant in the third period as the Celts prevailed in the initial contest 98–88. Pierce had sustained a strained meniscus, a painful injury but not one that ended his participation in the playoffs.

The attention began focusing more on L.A., with whispers of, "Can Kobe win without Shaq?" growing louder. He could not. Boston won the second game, and even when L.A. took the third one, Boston answered in Game 4 to lead the series 3–1. Again, not only did the starters bury the Lakers, but the bench came in to make the difference over a thinner L.A. squad. By then, pretty much everybody conceded the title to Boston, perhaps even some of the Lakers, as Boston won in six.

Ironically, the Celtics might have had their easiest time in the Finals as they matched up quite well against the Los Angeles Lakers. Kobe would prove he could win without Shaq, but not this year against this Boston team, as Pierce posted up against him on defense quite effectively when called upon. After 22 years of frustration, the championship had returned to Boston.

Causeway Street went as wild as it did during the '80s, back when Bird played and the MBTA trolleys still rode by overhead. Fans ran out to Quincy Market, some to drink while others lit up cigars and stuck them in the mouth of the statue of Red Auerbach. Captain Paul Pierce had had it roughest of all, playing for so many poor Celtics teams, but now even he could say, "I'm not living under the shadows of the other greats now." In the visiting locker room, Kobe Bryant paid Pierce a greater compliment, admitting, "Paul is one of my favorite players in the league. He's tough."

9 Chuck Cooper

Drafted out of Duquesne in the second round of the NBA Draft in 1950, Chuck Cooper broke the color barrier that had existed in the first five years of the league. Emboldened by the Celtics, the Washington Capitols selected Earl Lloyd, and the New York Knicks later signed Nat "Sweetwater" Clifton, other African American basketball stars; so when the nonsense of an all-Caucasian organization stopped, it happened abruptly.

A couple stories have surrounded the desegregation, both of them likely apocryphal. One has it that Abe Saperstein, owner of the Harlem Globetrotters, threatened Celtics team owner Walter Brown that if he drafted a black player, the Globetrotters would bypass Boston. This may have occurred, but desegregation occurred relatively quickly and in many cities thereafter, so if Saperstein did impose a ban, it did not remain in place very long. Another tale has it that other clubs were reticent about desegregating and relied on

Perhaps the Celtics have not retired the number of their first African American athlete, Chuck Cooper, because they are uncertain as to what his number was: the 11 on his jersey or the 20 on his shorts.

the Celtics to lead the pack in that direction. This one might have more substance, although it is hard to substantiate. On one level, the story is difficult to believe because in 1950 the Celts simply were not that good, and little in the way of an aura surrounded the club.

Strangely, the day after the draft, Cooper's selection merited a brief blurb in the *Globe*, so the breaking down of the barrier did not strike many people at the time. The paper spent more time on the Celtics' refusal to draft local college star Bob Cousy, who threatened, "I'll pass up pro basketball before I play for Tri-Cities." Cooper's first game also drew little attention, other than a line in the box score that he scored seven points in the opening game of the 1950–1951 season.

While desegregating basketball did not draw the type of headlines that accompanied Jackie Robinson's entry into major league baseball, Cooper still suffered in relative silence. In retrospect, the Celtics should have shunned exhibitions in segregated areas, but they did not, and once in North Carolina, Cooper had to take a train out of Raleigh past midnight after a game because he could not stay at the same hotel as his teammates. Bob Cousy, to his credit, stayed up with him and boarded the same train in solidarity, a small but touching step for a teammate.

Not that cities north of the Mason-Dixon line formed oases of tolerance, particularly the Celtics' home town. Years after his retirement, Cooper met up in graduate school with Wayne Edmonds (Notre Dame's first African American varsity letter recipient), and when the two shared their experiences, Cooper intimated that he did not like playing in Boston due to the eroding racial climate at the time.

Racial tolerance in Boston only worsened as the 1960s approached, but by then Cooper had left the team. His career lasted six years, with his rookie campaign proving his most successful, when he averaged 9.3 points a game. Although the Celtics were notoriously deficient in the forward position while he played for them, he still did not play as much as starting guards Cousy and Sharman, nor did he score as much as the team needed. At the end of four years, the Celts sold him to the Hawks, where he enjoyed a brief renaissance during his fifth year. In early 1956, after the

The Luck of the Celtics

The club's selection of Chuck Cooper in the second round of the 1950 draft was progressive and courageous and…potentially disastrous. Later in that round, the Washington Capitols chose Bill Sharman from USC, to this day one of the finest shooting guards in NBA annals. Sharman suited up for Washington for one year, then Red Auerbach finagled a deal that brought him to Boston to team up with Bob Cousy to form what many consider the finest backcourt ever. Back then Auerbach had a knack for plunging head-first into compost heaps only to come away smelling like fresh clover. The luck of the Celtics.

Hawks moved from Milwaukee to St. Louis, the team released him, at which point Cooper finished the season and his career with the Pistons.

After his career ended, Cooper continued his education and lived a very productive life in the Pittsburgh area, organizing to improve his community and the advancement of his race. He also had a knack for banking, but died too early, in 1984. His No. 11 has never been retired by the Celtics, but there is always time to rectify that oversight.

10 Hondo

Unlike their football team, the Ohio State Buckeyes basketball team has won just one national championship, that one occurring in 1960. Unlike many of the teams of that era, many yellow-dog basketball fans can recall not only the year the Buckeyes won the title, but can also rattle off several names of the players, such as Jerry Lucas, Larry Siegfried, and Bobby Knight. Of course, the greatest of them all was John Havlicek, nicknamed "Hondo" because he resembled John Wayne in the movie of the same name.

A boyhood friend of knuckleball major league pitchers Phil and Joe Niekro in Lansing, Ohio, he played baseball and other sports, but early in life his size earned him the nickname "Big John." Someday, an ecological study will determine how these athletes, who as children played in abandoned strip-mining areas, experienced such long professional athletic careers. Until then, one can marvel at their exploits and longevity without quite understanding the source of their success.

Bituminous elements aside, Havlicek nearly eschewed basketball for football, surviving as a Cleveland Browns tight end until

An astute Celtics observer can almost always tell from John Havlicek's hair style what era a photo of Hondo was taken. This photo was undoubtedly taken in the 1970s, judging from his long locks and the absence of fans in the upper decks of the Garden.

44

the last cut. Opposing linemen disabused him of this particular ambition, so Hondo took his still largely intact body to the Celtics' training camp.

Ridiculously stacked with talent in the early '60s, the Celtics made Havlicek their sixth man, a role he embraced as he waited for his more senior teammates to retire. At the professional level, Hondo played guard and forward, a considerable source of consternation to opposing coaches and players who had to find ways to defend him at both positions. That alone demonstrates the unique talent of Havlicek, a man seemingly too tall to play guard and too small for forward, he did not allow his size to hinder him at either position.

With the retirement of veteran guards and forwards, Havlicek largely shed his apprenticeship and matured into someone whose team required him to play as much as possible. After Red Auerbach retired from coaching at the end of the 1966 Finals, Bill Russell became the club's player/coach, and Hondo became a de facto assistant coach on the team. He rarely seemed to tire, flying down the court as he became one of the league's most proficient scorers, particularly in the clutch. He also played some of the best defense in the NBA, and when he drew fouls, he nearly always made his free throws.

Unlike many Celtics stars whose bodies wore down by their early thirties, Hondo continued to excel until the very late 1970s, outrunning many younger players and continuing to score. Despite putting up sick numbers every year, he largely escaped debilitating injuries. And while he served on six championship clubs in the dynasty years, he also helped lead them to two more banners in the 1970s, on teams not nearly as talent-laden as before.

In appreciating Hondo's durability, which translated into a 16-year career (twice pacing the NBA in minutes played), scant attention has been focused on the often debilitating pain he endured in accumulating his minutes on the floor. Havlicek did not merely luck out physically, he also played hurt and played quite effectively even in pain, seemingly always flying down the court. He forced himself to play hurt in the 1976 playoffs, for instance, and had he not made this sacrifice, it is doubtful the Celts would have won their title that year. Similarly, his injuries in 1973 kept his team from hanging up another banner at the conclusion of that campaign, despite accumulating an unbelievable 68–14 regular-season record.

He earned selection to 13 All-Star teams, habitually made either first or second All-Defensive teams, landed in the top 10 in scoring six times, and finished in the top 10 in free-throw shooting seven times. In addition to his keen shooting eye, he was an unselfish player who finished in the top 10 in assists seven times.

He retired with 26,395 career points, meriting induction into the Naismith Memorial Basketball Hall of Fame in 1984 and retirement of his No. 17 by the Celtics. Still, like Kevin McHale, Havlicek arguably has never received his proper due for the depth of his talent and for his achievement on the court, and probably never will. He never won an MVP award, maybe because he was too nice and unassuming, although he outplayed many recipients of the honor. Try arguing, for instance, that John Havlicek was a better player for the Celtics than Bill Russell or Larry Bird, and you will almost certainly lose.

And yet, if you attempt to argue that Russell or Bird was more valuable than Havlicek, it is likewise an extremely difficult argument to make. John Havlicek was that great.

11 Buy Something at the Pro Shop

In a Celtics bucket-list book, it is assumed that some day you will see the team play in Boston, but either before or after game time it is essential that you visit the Pro Shop off to the side as you enter

North Station from the old West End and get something for yourself or a friend or family member.

If you have not visited the Pro Shop since the old Garden days, you will notice that it is about a third of the size of its previous incarnation but still shelves some very attractive merchandise. These days you will rarely if ever see an actual Celtic shop there, although you might see a player's wife or girlfriend stop by. Since the club established a state-of-the-art training facility in the suburbs, individual team members only generally come to the Garden just before a game and do not linger to pick up gifts for themselves.

With or without Celtics, the shop is very busy, especially before a game, so you might want to get there on off hours or before the crowds come by, particularly if you are in town for the day. Of course, the worst time to patronize the Pro Shop is just after a title is won. After the team defeated L.A. to win the championship in 2008, the store stayed open well past midnight to accommodate fans wishing to buy official gear denoting the feat. The store became so crowded that police in riot gear had to come in to restore order and ensure that no one got hurt, as the number of people far exceeded the maximum allowed in the space.

The police cleared the store, permitting the shop staff to regroup and prepare for reopening later that morning. When the doors were opened to the eager fans, a wall of customers raced in to clean out the racks of what inventory remained.

A warning to purists: you will not simply shop around Celtics' gear and souvenirs, as the Bruins share the building and the hearts of many of the regular customers of the Pro Shop. Indeed, while you may never see a Celtic in the store, Bruins players still frequent the locale to scoop up merchandise. Since the city's hockey club preceded its basketball team by over two decades, its more historical jackets and jerseys might appeal to fans of the roaring '20s, so bring a bit more cash or extend your credit limit in the event you develop a crush for Boston's other winter franchise.

12 The Other Red

Celtics assistant GM Jeff Cohen caught everyone by surprise on November 10, 1976, when he strode into the press room an hour before game time and calmly handed out sheets of paper to the assembled writers. The copies he distributed contained the announcement that star center Dave Cowens had taken an indefinite leave of absence from the team due to "personal reasons."

While the club had not gotten off to a great start and had lost its last four games, the news shocked people because the Celtics were the defending world champions, having won two titles in the last three years, largely due to the contributions of their red-headed center. His teammates also seemed surprised, with Charlie Scott perhaps encapsulating it best: "Dave's an individual...a very lovable individual. I think we're human beings, and sometimes we don't think of people as individuals." *Boston Globe* sportswriter Ray Fitzgerald opined that Cowens "marched to a different drummer."

Over time, the "different drummer" label stuck, a simplification no doubt for a person who paradoxically placed basketball in perspective as just one element of life or one experience to be savored. And yet, while he played, no one matched him for intensity. For a career he seemed not to need, he cared about it more than anyone else on the floor every night he played. Hall of Fame guard Dave Bing once said of him, "When he first came into the league, I didn't think Cowens would last long, diving around like that. Big men didn't do those things." Well, most big men did not.

Red Auerbach scouted the collegian Cowens, a star at Florida State, famously leaving before the game had ended to create the false impression that he had seen enough. Internally, Auerbach

Celtics center Dave Cowens comes up big against Artis Gilmore. On the left, Jo Jo White has the best view of the greatness of his teammate.

knew he had to have this kid on his team to rebuild the Celtics in the post-Russell years, and he did choose him, fourth overall in the 1970 draft. An undersized center (his height has been variously listed from 6′8″ to 6′9″ on a good day), he scored an average of 17 points a game in his first year en route to Rookie of the Year honors. Far more important, the team won 10 more games than it did in the previous season and made it to the Eastern Conference Finals each of the two years after that. In the 1972–1973 season he was the Most Valuable Player in the NBA.

Returning to the issue of his intensity, he was one of the few stars of that era who dived onto the floor after balls or into the seats. Big deal, so does every player in high school who barely makes the varsity team. Well, in that era it was a huge deal, and Cowens matched his efforts not only with scoring but rebounding and, particularly in the early part of his career, fouls. Dave Cowens cared.

His efforts crystallized in a championship in the 1973–1974 season. He had by that time formed a strong partnership with Paul Silas, and Silas helped pull in rebounds and shove bodies around not only to take some of the pressure off Cowens but also to allow him to take some jumpers. The pairing in large part helped the club gain another championship after defeating Phoenix in the 1976 Finals.

Unwisely, the club unloaded Silas before the 1976–1977 season due to a salary spat, and whether or not that incident in part led Cowens to take a leave from the team the following fall, the Celtics never won another championship for Cowens. This development, together with the importation of some players not cut out of Cowens' mold, certainly made his decision to take a leave of absence not that difficult.

An extraordinarily popular player, Cowens seemed not that different from the average fan. He drove a taxi around for a while, tried to helped save some farm land in suburban Canton, and blended well with his community. By way of one example of many, during the Blizzard of 1978, Boston and much of New England came to a standstill as returning commuters abandoned their cars along the streets and highways, trudging their way back home. Hockey fans got stuck in the Garden, not able to navigate their way out during the storm. Fortunately, the Celtics did not play that evening, as it might have gotten very nasty in the old building if Sidney Wicks and Curtis Rowe had to stay overnight, but that did not mean that Cowens did not play a role in helping his fans.

Navigating his truck through a snowy downtown Boston, Dave Cowens made the best of the situation, providing rides to about 15 stranded people. At one point in Government Center in downtown Boston, as Cowens related, he "looked up and saw this man with a cast on one leg.… It was a big cast and his pants were split. His toes were sticking out of the cast. He was on crutches and having trouble standing up. I was worried about his toes. He'd have gotten frostbite." So Cowens invited the poor man into his truck along with the other guests and drove the man to his appointed destination in suburban Quincy, several miles away.

In Cowens' last season with the Celtics, he played on the same team as a rookie Larry Bird but passed up the opportunity to earn a lucrative salary by hanging on another year (imagine a team with Robert Parish and Dave Cowens as its centers). He tried a brief comeback with Milwaukee in 1982, largely at the urging of former teammate (and then coach of the Bucks) Don Nelson, but it did not work out, and the team waived him. No sentimentalist, Celtics GM Red Auerbach insisted that Milwaukee trade a player for Cowens, which explains how Quinn Buckner came to Boston.

Foul Indeed

Dave Cowens possessed a purist's view of basketball, an almost dogmatic distaste for acts and practices on the court that he deemed heretical. He particularly hated opposing players who faked fouls, flopping around like wimpy soccer players on the court for no reason.

Enter Mike Newlin, Houston Rockets guard, who on February 25, 1976, decided to try to act his way into drawing some cheap fouls at Cowens' expense. Cowens protested his innocence to no avail, of course, as no referee was going to admit that he had been suckered in such a manner. So Newlin got away with one.

Or so he thought until shortly after, when he dribbled the ball down the court, Cowens assaulted Newlin and sent the Rocket flying into space, depositing him somewhere around or upon the scorer's table. Looking at the ref, Cowens bellowed, "Now that's a fucking foul!"

Nicknamed "Big Red," Cowens was not a different drummer, he was one of us. He started a basketball camp, still in existence 40 years after its founding. As one of the friendliest Celtics, he later led the New England Sports Museum and served as AD at a small Catholic College, largely in an effort to procure the school better athletic facilities.

He pursued excellence on the court and earned recognition off of it, having his number retired by the Celtics and earning induction into the Hall of Fame for very tangible reasons. He played hard but also scored well, and remains to this day ninth all-time in the NBA for rebounds per game. He made seven All-Star teams during his too-brief career and a number of mythical All-Defensive and All-NBA teams, because few basketball players ever excelled like Dave Cowens did.

13 Johnny Most

Strange to say, but Celtics' broadcaster Johnny Most has been dead since 1993, an incredible fact considering how full of vigor he was when, for over three decades, he sat "high above courtside" announcing games. Taking over for Curt Gowdy, he handled Celtics' broadcasts from 1953 to 1990, his deteriorating health causing him to step down. His microphone has been symbolically retired by the team.

Listeners loved him if, of course, they happened to cherish the Boston Celtics. He almost transcended the personification of a homer as he consistently took the side of a Celtics' player or coach, no matter how dubious the call. By way of a partial explanation and not an excuse, at the beginning Most traveled with the team and engaged in regular card games with players like Cousy and

Sharman during long plane rides and layovers, so he literally covered his friends during his broadcasts.

Like an aggressive fan, at times he called out opposing players off the court for what he considered brutish behavior. Later, he became more of an uncle to the younger players and mellowed a bit, but as a younger man, he skirted being drilled through the parquet floor by opposing players. Undoubtedly, he reveled in the controversy he created—after all, his grandfather was the famed German anarchist Johann Most.

Had Most simply satisfied himself with the role of a buffoon, he probably would have eventually found his way to a career as an announcer for professional wrestling events, but he was so much more than the class clown. He knew the players on both teams and always called a well-paced game. Slanted, sure, but a radio listener knew what was going on when Most took the mike.

Fleetwood Sounds produced a marvelous LP (later reissued on CD) titled *Havlicek Stole the Ball*, which contains some audio highlights in the team's early dynastic years, including Bob Cousy's retirement speech. Interspersed are speeches by Walter Brown and John Kiley's tasteful organ interludes, but mostly it's Most. It's all audio, and it should be heard because it is carefully edited to show all aspects of Johnny's performance: humor; pacing; dramatic flair, certainly; but also a knack for vividly describing the action. No "fiddlin' and diddlin'" in this recording.

Along with Red Auerbach and Bob Cousy, he formed the third prong of a remarkable troika of native New Yorkers who popularized basketball in Boston. Everyone had their favorite description for Most's voice, Johnny himself conceded it sounded like he gargled with Drano. Truthfully, it only seemed this way, because most of the time he spoke in a much more modulated tone, but after a number of excited utterances, often during games against the Pistons, his voice became hoarse and took on the timbre that his fans remember him by.

He also possessed a depth born from serving as a war hero during World War II, earning several medals for valor as a gunner in almost 30 missions. In memoriam for the comrades he left behind, he penned the following:

I stood among the graves today and swept the scene with sight.
And the corps of men who lay beneath looked up to say good
night.
The thunder still, the battle done, the fray has passed them by;
and as they rest forever more, they must be asking, "Why?"

Johnny Most is buried in Boston.

14 The Truth

In 2001, after only a few years in the NBA, Paul Pierce received his nickname after Shaq uttered the following: "My name is Shaquille O'Neal, and Paul Pierce is the fucking truth. Quote me on that, and don't take nothing out. I knew he could play, but I didn't know he could play like this."

If Shaq did not fully appreciate Paul Pierce's talent, he stood in relatively good company, for nine NBA franchises passed on Pierce in the 1998 draft. Incredulous that Pierce had fallen that far, then president/head coach of the Celtics, Rick Pitino, barely concealed his glee after choosing him as the Celtics' first-round draft choice. While Pitino did not last much longer in Boston, Paul Pierce endured, often the lone star on some truly brutal teams.

He probably should have been a Laker—after all, he grew up in nearby Inglewood, hating the Celtics and sneaking into the Forum for games. But he was stuck with Boston.

One of the most intense players to ever don a Celtics jersey, captain Paul Pierce drives for the net. As he matured, Pierce augmented his game with an impressive presence on the perimeter.

A pet theory on why Paul Pierce is not anywhere near as appreciated as his talent and production dictate, is that the internationalization of the sport, particularly as seen in the Olympics, has affected how people perceive him. In the Olympics, of course, even with a Dream Team of NBA stars, a considerable accommodation with the international game has to occur, with an emphasis on a team having a roster of shooters heaving up three-point shots all over.

Traditionally, that has not been Paul Pierce's game. Early in his career, he stole the ball quite a bit, but throughout most of his professional life, his game has relied more on power and toughness, staring at his opponent and occasionally trash-talking, and then blowing by to the net. Even in that aspect, though, he has broadened his game, so much so that in 2009–2010 he lifted himself to a top 15 ranking in three-point field-goal percentage.

Most likely, Pierce simply came to Boston during the worst stretch in franchise history. An eight-time All-Star through the 2009–2010 season, Pierce was by far the best player the Celtics had since the heady winning days for the team in the 1980s. These repeated honors aside, he became the object of scorn from some segments of the media and the fans, many questioning his maturity.

The critics did not treat Pierce in a totally unfair manner, because even though he could not lead the team single-handedly to titles, he could improve and mature, and with Kevin Garnett and Ray Allen joining the team in 2007, he did. He listened to talented assistant coach Tom Thibodeau, watched Garnett, and developed into a better defensive player.

Yet Pierce's offense garnered the most attention during the long playoff run and drew comparisons to Larry Bird. For instance, in the final game of the Eastern semis, he came within four points of matching the Cav's LeBron James' 45-point performance. The Celtics won, prompting recollections of Larry Bird's matchup

No. 10

Unlucky for most of the decade, the Celts scored huge with the selection of Kansas' Paul Pierce as the 10th overall pick of the 1998 draft. Who was chosen before him? From first to ninth, the other teams selected:

1. Michael Olowokandi (University of the Pacific)
2. Mike Bibby (Arizona)
3. Raef LaFrentz (Kansas)
4. Antawn Jamison (North Carolina)
5. Vince Carter (North Carolina)
6. Robert Traylor (Michigan)
7. Jason Williams (Florida)
8. Larry Hughes (St. Louis University)
9. Dirk Nowitzki (DJK Würzburg)

against Dominique Wilkins in the seventh game of the 1988 Eastern Conference semifinals.

Similarly, in the first game of the Finals against the Lakers, Pierce injured his knee and had to be carted off the court in a wheelchair, only to return after the half (remember Larry Bird in 1991 against the Pacers) to outduel Kobe Bryant as the Celts won on the way to rolling over L.A. for the title. Deservingly, team captain Pierce won the Finals MVP award as he not only scored, but rebounded, stole the ball, fed his teammates shots, and defended better than he ever had. Even in defeat, in the fifth game of the Finals, he scored 38 points.

Unfortunately, Pierce probably will never shake the events that occurred on September 25, 2000, when at least two assailants attacked him with a bottle and a knife at a private club in Boston. One of the men stabbed Pierce 11 times in the chest, neck, and back, requiring immediate life-saving surgery on one of his lungs.

Despite all of the grave injuries he sustained, Pierce went on to play a full and very successful season for Boston that year, not missing one game.

That's the Truth.

1986

For many Celtics fans, 1986 was their favorite year, and it is not difficult to see why. If you had season tickets, you only left the Garden feeling bad once, as the team went on an unbelievable 40–1 tear at home; on the road, they were only slightly easier to defeat (27–14). The Massachusetts economy had been soaring for several years, the Bruins made the playoffs, the Red Sox almost won the World Series, and the Patriots participated in their first Super Bowl. Many of the social problems that had plagued the city had abated considerably, and as one bank's jingle went, "I got my BayBank card…life just keeps getting better."

The team started five players at the zenith of their powers: center Robert Parish, forwards Larry Bird and Kevin McHale, and guards Dennis Johnson and Danny Ainge; plus a newcomer, eventual Sixth Man Award–winner Bill Walton provided valuable contributions on the court and even leadership off of it. Five of these top six players eventually earned induction into the Basketball Hall of Fame. Adding to their bench strength were one-time All-Star Scott Wedman and guard Jerry Sichting.

In the playoffs, the Celtics opened with the Chicago Bulls, sweeping them 3–0, an extremely distorted statistic as Michael Jordan almost single-handedly led his team past the Celtics. In the second game, he reeled off 63 points, causing Larry Bird among others to tab Jordan as the greatest player who ever lived. In the other two games, M.J. also excelled, but unfortunately for Chicago, Scottie Pippen still suited up for the University of Central Arkansas, and Jordan could not carry his team past an extremely strong Celtics contingent. But he came very close.

By way of anticlimax, in the Eastern Conference semifinals Boston squared off against Dominique Wilkins and the Atlanta Hawks, a team that, like Chicago, still relied too much upon their superstar, even though they had other talented players such as a young Doc Rivers and Tree Rollins. Boston rolled, with only a bit of concern expressed when Bill Walton did not play in the third game due to injury, causing Robert Parish to play 45 minutes as the Celts won to lead the best-of-seven series 3–0. The Celts lost a sloppy Game 4 but zipped up the series in the fifth game, as they destroyed the Hawks by a 132–99 score.

Oddly enough, even that blowout tally misleads, as the Celtics outscored Atlanta 36–6 in the third quarter (the six Hawk points setting a record for least points scored in one period of a playoff game in NBA history), causing Dennis Johnson to observe, "It was the best quarter I've ever played in." At one point during the carnage, Danny Ainge leaned into the stands to high-five the fans.

In the Eastern Conference Finals, the Celtics swept Don Nelson's Milwaukee Bucks, led by Sidney Moncrief, Terry Cummings, Paul Pressey, and Ricky Pierce. Boston won the first game over the Bucks 128–96, and together with the previous Hawks game, this constituted the first time in league history that a playoff team beat opponents by more than 30 points in consecutive games. Other than that, the only other remarkable feature in the series occurred in the last game when Dennis Johnson racked up a number of fouls early and Larry Bird substituted for him at guard.

Old friend Bill Fitch coached the Houston Rockets, the team the Celtics had to defeat in the Finals. Armed with the Twin Towers of Hakeem Olajuwon and paper tiger Ralph Sampson, the Rockets promised to provide the Celts with more opposition than the last two playoff opponents had. Rather than upset Boston with locker-room wall material, Rockets guard Robert Reid gushed, "Whenever [Bird] gets in that rhythm, there isn't anyone who can stop him." He did not stop there, adding that Danny Ainge "should be a 6'10" center to go with his heart," while "Bird and everybody else knows they wouldn't be nearly as good as what they are now" without Kevin McHale.

Although Reid may have eliminated any animosity, Boston still cruised in the first two games, the second being a particularly steamy night in the old Garden, during which Bird scored 31 points with eight rebounds and seven assists. In Houston, the Rockets took advantage of a blown Celt lead to win the third game behind a particularly strong Sampson effort (24 points and 22 rebounds). Boston took a 3–1 series lead after the next game, one saved by Kevin McHale's key steal with 10 seconds remaining.

Boston lost the fifth game, the contest made famous by the giant Sampson getting into a fight with Celtics reserve guard Jerry Sichting. Sichting swung back, and then Dennis Johnson and Bill Walton joined the fray, attacking Sampson. Olajuwon then went in to help out his teammate, and the fans in Houston went berserk. Sampson got kicked out of the game, but the Rockets won ugly, to force a sixth game in Boston.

The Sichting fight might have gotten the Rockets energized to win what had been a close game, but the Boston Garden promised to be a most inhospitable place for Ralph Sampson. The crowd hooted him mercilessly, with M.L. Carr observing, "He looked terrified when he came on the court. I felt bad for him." Sampson tanked, and Larry Bird notched a triple-double to lead the Celtics to a 114–97 victory and another title, although Bird's best moment might have come when he observed that his sister could have beaten up on Jerry Sichting.

After the game, Kevin McHale exclaimed, "How much fun was that?" while K.C. Jones stated that Bird had "reached the pinnacle of basketball."

16 Boston 2010

Warriors they are not, these professional athletes who callowly compare themselves to the men and women defending this country. And yet gallant soldiers often justifiably receive credit for their feats in a losing cause, with the cavalry men of "The Charge of the Light Brigade" leading the way. Sports stars make poor warriors, but they also do not receive their full measure of acclaim and gratitude for coming close to victory without earning the final prize.

Hopefully, starting with the 2009–2010 edition of the Boston Celtics, this trend will change. From the earliest chapters of their season, the club seemed star-crossed, not self-assured. People questioned whether Kevin Garnett might ever return to his peerless form, while backup Glen "Big Baby" Davis broke a thumb horsing around with a friend and missed the first third of the season.

By mid-season, it appeared the Celtics had aged beyond usefulness, with their vaunted defenders always seemingly playing a step behind their opponents. Free-agent signing Rasheed Wallace appeared as disinterested as Sidney Wicks in the bad days of the franchise, apparently engaged only when firing up three-point field goals at a rate of futility virtually unmatched in league history. Embarrassing regular-season losses to the Nets and Grizzlies underscored the concerns of the fans, as the Big Three era of the Celtics seemed fated to come crashing down, with the team going 27–27 the last 54 games of the season, losing seven of its last 10. With the first round of the playoffs approaching against Dwyane Wade and the Heat, many prognosticators predicted a one-and-done scenario for the Celtics.

Coach Doc Rivers disagreed. While other teams posted much better regular-season records, he perceived that his club still possessed champion-caliber players and a dedication to achieving another banner. Most important of all, he entered the playoffs with a healthy Kevin Garnett, Paul Pierce, and Ray Allen, led by an exciting young star in point guard Rajon Rondo. The team had not lost a step, it had preserved them for a time they needed them the most.

Miami fell in the first round with embarrassing ease. Dwyane Wade fought mightily, and might have willed his team to one win, but the Celtics got the other ones behind a rejuvenated group of starters and some very effective bench players. Doc Rivers had coached the team better than perhaps any other Celtics coach in history, Red Auerbach excepted. Reserves Nate Robinson, Tony Allen, Davis, and Rasheed Wallace played exceptionally well when called upon, a trend repeated throughout the playoffs.

The series win versus Miami was nice, but few seriously believed that the Celtics had much chance of defeating their next opponent, the Cleveland Cavaliers led by LeBron James. During the regular season, the Cavs paced the entire NBA in games won, as LeBron had cemented his reputation as the greatest active NBA player. Surrounding him were veterans such as Shaquille O'Neal, Antawn Jamison, and Mo Williams.

In the Eastern Conference semis, the Celtics surprisingly tied the series at 2–2, but certainly expected the Cavs to come out strong in the fifth game. Instead, LeBron played perhaps the worst game of his career, appearing lost and enervated, and with his teammates unable to elevate their performances, the Celts romped. Game 6 became a coronation, because although LeBron tallied a triple-double, his teammates simply did not match up well against the Celtics defense, as the Cavs lost the game and the series. The Cavs had the best player, the Celtics had four of the top five best players.

The Celtics faced a more balanced Orlando Magic in the Eastern Conference Finals (a club that had yet to lose a playoff game in 2010), with star Dwight Howard at center and complementary effective long-range shooters, such as Jameer Nelson, Vince Carter, Rashard Lewis, and J.J. Redick. Howard may have been the finest center in the NBA, but Boston had a perfect antidote down low, with their own Kendrick Perkins. Often criticized for his lack of offensive scoring punch and less-than-soft hands, Perkins had become a very effective defensive presence and posted up well against Howard, allowing the Celtics the luxury of not having to double-cover Howard and allow the other Magic players to pick them apart from the perimeter.

Indeed, the Celtics quickly won the first three games of the series before Orlando found their groove and won the next two. The Boston Bruins had just blown a 3–0 playoff lead against the Philadelphia Flyers, and the fretful local fans began to worry that the Celtics might repeat the embarrassment of their hockey brethren. Not this Celtics team. Having lost the previous season's semifinal series to Orlando, the Celtics avenged themselves by winning the sixth game, ensuring another chance to "beat L.A."

The Lakers had changed for the better since their last Finals series with Boston in 2008, mainly due to the more physical presence of their center Pau Gasol. Boston managed to split the first two games in L.A., and Paul Pierce promised that his team would not return to L.A. in the Finals, with their next three games at the Garden. Unfortunately for Pierce's prognostications, the Lakers did win one game in Boston, but the Celtics looked very good with a 3–2 lead in the series, returning to Los Angeles with two more chances to win just one game and another championship.

It did not happen in the sixth game, as the Lakers blew Boston out. The Celtics not only lost that game but also lost the services of center Kendrick Perkins due to injury. Still, in Game 7, the Celtics played very well, ahead through much of the game, but coming up four points short in the end. Another banner would not be raised to the Garden rafters in 2010.

Basketball players are not warriors, but the 2009–2010 Boston Celtics were champions.'

 **Red's Run**

Especially today, with sports dynasties measured in five- or 10-year increments, the Celtics' run of eight straight NBA titles from 1959 to 1966 inspires awe, yet a year-by-year analysis almost cheats the team of a proper perspective of its accomplishments. Red Auerbach built and trained a team around some central concepts and stayed true to them, to the benefit of the franchise he served.

Having just won their first championship in 1957, the Celtics faced the St. Louis Hawks again in the Finals in the spring of 1958 and lost, principally due to Bill Russell's injury in the third game of the series. St. Louis avenged its loss from the previous year and remained a threat, with Boston facing more celebrated rivalries ahead with Philadelphia and Los Angeles. In response, the Celtics uncoiled a string of eight straight NBA championships.

That is one element of what makes the Celtics' consecutive run special, the fact that they faced very formidable opponents and always prevailed. Since the key personnel did not change suddenly or drastically, it is easy to blur the years together, yet therein lies a source of their strength. Once the club had obtained Bill Russell, Red Auerbach shied away from trades until September 1, 1966, when he swapped Mel Counts for Bailey Howell. The team that played together stayed together, and the continuity helped them to anticipate what teammates would do in certain situations and bonded them as a unit. Back then Red rewarded loyalty.

There are more iconic pictures of Bill Russell, but perhaps none demonstrate his dedication to the team concept more than this, as he leaps over the back of an opponent to assist a fellow Celtic under the basket.

The team prospered because individual honors did not mean that much to Auerbach; he wanted championships. In the 1958–1959 season, which ended with a Finals sweep against the Minneapolis Lakers, the Celtics placed three players on the All-NBA first team, Bill Russell at center and Bob Cousy and Bill Sharman at guards. And yet this proved an anomaly, as quite often during the dynasty, Wilt Chamberlain made first-team ahead of Bill Russell, once startlingly in 1961 when Bill Russell was voted league MVP. Celtics players played for championships, not All-Star selections or scoring titles.

They won because they had the best player in the league in Russell, but also because Red Auerbach coached them. For a while they were loaded, creating the sixth-man role for Frank Ramsey because they did not have the room for him in the starting five. By the same token, they sat players like Sam Jones and K.C. Jones until Bill Sharman or Bob Cousy tired, knowing that the Joneses would have their time in the future to start. It takes good players to win, but even better players to wait their turn.

Dedicated to defense, the team created many scoring opportunities off of their D, with Russell lofting long passes down the court after out-rebounding the opponent's center. Traditionally, the team ran only seven offensive plays, but basketball is not that static, and with an opportunistic defense, the Celts had several different ways to transition and score. Specific players besides Russell, such as Satch Sanders and K.C. Jones, subordinated their offense to sticking to the opponent's best player, keeping their points down, while better shooters like Sam Jones, Tommy Heinsohn, Bill Sharman, and John Havlicek put up the points.

Except for one year during Red's run, the team won the most regular-season games and often won the Finals with embarrassing ease, with only the Hawks in 1960 and the Lakers in 1962 and 1966 pushing the outcome to a seventh game. Conditioning mattered, and Red's insistence upon it produced remarkable results deep into the playoffs each year.

Continuity mattered, but the squad that won the Finals in 1959 differed significantly from the 1966 roster, because players waited their turn to star until veterans slowed up and later stepped down. Having been tripped up by the Hawks in the 1958 Finals, principally due to the loss of Bill Russell during that series, the Celts had proceeded to win championships the next three years. Once Bill Sharman retired, Sam Jones kept up his legacy as a shooting guard, while K.C. Jones at point guard and Thomas "Satch" Sanders at forward also established themselves. The team had largely rebuilt their bench, with the exception of still retaining the tough Jim Loscutoff, but a solid nucleus of stars who by then had played on four championship clubs remained: Bill Russell, Bob

Cousy, Frank Ramsey, and Tom Heinsohn. In all, the team had six future Hall of Fame players in 1962.

In 1962–1963 the Celts repeated as champions, welcoming rookie John Havlicek to the club and reluctantly saying farewell to Bob Cousy at season's end. Frank Ramsey retired after the next season, as did Tom Heinsohn two years later, but the team kept winning. As they had done in the late 1950s by adding stars transitioning into role players such as Arnie Risen, Andy Phillip, and Jack Nichols, Red Auerbach enticed other teams' players or rejects into valuable assets in the 1960s. Clyde Lovellette, Willie Naulls, Larry Siegfried, Woody Sauldsberry, and Don Nelson all signed up with the Celtics in Red Auerbach's later years as head coach and fit in, earning a ring, a watch, a Paul Revere bowl, or whatever else world champions won back then.

Celtics players exhibited certain traits and were coached by a unique individual, someone whose mold was broken at birth. And until he stepped down as the Celtics' coach at the conclusion of the 1966 playoffs, Red Auerbach and his men just kept winning.

First Dynasty's End

Burned out by coaching after the 1966 playoffs, Red Auerbach kicked himself upstairs, assuming the Celtics' general manager's mantel, and immediately faced the task of choosing his own successor. He most likely wanted Tommy Heinsohn to take over, but knowing Bill Russell had begun to tire of basketball, Red chose Russ to become a player/coach, the first African American to head up a team. Uncharitably, several commentators have suggested that the only person Bill Russell would play for at this stage of his career was…Bill Russell.

And Russ might not even have been the best choice, as John Thompson, future coach of the 1984 NCAA champion Georgetown Hoyas, had served as a backup center in Red's last year on the bench.

Though no longer roaming the floor of the Garden, Red left his successor with two very significant additions in center Wayne Embry and forward Bailey Howell. The Howell deal is still one of the greatest ever as the Celtics obtained him from Baltimore in exchange for a little-used backup center. Embry received a lot of minutes spelling Russell.

Even with these significant additions, the Celtics' string of successive championships finally came to an end the year after Auerbach ceased roaming the court, as the Philadelphia 76ers, led by new coach Alex Hannum, finally brought a banner to Philly. In the Eastern Division Championship, Philly's Wilt Chamberlain, Chet Walker, Billy Cunningham, and Hal Greer defeated the Celts 4–1.

Keeping his hand firmly off of the panic button, Red Auerbach essentially handed Russell the same team that had just come up short for the first time in the decade. K.C. Jones retired, and the club added first draft choice Mal Graham, who later became one of the most respected and beloved judges in Massachusetts, one day ascending to the Court of Appeals. Surprisingly, the club won a championship that year, as Russell got his sea legs as head coach and learned how to get his mates to listen to him.

The title in 1967–1968 appeared to be the Celtics' last hurrah. Sam Jones announced his decision to retire at the conclusion of 1968–1969, and privately Bill Russell resolved to do the same. The club sank to 48–34, fourth in the Eastern Division, actually losing six more games than the season before and dropping two more positions in the final standings. Two unappreciated developments had occurred, though, as Auerbach added guard Emmette Bryant to the team, and Larry Siegfried and Satch Sanders picked up some of the scoring slack. More important, the team had not overextended itself and still had some gas in their tanks for the playoffs.

Fortunately, in 1969 a team only had to defeat three opponents to earn a championship, and even though Philadelphia had finished higher in the standings than Boston, it no longer had Wilt Chamberlain on its roster, relying on the firepower of its core of guards and small forwards, Billy Cunningham, Hal Greer, Archie Clark, Wali Jones, and Chet Walker. It had no one suitable to post up against Russell, and the Celtics won the series 4–1.

Interestingly enough, the Celtics had prevailed as underdogs over Philly despite some rather sloppy play, particularly in the final two games of the series. In the fourth contest, the Sixers won despite being outshot by almost two dozen Celtics attempts. Similarly, in the fifth and last game, Boston had a dreadful first half but still managed to prevail 93–90 because they had superior talent and, as Bill Russell pointed out, Em Bryant made a critical free throw, rebound, and steal late to stave off defeat.

Next, the Celts had to defeat the New York Knicks for the Eastern Division Championship. The Knicks had finished only one place above Boston in the regular-season standings, but were rightly viewed as the team of the future with Willis Reed, Dave DeBusschere, Bill Bradley, Walt Frazier, and Dick Barnett. They had swept past the Bullets in their semifinal series.

New York dug a deep hole for itself, though, losing the first two games. Willis Reed candidly admitted, "As it turned out, we were intimidated by Bill [Russell]." The Knicks won the third in Madison Square Garden as Bill Bradley shut down Havlicek, but in a very smoky Boston Garden, the Celtics eked out a 97–96 victory to lead the series 3–1. New York won the fifth game, though Walt Frazier, too, tipped his hat to the Celtics' player/coach, affirming that "Bill Russell…he's the star of the show." The Knicks almost defeated the Celtics in Game 6 at the Boston Garden (with a seventh game at Madison Square Garden looming), but Walt

Frazier pulled his groin during the game, and again Boston escaped narrowly, 106–105, as Boston proceeded to the Finals against Los Angeles.

Certainly, this was the year for the Lakers to finally defeat Boston for the championship, and this outcome appeared assured as L.A. won the first two games. And then Larry Siegfried came alive and led the Celts to victories in the next two games, although in Game 4, it took an off-balance shot by Sam Jones from 17 feet out to seal the narrow 89–88 victory.

L.A. won the fifth with the Celtics prevailing in Game 6 behind Don Nelson's 25 points. Sam Jones enjoyed sustained applause at the Boston Garden, as his fans recognized him in this, his last game played at home before his retirement. In the deciding Game 7 in Los Angeles, Jones demonstrated how much more he had to contribute by scoring 24 points, just behind Havlicek's 26 points, as the Celts won their 11th title. After the game, the Celtics returned home to their first-ever ticker-tape parade.

Bill Sharman

Born and raised in New York, Bob Cousy has long since become a New Englander, ever since his starring at Holy Cross in the 1940s. He not only played for the Celtics but opened up a business in his adopted home of Worcester, where he has resided since. He remains in fans' consciousness because he has broadcast Celtics games well into the new millennium and his ball-handling and passing magic is still displayed on Jumbotrons and television sets (primarily for commercials or trailers). Even younger Celtics fans who never saw him play at the Garden usually know of the Cousy legend. Although he retired as a Celtic in 1963 (he made a brief comeback as a player/coach with the Royals), there remains a freshness about him and his game that every fan can appreciate.

Contrast this with his partner in the backcourt, Bill Sharman, a Californian who returned to the Left Coast after retiring in 1961, and in a later incarnation coached the Los Angeles Lakers for five years, once bringing them a championship. Relatively few fans remember him either because they never saw him play or even if they have viewed old footage of the team, they probably did not notice him. Most people focus on the Cooz, and Sharman did not possess the same ball-handling skill that still translates today. Worse yet, when he shot the ball, he did it with a one-handed set shot, a growing anomaly even in his day.

In 1948 legendary basketball coach Clair Bee had already begun writing his *Chip Hilton* series of sports books, a modernized adaptation of the Frank Merriwell model of the perfect young American sportsman and gentleman. Few athletes have ever approximated the Hilton/Merriwell ideal, but Sharman may have come closest. Probably no Celtics player ever had as much natural athletic ability in so many different sports as Bill Sharman did. When one considers the number of players who played on championship teams in Boston or played two professional sports to some extent, this is a bold statement, but an accurate one.

Folklore has it that in high school Sharman started out one day competing in a tennis match, then went to a track meet where he won the javelin and shot put events and placed in the hurdles. After polishing off these appetizers, he cleaned his plate that evening by starting in a baseball game. This might not sound so unusual today with the plethora of youth travel teams and AAU opportunities, but back then few operated on such a schedule. In his senior year of high school, he lettered in five sports: tennis, football, basketball, track, and baseball, doubling up some seasons.

After graduation, Sharman entered into the naval service during World War II, serving mainly in Shanghai, China. Before he

The sportswriter to the right is Colonel Dave Egan, a columnist who possessed an almost bottomless reservoir of disdain for the Sox's Ted Williams. Here, he seems to radiate nothing but respect for Celtics guard Bill Sharman.

began his tour of duty, just one week after graduation, he won the Central California tennis tournament and married his girlfriend. Surprisingly, in all of the articles written about Bill Sharman, it is never pointed out that neither the Japanese Empire nor the Red Chinese insurgents captured Shanghai during his watch.

Post-service, he pursued basketball at the University of Southern California, earning All-America honors and selection as conference Most Valuable Player his final two years. Despite his success on the court, he continued to excel in baseball, and as professional baseball beckoned, he signed with the Brooklyn Dodgers farm system. In 1951 he was called up to the majors but never got into a game, as the Dodgers collapsed after posting a 13½-game lead over the New York Giants late that summer. Sharman sat helplessly in the dugout when Bobby Thomson hit the "Shot Heard 'Round the World," the home run that clinched the pennant for New York, concluding a three-game playoff. Although he never played, Sharman did enrage an umpire enough during one game to merit an ejection along with several of his teammates.

Although baseball vied for Sharman's affections, he led the NBA's Washington Capitols in scoring under coach Bones McKinney in 1950–1951. He became a Celtic before his sophomore season in the league after a convoluted set of circumstances played out, commencing with the Fort Wayne Pistons gaining his rights once the Capitals ceased to exist. The Pistons received center Charlie Share from the Celtics in exchange for him; since Sharman also played for the Brooklyn Dodgers chain, the brain trust in Fort Wayne may have thought that he had no intention of playing basketball and meant to dedicate himself full-time to his first love, baseball. Craftily, Red Auerbach did nothing to disabuse them of this belief, probably in part because even Red did not know exactly what Sharman intended to do.

To their credit, when Fort Wayne's management felt that Sharman might have divided loyalties, they were right. Unfortunately for Sharman, the Dodgers kept him in the minors as the team finally thrived in those precious last years in Brooklyn. Since the Dodgers had not made a solid commitment to Sharman to keep him in the major leagues and play him, he eventually dedicated himself to his role as a shooting guard with the Celtics.

He did not merely start, he excelled, participating in eight All-Star Games and, even more important from the Celtics' perspective, helping to lead them to four championships after Bill Russell came aboard. In his relatively short career, he posted top 10 finishes in average points per game in seven seasons and in field-goal percentage six times.

Do not look for Sharman's name on any all-time shooting percentage lists, though, as he played in conditions adverse to such statistics. The rims and backboards were inferior, and without a 24-second clock for part of his career, offenses lagged league-wide. His shooting skills from the field, in comparison to his peers, provide better perspective.

To better gauge Sharman's excellence, review his performance in free-throw shooting, an area in which he surpassed almost anyone who ever played in the NBA. His .883 percentage still ranks 11th best all-time, and he paced the NBA in this category on seven occasions. If one accepts that shooting percentages must be adjusted up or at least better understood in some way to account for the type of equipment available to ballplayers at that time, Bill Sharman might be the greatest free-throw shooter ever.

As skilled a shooter as Bill Sharman was, he might have been a better fighter. A generally very mild-mannered man, he used his natural athletic ability on a number of occasions to pugilistically vanquish a foe, a fact about which he was never proud, but which he knew he earned. Particularly since his bread-and-butter was the one-handed set shot, he tolerated no excessive contact from the opposition, explaining, "You have to show them you're not going to let them push you out of the league." The Lakers' Jerry West once said, "Bill was tough. I'll tell you this, you did not drive by him. He got into more fights than Mike Tyson." In one famous fight, Richie Guerin broke his thumb after a mêlée with the gentlemanly Sharman. Gentleman Jim Corbett is more like it.

Due to some time lost to military service, Sharman got a late start in basketball so that by the end of 1961, even though he had only played 11 years, he retired rather than start the next season as a 35-year-old guard. The much younger Sam Jones had spelled him for four years and, by the end of his apprenticeship, deserved the starting position more.

Given the intense rivalry between the Lakers and Celtics, it is not surprising that the two dominant NBA franchises have shared few players, for much the same reason that in baseball, the Red Sox and Yankees rarely swap players. Although he never laced up for L.A., Bill Sharman did join them as a coach several years after retiring (with broadcasting and other coaching stints in the interim).

Following his own regimen of preparation as a player, he instituted the game-day shootaround, which even a laconic player like Wilt Chamberlain reluctantly bought into. At his most successful, Sharman guided the Lakers one year to a 33-game winning streak en route to a title. He later served as the club's general manager and then president during the 1980s, when, under his supervision, the Lakers won five more championships. Even though he served only as an administrator, he was not above showing then-superstar guard Earvin Johnson a thing or two, once beating Magic in a free-throw shooting contest, netting 28 out of 30 (Johnson made 23 of his attempts). Sharman was 54 years old at the time.

The Celtics retired his number, and the Basketball Hall of Fame inducted him as a player and a coach, one of only three people so honored. Curiously, though, the Hall did not select him for his ballplaying until 1976, underscoring that despite his excellence and his continued contribution to one of the other leading franchises as a coach and front-office man, he was forgotten too soon.

Dollars and Defense

In 1965–1966 the 76ers seemingly had become the dominant team in the league. Led by Wilt Chamberlain, Chet Walker, Hal Greer, and Billy Cunningham, they had edged out the Celtics in the regular-season division standings by one game. Yet, in the playoffs, the Celtics defeated them in five games, setting the stage for another Finals series between Boston and L.A.

In their classic seven-game series in 1962, L.A. largely relied on the performances of their two superstars, Elgin Baylor and Jerry West. Four years later, they still remained with the club but had been joined by some very good players—Gail Goodrich and Walt Hazzard at guard and Bob Boozer at forward. They had closed the depth gap with the Celtics.

In that interim, Bob Cousy, Tom Heinsohn, and Frank Ramsey had retired, but newcomers Havlicek, Larry Siegfried, and Don Nelson had helped fill the breach, with Mel Counts and John Thompson spelling Russell at center. Russell still played too many minutes per game. The team had even added Sihugo Green, the first draft choice of the Rochester Royals in the year the Celtics drafted Tom Heinsohn and Bill Russell.

The minutes had added up on Russell, who considered retirement, and even though Red Auerbach had won seven straight championships going into the season, he had begun to burn out and ceased coaching at the campaign's end. The Celtics were not a team in transition, because strictly speaking every year they changed and luckily added stars to replace departing ones, but Red certainly did not want to lose his last game.

He thought his team had won it in the fifth game of the series, only to witness a nine-point lead blown. His starters largely looked like a recreation of the Revolutionary War–inspired painting, *Spirit of '76*, as John Havlicek came out on the floor for the national anthem with fellow starters Russell, Satch Sanders, Sam Jones, and K.C. Jones with bandages all over their respective knees, ankles, and thighs.

Bad officiating worked against the team in the end, as Red Auerbach had his head in his hands during and after the game. Two of the referees were attacked afterward by irate fans, and speaking to the press after the game, Red did not even attempt to masquerade his sense of deep frustration. After questioning the officials, admittedly a favorite pastime of his, he barked at a reporter holding a tape recorder, "Please turn that thing off. Don't do that unless you let me know first."

Energized, the Lakers won the sixth game at home, with the deciding game in the Boston Garden on April 28.

In his pregame pep talk, Red gave his best Knute Rockne rendition, his last ever as a coach, emphasizing repeatedly the mantra of "dollars and defense." If the Celtics stuck to their dynasty-long devotion to defense, they could beat the Lakers and earn the big money set aside for them as their championship share.

The defense performed superbly early, holding the Lakers scoreless for the first four minutes as West, Baylor, and Goodrich drew defenders as soon as they touched the ball. Boston led by seven at the conclusion of the first quarter and by 15 at the half. The Lakers' three most effective scorers accounted for only a collective 13 points as the teams walked to the dressing rooms.

Even though L.A. played better ball in the second half, they trailed by 10 points with 45 seconds left to play in the game. Then, seemingly, the Garden roof began to cave in.

With fans lining the court and Auerbach smoking his cigar, the Celts coughed up the ball and Russell got stuffed. Then K.C. Jones committed an offensive foul trying to beat the 10-second clock to half-court and Sam Jones had a pass stolen followed by another L.A. basket, and the Celtics led by only two.

It all came down to the inbound pass, and this time, the Celtics held with K.C. Jones heaving the ball over the center stripe to Havlicek, at which point the old buzzer went off, and the Celtics had won their eighth straight championship, and ninth overall, by a 95–93 tally.

Panic broke out on the floor as young fans lifted themselves onto the hoops and others ran after Red Auerbach and their favorite players. The Celtics had nearly blown it, but the Lakers did not fully capitalize on the mistakes, plus their offense woke up too late to make the difference.

In their locker room, Auerbach kissed the game ball and jumped on a bench next to Russell to yell, "You are the greatest!" A photographer asked Russell to kiss Red, but the center demurred, saying, "Red and I may be close, but we're not funny." For his part, Auerbach dropped an ash from his cigar onto Bill Russell's head.

Given an opportunity to review the remarkable run by his teams and their latest triumph, Red maintained, "This team was the shortest on ability, but the longest on heart of all the championship teams."

Oddly enough, as future Finals stretched into June, and complaints arose about the Garden resembling a sauna with close to 100-degree temperatures, most of the gripes this time centered around the old arena being too cold. Asked about this, Jerry West deadpanned that it only seemed chilly "when I shot the basketball." Both teams played in the same temperature, only Boston played better defense. It had to because L.A. had the better guns; but once again, Boston had the better team.

Defense had accounted for another title for Boston, and now each player lined up for his winners' share, a whopping $800 per man.

Unlike many Celtics stars, who gravitated to basketball as youngsters and shot baskets for an obscene amount of hours in their free time, Robert Parish had little interest in the sport, later confessing, "I really didn't like basketball growing up, but I was able to make a career out of it." One junior high teacher had to beat the love of the game into Parish, literally, if the story is accurate, at which point the young native of Shreveport, Louisiana, began to participate and quietly work on his game.

Though his prowess on the court continued to grow into his high school years, his grades kept most Division I programs away, with tiny Centenary taking a shot at him, an act that swiftly brought the wrath of the NCAA down on the college. In spite of the controversy that surrounded the recruitment and retention of Parish, he earned his degree and was chosen as the eighth overall pick in the 1976 draft by Golden State.

Strangely, the Warriors seemed perplexed concerning what they had in Parish during his four seasons with the franchise. He blocked shots and rebounded well and had a decent scoring touch, but never seemed to fit in. He detested resident star Rick Barry for his perceived arrogance, but disliking Barry did not necessarily disqualify anyone in the NBA. League-wide he also failed to build up much respect, never making an All-Star team as a Warrior, so his team began to shop him around.

Robert Parish came to Boston along with Kevin McHale in the providential "Joe Barry Carroll" trade with Golden State, having already amassed some impressive statistics in his first four seasons. In Boston, he began accumulating titles and acquired the nickname of "the Chief" because he reminded Cedric Maxwell of the Chief in *One Flew Over the Cuckoo's Nest,* and one Boston scribe compared Parish's gaze to that of a cigar-store Indian.

Although Cedric Maxwell initially started at forward over McHale, the Big Three nucleus of Bird, McHale, and Parish had begun to jell. By 1981 Parish had made the first of nine All-Star appearances, as he played within himself, content to facilitate McHale in the low post and Bird along the perimeter. By 1985–1986 he had entered the top 10 in the NBA for field-goal percentage with his beautiful rainbow jumper, a feat he achieved for five straight years after that. To this day Parish sits within the top

It's too late, Kareem, Robert Parish has already beaten you. They did not call him "the Chief" for nothing.

25 all-time for shooting percentage of NBA/ABA players, a tribute to his ability to not simply jam in shots. More elegiacally, Bill Walton, in assessing Parish's scoring touch, opined, "He's probably the best medium-range shooting big man in the history of the game."

His growth as a player and the team titles did not translate into an accelerated respect for his game, as Parish often picked up some votes for league MVP consideration, but never seriously challenged for that award and only finished once in the second-team All-NBA and once on the mythical third-team. This, despite compiling 10 years of averaging double figures in points and rebounds and also exhibiting unusual dexterity for a big man in stealing quite a few balls from opponents.

Although he did not generally get into fights with opposing players, he saved his best for the Pistons' Bill Laimbeer in a classic confrontation in Game 5 of the 1987 Eastern Conference Finals. The Pistons had largely eschewed finesse for intimidation, and they drove Johnny Most and most Celtics fans crazy, but Boston had some pretty intense players of their own, the Chief among them. When angered, the Chief looked like he could unscrew someone's head like the top of a can of stewed tomatoes, and for his attack on Laimbeer he incurred a fine and a one-game suspension, although strangely enough, he did not draw a foul.

The Celtics let him walk after the 1993–1994 season, the same year he became a grandfather, but he played two years thereafter for the Hornets and then spent his final season with the Bulls, earning a last championship ring. He retired with the most games played in NBA history, together with second place in total offensive and defensive rebounds. The Celtics retired his No. 00, and he walked into the Hall of Fame in 2003.

22 Greatest Game in NBA History

Logically, there never should have been a Suns-Celtics Finals at the end of the 1975–1976 season. The Celtics had posted the best record in the East, but in the West the defending NBA-champion Warriors had cruised behind Rick Barry, Jamaal Wilkes, and Phil Smith with a league-best 59–23 record. While the Warriors had finished 16 games ahead of the Supersonics and 17 games ahead of the Phoenix Suns in their division, the Suns turned the tables on the defending champs in the playoffs, earning their spot in the Finals against Boston.

The Celtics alloyed youth and experience on their roster, led by center Dave Cowens, guards Jo Jo White and Charlie Scott, forwards Don Nelson and Paul Silas, and swingman John Havlicek. The Suns had a spottier roster, with former Celtic Paul Westphal at guard and Rookie of the Year Alvan Adams at center as their top offensive threats, utilizing wounded veteran Keith Erickson primarily on defense. The Suns appeared hopelessly outmatched.

The teams played to script in the first two games at the Boston Garden, with the Celtics winning both contests as most everyone expected. But then back in Phoenix, the Suns won a rather chippy third game and then a more sedate but no less shocking fourth game by two points. The series had inexplicably evened out as the two clubs headed east for the fifth game at the Garden on Friday, June 4, 1976.

With thousands of New England high schoolers deciding whether to turn in early to bed for their SATs the next day, the two teams warmed up on the Garden parquet. The commentators and network analysts diverted the attention of both teams: Brent Musburger dressed appropriately, but his color commentator, Rick Barry, went for pornstar chic with an open shirt and huge crucifix on his chest, while Mendy Rudolph's suit looked like a picnic tablecloth.

Eschewing their own garish uniforms of the past (and sadly, the future), the Suns looked great in their blue uniforms with red-and-white lettering, but did not play as well as they appeared. Across New England, it looked like most concerned future collegians might safely turn in early for bed, knowing that the Celtics jumped out to a 36–18 lead in the first period as Cowens' backup Jim Ard sank a jumper to beat the buzzer. His squad played so well that coach Tommy Heinsohn could spell Cowens with Ard and otherwise keep his starters fresh. The only negative lay in Charlie Scott ringing up three quick fouls, but that seemed inconsequential at the time, given the healthy lead at home.

The Suns came out racing to start the second period, and for a while they had the Celtics on the ropes, closing the gap to seven points. The Celtics' own fast break appeared frantic as Chaney rang up his fourth foul and Silas his third, but the Suns were also committing enough fouls to force coach John MacLeod to sit out his star, Westphal. The Celts stabilized, largely due to the contributions of Jo Jo White. Don Nelson, sinking two free throws and looking like he was shooting a shot put, closed out the scoring for the half, as the Celtics regained momentum, holding a 61–45 lead.

To this point, the Celtics had held off the Suns en route to an apparent blowout. Unfortunately for Boston, in the third quarter their shooters went cold as Phoenix closed the gap and, at one juncture, knotted the score. The Celtics tightened up their offense, restoring the lead at the end of the third to 77–72, but the fans had grown quiet, as it seemed a real game was afoot.

And yet, it was still the Celtics against the lowly Suns in the Garden, and for most of the fourth period, Phoenix struggled until Westphal resuscitated them with some timely shooting. Still, the Suns trailed by five points with less than a minute to play. And then Westphal scored on a turnaround jump shot, double-covered the whole time. Bringing it down the floor, Charlie Scott let Paul Westphal get a hand in, batting the ball away to Adams, who then heaved it down to Westphal on the fast break. Westphal had a clear layup, which he scored with Jo Jo White conceding it. But Charlie Scott made contact and fouled out. Westphal then sank the free throw to tie it. After Jo Jo White missed a jumper, Cowens was called for a cheap rebounding foul against Curtis Perry. Perry converted the first free throw to put Phoenix ahead by one but clanged the second.

Behind by one point now with 22 seconds left, the Celts inbounded at halfcourt with Havlicek getting the ball in crunch time. Adams slapped Hondo, fouling out in the process. Havlicek sank the first free throw to tie it, missed the second, but the Celtics came up with the rebound. Unfortunately, Havlicek then took a bad shot with too much time left, and Phoenix got the ball back with three seconds remaining in regulation (it should have been five seconds when time was actually called by Phoenix, but this is Boston).

On the inbound Gar Heard heaved it in, but Cowens intercepted with one second left, at which time Paul Silas called timeout. But Boston had no more timeouts left, meaning a technical foul should have been called, with Phoenix putting their best shooter on the line to win the game. But the timeout request was either not seen or ignored (referee Richie Powers looked at Silas as if the Celts' forward were the invisible man), and time ran out with the game going into overtime, 95–95.

In OT Westphal collided with Cowens, temporarily injuring the Suns' star and forcing him to sit. The Celts took advantage of his absence, but when he returned to the game, the gap closed. With the score tied at 101, Phoenix inbounded it with 29 seconds left, and Dennis Awtrey, Adams' replacement, was fouled. No big deal on one hand, the Celts had one to give, but Phoenix could now play for the last shot. Oddly, they did not, and when their shot missed, Silas rebounded it with three seconds left and promptly called timeout. Nelson then inbounded to Havlicek, who shot from the corner, a clear shot after he faked out defender Heard, but the ball missed as Don Nelson vainly ran through the baseline to tap it in. Double overtime.

When play resumed, Cowens and Suns backup center Awtrey fouled out, but Jo Jo White, who was shooting lights out in the clutch, later sank a basket to make it 109–106. Phoenix scored on their possession, but Boston seemed prepared to kill the clock until they inbounded, and Westphal scooted in and stole the ball. Hanging on the sideline, he swatted it in, and although the Suns did not score at first, they eventually sank their shot and led 110–109.

The Celtics had one chance, and with five seconds remaining, Havlicek heaved the ball, looking as if he would fall over forward in

Greatest Thing Anybody Ever Saw

Skeptical that the Celts-Suns playoff game was the greatest ever? Go no further for contrary evidence than the quadruple-overtime playoff game between Boston and the Syracuse Nationals on March 21, 1953. Bob Cousy scored 50 points, half of them after regulation, including a 30-for-32 performance from the charity stripe. Celtics enforcer Bob Brannum got into a huge scrape with the Nationals' star, Dolph Schayes, a donnybrook that escalated to such an extent that Boston police and Garden ushers had to help break it up. The referees called an astounding 106 fouls during the contest, as 14 of the 20 players were ejected (refs had to allow some of them back in the game in order to give each team five players). At the end, *Globe* columnist Jack Barry noted that Red Auerbach "nearly lighted his nose instead of a cigar." Commenting on the performance of his star guard, Auerbach gushed, "Cousy, you ask? Don't get me started. I could go all night on what that kid did. He's only the best." With a new stitch or two over his face, instigator Bob Brannum grinned and observed, "Greatest thing anybody ever saw."

the process, and his shot swished in. Pandemonium broke out in the Garden, as Celtics players ran roughshod for the exit and the relative safety of the locker room to celebrate their narrow victory while the fans carpeted the parquet.

Problem was, once the shot had gone in, there was still time remaining on the clock, a point made by referee Richie Powers, who held up two fingers, signifying his belief that the game had not ended and two seconds remained in overtime. An irate fan pummelled Powers, but the game had clearly not yet ended, so slowly the fans returned to their seats, and the players trudged back to their benches.

Out of timeouts, Paul Westphal called time for Phoenix anyway to incur a technical foul in order to get the inbound pass at half-court. (This would never happen again in the NBA; the rule was changed in the off-season.) As he had done all night, Jo Jo White sank the T, giving the Celtics a two-point lead, but now Phoenix had the inbound. Unbelievably, Phoenix's Gar Heard took the inbound pass, turned around, and drained the shot just before time expired. Triple overtime: 112–112.

At 3:23, Paul Silas fouled out, a seeming catastrophe, but a blessing as reserve Glenn McDonald entered the game and Celtics lore. He proceeded to score six points in the third overtime and made a key rebound. While the Suns' starting and backup centers sat with six fouls, Dave Cowens' replacement, Jim Ard, converted two crucial free throws to pull his team ahead 128–122. Paul Westphal almost spoiled the anticipated party by making two baskets to pull the Suns to within two points, but on the last inbound, Jo Jo White dribbled the remaining time off the clock to finally win the game for the Celtics. Fittingly enough, he was the last player touching the ball as he had carried his team to the win and the series lead with his 33 points and constant presence on the court.

Phoenix Suns coach John MacLeod admitted after the game that he had "never been in a game like this in all my years of coaching. It was great, great basketball." Jo Jo White had the final word: "No two teams ever shot so well in overtime. That's the kind of game that you'd like to have to end a series. The funny thing is that we've got another one to play Sunday." There was the matter of that final game, but juxtaposed with Game 5, it paled, as the Celtics marched away with the victory and the championship.

23 Rivals and Rivalries

Think of the Boston Celtics' greatest rival, and the Los Angeles Lakers reflexively come to mind, not a bad impulse since the two clubs have faced each other in 12 NBA Finals (including the Minneapolis Lakers in 1959), with Boston losing the most recent series in 2010 but still owning a 9–3 series advantage.

Historically, though, Boston's first two rivalries involved the St. Louis Hawks and the Syracuse Nationals, two defunct franchises. The Hawks became the Celtics' nemesis largely due to the trade that brought Bill Russell to Boston at the expense of future Hall of Famers Ed Macauley and Cliff Hagan. Mainly, though, the Hawks prospered because they had Bob Pettit at forward, a great leader and scorer. Boston won the championship during the 1956–1957 season, with St. Louis turning the tables the next year. Thereafter, the teams met again in the Finals two more times, with Boston prevailing. St. Louis had Pettit and some very good complementary players, but the Celtics always had a bit more depth, and they had Bill Russell. After 1961 the Hawks did not pose much of a challenge to Boston again until the club moved to Atlanta and fielded Dominique Wilkins.

The Syracuse Nationals became the Celtics' rivals more because the Eastern Division championship hinged mainly on who defeated the other. Plus violence. The two teams just never seemed to get along, and an enforcer like Jim Loscutoff served a useful purpose in protecting his teammates and intimidating the opposition. The Nationals answered in kind until the team moved, metamorphosing into the Philadelphia 76ers after the conclusion of the 1962–1963 campaign.

Philadelphia became a huge rival to Boston in the 1960s, as their center, Wilt Chamberlain, squared off against Bill Russell. Wilt also had a very strong supporting cast, with Hall of Fame players such as Hal Greer and Billy Cunningham, and other top talents such as Chet Walker. Again the Celtics dominated the rivalry, although Philly did win the championship in 1966–1967, Bill Russell's first year as a player/coach. But Russell did not repeat that mistake, and the rivalry petered out a bit after Chamberlain became a Laker. It did revive during the early 1980s, with Julius Erving, Andrew Toney, and Bobby Jones battling the early Bird-era Celtics, a rivalry that oddly one day simply seemed to die.

Spiritually, though, the 76ers' rivalry generally did not match the intensity of the Boston-Syracuse rivalry; that ill feeling did not manifest itself to that degree until the Detroit Pistons battled the Celtics in the 1980s. Joe Dumars was a decent guy, but Detroit thrived at that time on their "Bad Boys" image, with center Bill Laimbeer chipping away at opponents in each game and Isiah Thomas and Dennis Rodman driving everybody crazy.

Most Celtics fans continue to view opposing players like the late Johnny Most did, as the enemy. Occasionally, a grudging respect emerges for certain players, sort of like how Red Sox fans think the Yankees (stink) but admire Derek Jeter and secretly wish he had played his whole career at Fenway. Many Celtics' opponents fit this bill.

It is hard not to respect Magic Johnson, a guard who once led his Lakers in the playoffs as a center. He did not cheap-shot the Celtics, and after he and Bird filmed a commercial together in the mid-1980s, he became a lifelong friend of Larry Legend. When the club retired Bird's number, Magic showed up for the event and thrilled all by donning a Celtics jersey. The Lakers' Jerry West and Elgin Baylor were honorable opponents, as was former Lakers coach and front-office figure, Bill Sharman, himself a Hall of Famer with the Celtics.

The fans both inside and outside of the Madison Square Garden abused the Celtics terribly, perhaps worse than any other city's faithful, but most fans in the real Garden would have loved to see Knicks stars Reed, Frazier, DeBusschere, Bradley, Monroe, and Barnett in green. Not to mention Patrick Ewing, who grew up across the Charles River in Cambridge.

Few if any of the post-Pettit Hawks qualify, although Dominique Wilkins performed magnificently during his notori-ously epic battle against Larry Bird in Game 7 of the 1988 Eastern semis. By the time the Celts signed him, he had largely lost his game on his way out as a free agent for a number of teams—

Panathinaikos, San Antonio, Bologna, and Orlando. For most Celtics fans who saw 'Nique in his year in Boston, it was a case of "be careful what you wish for."

24 Havlicek Stole the Ball!... Then Henderson, Then Bird

It's the Eastern Conference Finals on April 15, 1965, at Boston, and the Philadelphia 76ers of Wilt Chamberlain, Hal Greer, Luke Jackson, and Chet Walker have the ball. The Celtics lead 110–109 and had seemingly iced the game just a moment ago when they had possession, but when center Bill Russell inbounded, the ball hit a support wire, causing possession to revert to Philadelphia.

In the huddle, Russell intones, "We've got to do something."

All Philly has to do is successfully inbound the ball, set up their play and score a field goal with little time left, and they advance to the Finals against the Los Angeles Lakers.

As Johnny Most called it: "Greer is putting the ball into play. He gets it out deep...Havlicek steals it. Over to Sam Jones. Havlicek stole the ball! It's all over! Johnny Havlicek stole the ball!"

The call remains a classic today, with Most's gravelly voice cutting through the smoke of the old Boston Garden. The quality of the film is not good, a grainy black-and-white that looked as if it might have been produced circa the crowning of Charlemagne as Holy Roman Emperor.

Leading up to this most famous play, the Celtics had an advantage, knowing that the great Wilt Chamberlain did not want the ball in his hands at crunch time. If he got fouled, he had a notoriously poor touch at the line, but even worse, he simply did not possess the killer instinct required to want it in that situation and have the outcome of the game revolve around him. This, despite the fact that he had just single-handedly reeled off six unanswered points to bring his team to within one of tying it.

After Havlicek swatted the ball to Sam Jones, Jones dribbled it down the court, guarding it, until he passed to Havlicek, who shot the ball up. The game had ended and fans had begun to flock onto the parquet, with some fans lifting up Havlicek on their shoulders. As the ball fell, an alert young fan ran straight over to the ball, rebounded it, and ran it off the court, against the grain of fans running over to Havlicek.

A couple notes on the series: even though the 76ers had a number of very talented players, they only managed a very mediocre 40–40 record during the regular season (the Celtics posted a 62–18 record). The Celtics went on to the Finals and won their seventh consecutive championship, quite convincingly, 4–1 over a talented Lakers team.

Nineteen years later, another famous steal saved the Celtics. The club had already lost the first game of the 1984 Finals at the Garden against the Los Angeles Lakers, and Game 2 looked similarly perilous. Lose the first two at home, and the series would be extraordinarily hard to win, as the next two games would then go out to L.A. With 18 seconds left and L.A. set to inbound the ball guarding a 113–111 lead, the fans anxiously hoped for a small miracle.

They got it. James Worthy inbounded it to Magic Johnson successfully, and once Worthy came onto the court, Magic returned the ball to him. So far so good. Then Worthy passed the ball to Byron Scott at the other side of the court, and in scooted Gerald Henderson for the steal. Henderson layed it up as Johnny Most screamed, "And it's picked off…*goes to Henderson, and he lays it in!*" Henderson himself swore afterward that he could hear Most blare out, "Henderson steals the ball!"

Like the more famous steal by John Havlicek in 1965, Henderson bailed out a fellow teammate, this time Kevin McHale,

Gerald Henderson made one of the greatest thefts in NBA history, but the club later rewarded him with a trade out of town.

who had just missed two free throws. The Celtics won in overtime, and though it took them seven games to do it, they won the series and the championship.

Whatever happened to Gerald Henderson? He got into a salary dispute with Red Auerbach in the off-season, which prompted his trade to the Seattle Supersonics for a first-round draft choice in 1986. The club used the pick to draft Len Bias from Maryland. Although Henderson had his highest season scoring totals the next two years and remained in the NBA until early 1992, he tailed off considerably a few years after the trade. Danny Ainge replaced Henderson with the Celtics.

Many of the same players were adorned in the Celtics green when the third famous steal occurred. In Game 5 of the Eastern Finals on May 26, 1987, the Celtics were behind by one point with five seconds remaining in their series against the "winning ugly" Detroit Pistons. The teams had already split the first four games, and it appeared likely the Pistons would soon lead the series 3–2, with their guard Isiah Thomas inbounding. He had an open man, Bill Laimbeer, under his own net with Larry Bird in the perimeter guarding another Piston.

Intuitively, Bird began gravitating toward Laimbeer, as Chuck Daly began furiously yelling, admitting afterward, "I was trying to get Isiah to call timeout." A timeout made perfect sense—they could reset at halfcourt—but the call went unheard and unheeded. Thomas then lofted the ball under the net toward Laimbeer. Bird anticipated the play and ran in with the initial intent to foul the Pistons' center, but then seized an opportunity to steal the pass. Teetering on the foul line, he spied Dennis Johnson running into the paint and threw him the ball for the open layup.

Of course, Johnny Most went berserk but again, so did all of the Celtics fans at the game or watching the game on television or hearing the play unfold on the radio. After the game, Thomas reasoned, "You can look back and say any number of things. You can say I should have called timeout." For his part, Bird sort of let Thomas off the hook, opining, "The ball just hung up there. It seemed to take forever to get to Laimbeer....It was a lucky play."

In order to reach the Finals, the Celts had to win a seventh and deciding game, which they did, but unlike the past memorable steals by Havlicek and Henderson, a championship did not await the team at the end of the season. A banged-up Celtics squad faced the Lakers in the Finals and lost to L.A. in six.

Another odd factor somewhat obscured the Bird steal. Having lost the seventh game, the Pistons' Dennis Rodman and Isiah Thomas mused on the relative merits of Larry Bird, with Thomas stating, "Larry Bird is a very good player. An exceptional talent....But...if he were black, he'd be just another good guy." Not only did the comment come off as the sourest of grapes, it brought to the surface an ugly misconception that, because Bird was white, too many people had overrated him.

Thomas had to later give a press conference to sort of apologize, at which time Bird appeared graciously to bail him out.

The steal? Thomas had been outsmarted by the better guy.

Havlicek Stole the Ball, Schlaf Lost It

We all know that Havlicek stole the ball, but what happened to the ball afterward? As time ran out, the ball was heaved toward the basket as fans rushed the floor to lift Havlicek onto their shoulders. Naturally, that was where the focus was properly directed. But if you look closely, a young man ran after the ball, rebounded it, and ran out of the building. The identity of the young fan? Future ABA and NBA referee Mark Schlafman. Where is the ball today? It is not known. "Schlaf" gave the ball to a cousin in 1975 and cannot vouch for its current location.

25 Sam Jones

Red Auerbach never had a sophisticated scouting combine or system in place for judging collegiate talent during his coaching tenure, so to a considerable extent, he relied on the recommendations of people he knew and trusted in this evaluative area. One of the friends with whom he consulted was Bones McKinney, a former Celtic and later a coach himself at Wake Forest.

One day Red called up Bones, who was going to a ballgame featuring a highly touted college ballplayer: "Bones, there is a *schvartze* [Yiddish term for black] player that you are going to see next week, and I want you to tell me if he's any good." Bones agreed to serve as the scout, but when the game finally arrived, he had to tell Red that the prized player was a stiff, someone unlikely to fit into the Celtics' team concept.

He had, however, seen a player on the opposing team who he knew fit all of Red's criteria for a professional and passed on to Red the name of Sam Jones. Red wrote down the name on a scrap of paper, which promptly got lost in the maze of disorganization in the Boston coaches' office.

On draft day in 1957, people did not sit around with live cable feeds recording their historic selections of rookies; rather, the league phoned in the information for each team. When the time came for the Celtics to choose, Red Auerbach scrambled everywhere to find the piece of paper with Jones' name on it because he could not remember much else about him. He turned over stacks of paper and finally found the scrap that he had searched for in an increasingly panic-laced state. The league official asked him whom the Celtics had decided to choose, and acting all the while as if he had

had the information just ready to pop out for several months, Red barked, "The Celtics choose Sam Jones from North Carolina Central University." And that is how Sam Jones came to Boston.

Once described by sportswriter George Walsh as having "somewhat elongated features [that] recall the haunting sadness of a Modigliani portrait," Sam Jones had his moods, but never lost his shot. Starting out as a player who preferred to bank his shots off the backboard, he later perfected his scoring from all combinations. Early in his career, Jones watched aging guards Bob Cousy and Bill Sharman start, while he came off the bench. With his swiftness, he rejuvenated the team while giving the veterans their rest. Anywhere else in the NBA, he would have started, a fact that he seemed to appreciate even on the night he was drafted, admitting, "I was a little mad, a little glad." The Celtics instantly found a place for Sam on the team, mainly by playing Frank Ramsey more at forward, and then groomed him for his eventual starting role.

Interestingly, though, even after he and K.C. Jones served their apprenticeships waiting for guards Bill Sharman and Bob Cousy to retire, Sam never played all that many minutes. He topped off with an average of 36.1 minutes per game in 1964–1965, the only year he scored more than 2,000 points, an average of more than three minutes per game more than his next highest season. He optimized his time on the floor, placing in the top 10 in the NBA for points per game on four occasions, earning selection to five All-Star Games in his 12-year career. He also made good on a high percentage of his shots, again ending three seasons in the top 10 for field-goal shooting percentage and four times in free-throw percentage. Like most Celtics in the dynasty years, he also defended his opponents well.

Having played on numerous championship teams, he fittingly left the game after the 1969 Finals, just as the great dynasty ended. The Celtics retired his No. 24, and in 1984 he was inducted into the Basketball Hall of Fame.

26 Tommy Heinsohn

Many Celtics players have left Boston after a trade or once their careers ended, rarely if ever to return. Then some, like Bob Cousy and Tommy Heinsohn, seem as if they never left. Like the Cooz, Tommy Heinsohn played for the Holy Cross Crusaders in college, although a number of years separated the two. While Red Auerbach at first rejected Cousy, he overcame any trepidation in bringing a local collegian onto the team by making Heinsohn the club's territorial pick and starting him immediately in the 1956–1957 season.

To fully appreciate Tommy Heinsohn, he served with the Celtics in three distinct incarnations: the first, as a "gunning" forward with a crew cut; the second, as a championship-winning head coach with much longer hair and louder suits; and the third, as a television game announcer, perhaps as beloved by the fans as the late Johnny Most.

The crew-cut Heinsohn won Rookie of the Year in 1956–1957, averaging 16.2 points per game. Since Bill Russell also started his professional career the same season, this fact often trips up the casual NBA trivia fan, but Russ had other obligations to fulfill for the first part of that season. Heinsohn also played in the All-Star Game that year and starred in the seventh game of the championship, leading the Celtics to their first title ever.

Despite these honors, quite early Heinsohn's flaws emerged, leading a teammate to quip that Tommy "only shoots the ball when he has it." Alarmingly, he shot his field goals at less than a .400 clip in his first three seasons in the league, causing him to never play in another All-Star Game in the '50s. He also smoked and looked winded at times, causing Auerbach to get all over him in practices and games.

The banter between coach and player extended outside of the practice facility, with Auerbach playing pranks on his star forward at every possible opportunity. Heinsohn usually waited to get back at Red, but he always did even the ledger, usually with an exploding cigar.

On a technical level, in the '50s Heinsohn earned the reputation as an unreconstructed gunner, and yet the new decade brought a greater appreciation of what he brought to the court. His defense and rebounding skills improved, and with Sam Jones increasingly assuming scoring responsibilities, Heinsohn's shooting percentages improved.

Shocking to many, after the 1965 championship, having played in the past five All-Star Games (six total), Tommy Heinsohn retired at age 30. Many fans expressed surprise, but he foreshadowed his exit in a *Sports Illustrated* article the previous fall in which he spoke about the intense pain he felt due to the many knee and ankle injuries he had sustained in the past: "There comes that autumn morning when I throw that first leg out of bed and a shocking pain runs all the way up to my ears." Tommy Heinsohn turned his attention to a successful business career, and though he remained in Massachusetts, he never attempted a comeback.

The next phase of Tommy Heinsohn's association with the Celtics occurred after the 1969 championship season, when Bill Russell retired as player and head coach, causing general manager Red Auerbach to tab Heinsohn as the new head coach.

It was a thankless and futile task that first year: not only had Russell retired, but so too had shooting guard Sam Jones, and with other players aging, rather large gaps were exposed and exploited by rival NBA franchises. Further, while the Celtics did win the title in 1969, they only won 48 regular-season games, literally saving their best for the playoffs. During that first year as head coach, Heinsohn managed only a 34–48 record as the team missed the playoffs.

Matters improved rapidly afterward, as the Celtics drafted sagely, complementing existing veteran talent. By 1971–1972 Heinsohn and his men had begun to establish their team as the premier entrant in the Atlantic Division, winning NBA titles in 1974 and 1976.

Sadly for Heinsohn, there developed a popular opinion that the Celtics won despite him, not due to his great coaching skills. One of the most popular stories that circulated at the time concerned an incident where he kicked his leg up high, which caused one of his shoes to shoot loose and land in the stands. This and other tales and whispers contributed to the sense that the deckhands no longer listened to their captain. Yet the team kept winning under Heinsohn until Red Auerbach unwisely tinkered with the team chemistry and dealt Paul Silas away, bringing in Sidney Wicks and Curtis Rowe. After that, the team spiraled wildly and rapidly down, with Heinsohn fired during the 1977–1978 season. The termination accomplished little, and the club foundered until Larry Bird joined the team two years later. It turned out that Tommy Heinsohn coached very well.

Tommy's termination completed the second act of his tenure with the Celtics, but he had one more life left in him as a very popular television color commentator. The experience was not a new one for him, as he had announced games for the team between his previous playing career and the start of his coaching tenure, but back then broadcasts did not come to as many homes or nearly as often as they later would. When he started in 1981 with partner Mike Gorman, the NBA stood on the cusp of a huge increase in popularity, and Tommy's effusive personality and knowledge of the game dovetailed perfectly with the exciting era that lay ahead for Boston in that decade. He remains to this day a very popular figure and a genuine Boston legend.

Tommy Points

"Tommy Points" are the invention of Celtics television announcer Tommy Heinsohn, who awards them during his telecasts to Celtics players who make smart plays, the type of effort that typically does not show up on a stat sheet. Smart opportunistic play, along with hustle, is rewarded. Sometimes, even a fan earns a Tommy Point.

27 The Celtics Enter the Stock Market

Beginning in December 1986, a Celtics rooter not only could cheer for the home team but also literally own a share of it by buying publicly traded stock in the team. The idea was the brainchild of the Celtics' ownership at the time, Alan Cohen, Donald Gaston, and Paul DuPee. It quickly became an extraordinarily popular gesture that permitted the owners to sell stock and make money and yet still retain practical control of the team under a limited partnership agreement, whereby this triumvirate controlled the majority of stock.

It worked. Fans opened up birthday and Christmas packages to find their share of stock, an item that usually found itself proudly framed on the recipient's home or office wall or next to a portrait of dogs playing poker in the billiard room. The Celtics' managing owners made money and reduced tax liability, while publicly traded owners proudly viewed the stock quotes each day in the newspaper (listed as "BOS") to see how their investment had fared since the day before.

In Boston and surrounding suburbs, it became rare for a week to pass without someone crowing that they owned part of the Boston Celtics or that Larry Bird worked for them. Stockholders received reports and tiny dividends, and the single-share owners generally did not trade their share, preferring to keep it framed proudly on their wall.

Had this practice continued, buying a share of Celtics stock would have definitely been recommended as something a fan should do before they die, but unfortunately, when new owners purchased the team, stockholders received notices informing them that they must either redeem the shares or in effect lose them. Some went down with the ship and kept them, but others made copies and redeemed the original, ending the wild days of speculation on the big board for Celts fans.

28 Another Banner Is Raised: 1974

It bugged Bill Russell that some people proclaimed the New York Knicks a dynasty in the wake of the Celtics concluding their run of 11 titles in 13 years, and yet even in the absence of a proper perspective, the Knicks possessed a very powerful team. They had just won their second championship in four years at the close of the 1973 Finals, led by five future Hall of Fame starters, Willis Reed at center, Bill Bradley and Dave DeBusschere at forwards, and Walt Frazier and Earl Monroe at guards. Coached by the legendary Red Holzman, the club also had some very good reserves with Jerry Lucas (another Hall of Famer), Phil Jackson, and Dean Meminger.

During the 1973–1974 campaign, though, the Knicks faltered a bit due mainly to injuries to Reed and Monroe, finishing second in the Atlantic Division with a 49–33 record. Call it the luck of the Irish, but the Celtics won the division title despite having a significantly less successful regular season than the previous one, ending up at 56–26, rather than the stellar 68–14 season of the year before.

Both Celtic editions won the Atlantic Division with virtually identical rosters, the lone exception being that Satch Sanders had retired after the end of the 1973 campaign, but that should not have accounted for that much of a difference. The previous year in the playoffs, the team lost John Havlicek in the third game of their series against New York, and that effectively ended their season.

Center Dave Cowens, swingman Havlicek, and guard Jo Jo White again led the squad, with significant contributions from Paul Silas, Don Chaney, Don Nelson, and Paul Westphal. Westphal added a few more points a game to his average, but otherwise the two Celt teams appeared to be mirror images. The exception was one team won more in the regular season but lost in the playoffs, while the newer one saved their best for the playoffs. Former Celtics star Tommy Heinsohn coached the team.

In the first round of the playoffs in 1974, the Celtics faced off against the Buffalo Braves, then concluding their fourth year in the NBA, almost exactly midway through their active existence as a professional franchise, awaiting their future incarnations in San Diego and Los Angeles as the Clippers. During the season, Buffalo barely finished above .500 at 42–40, but they possessed a number of dangerous gunners in Bob McAdoo, Jim McMillian, Randy Smith, Gar Heard, and Ernie DiGregorio. To provide ballast, center/forward Bob Kauffman had once famously fought Dave Cowens and had given the Celtics' center a shiner.

Shockingly, the teams split the first four games of the Eastern Conference semifinals. The Celtics then eked out a tough win at home, 100–97, to pull ahead in the series. But the Celtics did not seal matters until they traveled to Buffalo, where they won narrowly, 106–104, to finally advance. The Celtics won ugly in that last game, scoring just one field goal in the last 8:12, only icing it when Jo Jo White sank two free throws at the end.

Arguably, the Celtics had an easier time in the Eastern Conference Finals against the Knicks, where some of the worst abuse heaped on the team emanated from the 100 to 200 youngsters who screamed at them outside Madison Square Garden, many of whom accused stars like Dave Cowens of feats normally attributed to Oedipus. Hobbled by the injuries to their stars, the Knicks fell in five games, thus ending the shortest dynasty in NBA history.

In the Finals, the Celtics had to battle the much more formidable Milwaukee Bucks, showcasing Kareem Abdul-Jabbar, Oscar Robertson, and Bob Dandridge. Like the Buffalo series, the Celtics split the first four games, as unlikely candidates such as Milwaukee's Cornell Warner and Boston's Hank Finkel played key roles to keep the teams even. Strategically, the Celtics' Jo Jo White and Don Chaney harassed Oscar Robertson (due to an injury to Lucius Allen, Robertson in effect became the Bucks' point guard) while Cowens played a very physical game against Kareem.

Indeed, the Boston press fueled a 96–87 Celtics win in Game 5, as Cowens inadvertently but literally butted heads with Kareem, and Paul Silas assisted under the basket. After the game, Cowens gushed, "We've never pressed like this before. It's phenomenal." In the most exciting game of the series, Milwaukee won 102–101 in double overtime as Kareem swished a running hook from 15 feet for the win. The Celtics had just taken the lead due to a clutch Havlicek shot, and had defended the anticipated final bid by the Bucks just as they wished, but Kareem still sank his difficult shot as the series was knotted at three games apiece.

Game 7. In Milwaukee, Celtics coach Tommy Heinsohn let Dave Cowens loose, and it worked, with the team's nominal center hitting jumpers all over for 28 points. As Heinsohn later pointed out, perhaps with a bit of hyperbole, "It's never been done. To play a center like a guard and move him outside. It's never been done." The guards kept swarming Robertson, and Paul Silas outrebounded everyone. Although Milwaukee narrowed Boston's lead to 71–68 at one point, the game evolved into a blowout, as the Celtics won the game and the title 102–87.

Dave Cowens had played at least as well as Kareem, while the estimable Oscar Robertson (who had just played his final NBA game) was hounded the whole series. Paul Silas kept Cowens' back and rebounded with furor while Havlicek shot well throughout. And yet the team spirit swept the Celtics into their 12th championship; as the Bucks' Jon McGlocklin commented, "They're the most emotional team in the league. They have a great team, and we really respect them. They played harder in this series than any other team I've ever seen."

The Celtics had ended their drought from their last dynastic title, Tommy Heinsohn won his first championship as a head coach, Red Auerbach was a genius again, and Dave Cowens celebrated by sleeping on the Boston Common that evening.

29 Celtics Trade Ice Capades for Bill Russell

In 1956 the Rochester Royals were a hurting franchise, so awful that they naturally had the first choice in the draft that year. On the West Coast, center Bill Russell, along with K.C. Jones, had led a small Jesuit school, the University of San Francisco, to two straight NCAA championships. Even in that relatively unsophisticated period in NBA drafting history, few challenged Bill Russell's status as the finest collegiate basketball player in the United States.

The problem for the Rochester Royals was that the perceived price to procure the services of Russell exceeded their means, so their front office was amenable to a deal, ideally one that let them keep their first pick and also reap some additional financial windfall. Into the fray came Celtics owner Walter Brown, who also had a controlling interest in the Ice Capades. In order to give the Rochester owners some revenue and some credibility with their city,

You've Got to Give Some to Get Some

One more piece of the puzzle had to fall into place.

Having rid themselves of the possibility of losing the rights to Russell to the Royals, the team then had to face the prospect of the next club in the drafting order, the St. Louis Hawks, choosing Russell. If the deal to have the Royals pass on Russell for some Ice Capades shows proved a great fleecing, the deal with the Hawks was the team's finest transaction.

On April 30, 1956, the Boston Celtics made their greatest trade by swapping Easy Ed Macauley and the rights to Cliff Hagan to the St. Louis Hawks for the second pick in the draft, Bill Russell. The team's best trade does not necessarily make it one of their biggest ripoffs of another franchise, though, as both Macauley and Hagan made the Basketball Hall of Fame. Also, they combined with other Hawks stars, such as Bob Pettit, to win the NBA championship after the 1958 season, the last time the Celtics failed to capture the prize until the 1966–1967 season.

Despite their qualities, Macauley and Hagan combined could not improve on that one championship, while Russell represented the keystone to the great Celtics teams during his entire career. The Celtics parted with quality to get quality, and this remains their wisest transaction, even if they parted with value.

the Celtics' owner sent the figure skaters on an extended run in that central New York burg, while the Royals supposedly passed on Russell.

The Royals duly chose Sihugo Green instead of Russell, and the Ice Capades extended their residency the next winter in Rochester.

If true, it was a huge swindle by Brown and Auerbach, akin to the Yankees repeatedly ripping off the Red Sox in the Harry Frazee years, or the Kansas City Athletics in the 1950s. What makes it a bit implausible is that if the Royals were that hard up, why did the Celtics not trade them a couple of stiffs, the Ice Capades, and a bag of cash for the first choice? The Celtics never reaped terrific sales in this era, but compared to the Rochester Royals (later the Cincinnati Royals, Kansas City Kings, and Sacramento Kings), they were flush. And if the Celtics wanted Russell so badly, which they clearly did, why not give the Royals what they needed the most, revenue? Why not trade them the Ice Capades even up?

Other Steals

1. Robert Parish and Kevin McHale for Joe Barry Carroll and Rickey Brown

June 9, 1980, is a date that will live in infamy in the Bay Area because Golden State traded center Robert Parish and a first-round pick for two Celtic first-round picks at that time. The key for Golden State was the first choice in the draft, which they coveted as they had fallen in love with Purdue's center, Joe Barry Carroll. As expected, they chose Carroll the moment that the draft commenced.

In order to move up from third to first, the Warriors had of course given up their original place to Boston, at which time Red Auerbach chose Kevin McHale from Minnesota. Later, with the 13th pick (Boston's second first-round pick before the trade), Golden State went after another center, this time getting Rickey Brown from Mississippi State.

From the outset, the Celtics had fleeced the Warriors, as Robert Parish had already established himself in his four years in the NBA as a potent shot blocker, offensive and defensive rebounder, and a decent scorer. He needed to mature, which he did, and with this maturity "Chief" thrived in Boston as the team set him up with not only draft choice McHale, but a young Larry Bird. A physical marvel, Parish played well into his forties, earning nine All-Star selections after he came to Boston, on his way to a Hall of Fame career.

At 6'10" (some say he was an inch taller) Kevin McHale may have reminded some longtime Celtics fans of Easy Ed Macauley, but with Parish, the team did not need a fierce center. In Larry

Bird and McHale, the Celts had a peerless pair of forwards. McHale did not have as long a career as Parish, although he also made the Hall of Fame and earned recognition as one of the 50 greatest players ever.

In return for providing the Celtics with two future Hall of Famers, the Warriors got little back with Rickey Brown, as he played only five years and retired with the Atlanta Hawks with less than 1,500 points as a center/forward.

Celtics mythology has made this trade worse than it was by ignoring the accomplishments of Joe Barry Carroll, whose career hardly mirrored that of Sam Bowie or some other player who accomplished little or nothing. He earned selection to an All-Star Game, and in his third year scored 1,907 points, making him more like the Bob Rule of his generation. Over the following three and a half years, his production slid precipitously, all the way to retirement.

Still, even if Joe Barry Carroll did not become a complete bust, Robert Parish far outplayed him, and between McHale and Rickey Brown, the comparison is laughable. Even when judged with some perspective and a fairness not accorded to Carroll, the trade constituted a Celtics steal.

2. Bailey Howell for Mel Counts

Those who believe that Celtics basketball only began with the drafting of Larry Bird have missed out on a pretty interesting franchise. One of the most important transactions the club ever made kept the team in contention for championship banners three years after their anticipated expiration date, and this occurred on September 1, 1966, when Boston swapped backup center Mel Counts to the Baltimore Bullets for forward Bailey Howell.

Chosen as their first-round pick in the 1964 draft, the 7' Counts had competently spelled Bill Russell at center, but otherwise provided Red Auerbach with little indication that the young man might someday take over the job. Unfortunately, the Celtics had not drafted well after 1962, so as stars retired or grew older, the team lost talent and depth.

Howell had starred at Mississippi State and had distinguished himself in his seven professional seasons, playing on five All-Star teams while finishing among the league leaders in rebounds and field-goal percentage. Again, Counts served capably as a sub, not as a starter, an observation the Bullets soon made, trading him in the middle of his sole season there to L.A. as part of a three-team deal.

The deal having been struck, Howell rang up points-per-game totals for the next three seasons of 20.0, 19.8, and 19.7, before trailing off in his fourth year to a 12.6 average, on his way to eventual induction into the Hall of Fame in Springfield, Massachusetts.

The deal for Counts turned into a gift that kept on giving for Boston. In the seventh and deciding game of the NBA Finals in 1969, Counts played the last 5:19 in lieu of Wilt Chamberlain because L.A. coach Butch van Breda Kolff had lost faith in Chamberlain. Although Counts played well under the circumstances, he was no Wilt and certainly paled next to Bill Russell, as the Celtics won their 11th title, in the newly constructed Forum, no less.

The Lakers had the last laugh, though, eventually trading Counts for prodigal son Gail Goodrich the next year. But Boston had two championships, one at the end of 1968 and one the next year, largely due to the infusion of talent that Bailey Howell brought to the team—all thanks to the Mel Counts trade.

3. Dennis Johnson for Rick Robey

Disappointed by their quick exit in the 1983 playoffs after Milwaukee swept them, the Celtics swept out head coach Bill Fitch and also made one of their more remarkable trades by shipping out backup center Rick Robey for Phoenix Suns guard Dennis Johnson. (Each team also gained two draft picks, but they had little impact on the transaction.)

The Suns had made the same mistake the Bullets made in the Counts-Howell trade, relinquishing an All-Star player for a backup center, and the Suns got little out of Robey, who played only about 100 games for them in three years before they released him in 1986. The highest draft pick they received from Boston was used by the Suns to pick Rod Foster from UCLA, and although Foster showed some promise in his first two years, his career ended a couple months earlier than Rick Robey's. The Suns' other pick obtained in the deal went nowhere.

4. M.L. Carr and Two Picks for Bob McAdoo

Then–Celtics owner John Y. Brown dumped a bunch of picks to obtain Bob McAdoo, supposedly because his wife, Phyllis George, liked the high-scoring center/forward. McAdoo did nothing in Boston in his one partial season on the parquet (1978–1979), and soon after John Y. Brown left town. With Brown and his wife gone, McAdoo found his shelf life limited, and Auerbach swapped him soon thereafter.

Prompting the trade, the Celtics had signed guard M.L. Carr from Detroit in July 1979, and a huge row erupted over compensation. Within two months, the controversy subsided when Boston closed this divisive issue by convincing Dick Vitale in Detroit to take McAdoo and let go of two draft picks. As he left Boston, McAdoo exulted, claiming, "I wasn't part of the Celtics team....It's one of the best things that has happened to me. Detroit made a good deal. They're getting a proven player. The Celtics will be getting two unproven players."

Detroit in fact had made a dreadful deal, waiving Mac less than two years later. The Celtics closed the books on their signing of M.L. Carr, who played well for them and was as positive a presence on the club as Mac was a negative one. As far as the draft picks, one did not pan out for the Celts, but one did, used in the deal that brought McHale and Parish to Boston.

Last Man Standing

The Celtics utilized a pick obtained in the Dennis Johnson–Rick Robey trade to draft center Greg Kite out of BYU. Kite had no scoring touch, and it seemed like he always only put up a point or two in each game he played. Still, he played for 12 years in the NBA, retiring with a 2.5 points-per-game average, outlasting every other player involved in the original Suns/Celtics transaction.

5. Kevin Garnett for Al Jefferson, Ryan Gomes, Gerald Green, Theo Ratliff, Sebastian Telfair, and Two Draft Picks

Having not won an NBA title in more than 20 years, this trade by Danny Ainge made the Celtics the prohibitive favorite to win the crown in 2007–2008, a feat the team eventually accomplished. Having previously traded for Ray Allen, the Celtics now had their first Big Three (Paul Pierce, Allen, and Garnett) since Ainge played for Boston.

Still only 31 years old at the time of the trade (July 31, 2007), Garnett had starred for several years on Timberwolves teams that never went anywhere. The forward rebounded better than anyone on defense, blocked shots, scored points (more than 19,000 at the time of the trade), thrived on defense, and played with an intensity that often translated in a torrent of expletives emanating from him at key moments in the game. No Curtis Rowe, this man came to win, and when he saw how committed the Celtics were, he gladly joined the franchise. When they won the championship his first year in Boston, Garnett screamed out, "Anything is possible!"

In return, Timberwolves GM Kevin McHale eventually got himself fired. Al Jefferson and Ryan Gomes certainly played very well for Minnesota, but neither one was Kevin Garnett. Telfair, Green, and Ratliff left town shortly after the trade, each by different routes, each with little fanfare. The draft choices did not fail, but again, trading a star player in basketball is not done on a ledger sheet where one man's statistics lend themselves to a counterbalance when balanced against the numbers put up by the players exchanged for him. In a superstar-driven league, Kevin Garnett, Paul Pierce, and Ray Allen had the potential of bringing a banner to Boston, and they did. The players received by the Timberwolves did not exceed the sum of their parts, and the team probably ended up weakened rather than strengthened.

Red Auerbach used to make trades like this.

31 All-Time Winning Streak

After capturing the 2008 NBA title, the party did not seem to end for the Boston Celtics, as they began their next season with a 27–2 record, punctuated by a 19-game winning streak, the longest in franchise history. The starting unit of Kendrick Perkins at center, Kevin Garnett and Paul Pierce at forwards, and Rajon Rondo and Ray Allen at guards grew even more at ease working together as a unit, and while the club did not re-sign James Posey, much of their strong bench from the previous season remained intact.

On November 14, the Celts lost to the Denver Nuggets, but they quickly revived, commencing a streak that they maintained right through December 23, when they defeated the 76ers. By the end of the Sixers contest, fans at the Garden began shouting "Beat L.A.!" in recognition that the next game fell on Christmas against the Lakers at the Staples Center. Along the way, the team won 10 road games and got off to the greatest start in NBA history, shattering the previous mark shared by the 1969–1970 Knicks and the 1966–1967 Sixers.

On Christmas Day, Pierce, Allen, and Garnett all played well, but the Lakers played a bit better behind a great effort by Kobe Bryant, as Phil Jackson won his 1,000th game as a head coach. Summed up by Garnett, "Unless you win it all, it's pretty much just steam in the air." Coach Doc Rivers promised, "We'll see them again."

Unfortunately, the teams did not meet again in the Finals, as Kevin Garnett sustained a right knee sprain in February and only played in 57 regular-season games, missing the playoffs entirely. The Celts did not get past the second round of the playoffs that year without their star, but still finished with a strong record, and, for the first 30 games, accomplished something no team has done before or since, propelling themselves to the greatest start ever.

32 Visit the Boston Sports Club at HealthPoint

Located in the suburban town of Waltham, Massachusetts, the Celtics' training facility is a must-see for any Celtics fan. For many years the team practiced at Hellenic College in Brookline, a short drive from Larry Bird's house, a perfectly adequate court far from the madding crowd around the Garden.

The Celtics moved their training and practices in 2002 to the state-of-the-art HealthPoint Training Center to permit players access to not only a court but also the weight rooms and sports-medicine facilities there. Technically, the Celtics' basketball court and fitness machines are restricted to the team, but occasionally a player might use one of the pools open to club members or be seen grabbing a snack at the café inside the building. In addition, there are six MDs on the premises with a platoon of physical therapists, so in the event one wishes to become a patient, the finest in health care is available, the same the pros use.

For members, the club houses more than 80,000 square feet and contains considerably more than 100 cardio and strength machines, a lap swimming pool, a separate therapeutic pool, a running track,

> ## Practicing at the Y
> Ensconced in a beautiful and very useful facility today, the Celtics can practice, train, and recuperate from injuries in peace and a degree of anonymity. It was not always so. Particularly in the team's early years, they practiced where they could. For instance, they once worked out at the Downtown Boston YMCA and the Cambridge YMCA, where the players and coaches had to suspend practice each day to run outside and feed their parking meters.

three squash courts, and its own NBA-sized basketball court. Practices are closed to the public, but members may view the Celtics' training court at all other times, an authentic facility right down to its parquet floors, logo at halfcourt, and championship banners. Limited opportunities also exist for members to occasionally attend a media event.

Club members understand that the site is not an autograph opportunity, but rather a top-flight facility for people serious about staying healthy, and if everyone respects each other's space, you might find the Celtics and the team management staff very friendly.

33 Celtic Mystique

Celtic mystique. Every basketball fan has heard the phrase, but few can pinpoint when the term first gained vogue. Certainly, in the 1940s, when the team barely remained afloat with a surfeit of despair and no swagger, no one used the term. Nor did it gain any use during Red Auerbach's first five years of coaching the team, as he slowly built his eventual dynasty. It certainly predated the Bird era of excellence, although it is very difficult to ascertain who coined the term and when it was first used. By 1988, when Bob Cousy and the *Boston Globe*'s Bob Ryan cowrote *Cousy on the Celtic*

Mystique, it had become accepted doctrine, even as the team itself stood poised to embark on a long malaise.

Like the British Empire at its height, this aura of near invincibility had to sustain itself equally with force, diplomacy, and smoke-and-mirrors. Without all of these elements, the franchise most likely would have wallowed in a hazy fantasyland. In fact, once undeniable and irreversible decline had set in by the early 1990s, Celtic mystique had become laughable.

The foundation for greatness had been laid of course by Walter Brown and Red Auerbach, and even after Brown's untimely death in 1964, Auerbach personified the magic that seemed to surround the club. During periods when later owners patronized Red or figuratively placed him in the back of the bookshelf, the mystique faded, only to brighten once the natural order had been restored.

Auerbach needed stars, but he also needed players on the floor and on the bench who understood their roles on the team and followed them, people who bought into something larger than themselves. Selfish or moody souls rarely lasted in Boston, while those who treated their teammates like members of their own family thrived.

Opposition coaches and players imply that they at least have an awareness of the concept of the team's mystique, shown mainly in their efforts to deny its existence. In anticipation of his team's upcoming playoff series with Boston in early May 2009, Magic coach Stan Van Gundy had this to say about his opposition and their tradition: "For opposing players now, I don't think the Celtic mystique carries much sway. That's something guys our age [49] are aware of, but when these players grew up, the Celtics weren't the Celtics. They weren't Red Auerbach's Celtics, or even Larry Bird's Celtics. Our guys didn't grow up thinking the Celtics were anything above the rest of the league."

Interestingly enough, Van Gundy did not deny the past existence of the mystique, he simply opined that it no longer lived and breathed. Van Gundy's sentiments hark back to comments made by then-Knicks players Marvin Webster and Rory Sparrow, after their team defeated Boston in a game during the 1983–1984 season:

Webster: In the past, playing Boston, we always came in scared to lose. It was a psychological thing. Now we know we can beat them.

Sparrow: We're no longer in awe of the Celtics' mystique.

Again, by their own opponents' admission, there was once something called the Celtic mystique, but like Camelot, it perished.

But it never truly disappears completely, because when the Celtics become competitive again, as they did in the fall of 2007, it is because the elements that have contributed to their past success have returned, and as a consequence, the team rolls over its opponents. Bob Cousy never doubted its existence, but when he cowrote *Cousy on the Celtic Mystique* in 1988, he said very little tangibly about the mystique, although certainly the phenomenon owed much of its existence to the hiring of Red Auerbach and the drafting of Bill Russell.

The key components in Cousy's mind lie in "a basic approach to how the game should be played." Auerbach brought in players who subordinated their goals to the attainment of titles and cut those candidates who did not understand this. He instilled the fundamentals of winning basketball in his players, who, because of their individual characters, executed the wishes of their coach. Not mentioned often, Auerbach also liked smart players, like another successful local professional coach, Bill Belichick of the Patriots.

Unfortunately for the team, Red Auerbach advanced to such an age as GM or president that he no longer exercised the control and influence he once did, nor did he have the ability to stay one step ahead of his opponents. His disciples tried, but they exhibited an ambivalence between old-school and new-school solutions. For example, in the *Celtic Mystique*, Cousy and Ryan observed, "Think of all those great players who only performed for Boston.... From today's crop you can include the names of Bird and McHale, not to mention Ainge. And you know neither Robert Parish nor Dennis Johnson will ever play for another team."

And yet as the club continued to decline, it shipped out Ainge and Parish, and arguably if the front office had made deals to other teams involving Bird, DJ, and McHale, they could have enjoyed success throughout the 1990s and the early part of the millennium. In part, the administrators stayed with a pat hand until they drove their stars into the ground, while dealing others and receiving in return either inadequate value or players who did not understand the tradition of greatness that preceded them.

Without wins, the mystique evaporated, but when Danny Ainge brought together a club dominated by Kevin Garnett, Ray Allen, and Paul Pierce, it returned with a vengeance—as if by magic, but Celtics fans know better.

34 Bailey Howell

It is possible that not one American young man had a poster or basketball card of Bailey Howell nailed to the wall of his room, not because the forward did not play basketball well, but mostly because Howell probably never spent one moment of his life considered by anyone to be cool.

During the late 1960s as hair styles grew out, Bailey largely kept a traditional haircut unchanged from the days before Elvis, only letting his hair down a bit toward the end of his career, and even then it did not look right. A very religious person from Middleton, Tennessee, he seemed to personify solid, traditional values. It seemed that if you bumped into him on the streets of Boston, he would have been in the same black-and-white hues seen in most television sets of the day. It is not known if Fred Rogers from *Mr. Roger's Neighborhood* ever met him, but if he did, Fred might have found Bailey Howell too square for his taste.

Appearances deceived because Howell rivaled perhaps only Bill Sharman in team history for the "He Looks Like the All-American Boy But Plays Ball Like a Hockey Player Award." For such a mild-mannered and harmless-looking guy, Howell absolutely hammered opposing players, leading the NBA in personal fouls in 1964–1965 and finishing in the top 10 in this category on seven other occasions. As of 2010, he still falls within the top 25 all-time with personal fouls, totaling 3,498. Howell attributed this to his hustling: "When I was younger, I used to go barreling in on everything, even when I had only one chance in a hundred of getting the ball." He might not have been handy with his fists like Sharman, but he certainly did not turn the other cheek on the court very often.

Similar to Sharman, he also stood out for his shooting accuracy, finishing in the top 10 for field-goal percentage for seven years and free-throw percentage on one occasion. The second player selected in the 1959 draft, he played five years in Detroit and two in Baltimore before coming to Boston. The Bullets' owner wanted him to become a player/coach, a post Howell declined, but when the club signed a new coach, Phil Seymour, Howell found himself under suspicion. After his second year in Baltimore ended in 1966, the Bullets traded him to Boston for Mel Counts.

Bailey Howell welcomed the change, finally getting the opportunity to play for the Celtics in their dynastic years. As a white southerner, he seemed an odd fit playing for Bill Russell, the league's first African American coach, but it did not affect him negatively at all. In fact, he respected Russell more than any coach he had ever played for in the past. True to his steady nature, he scored the exact amount of points in each of his first two years with the Celtics: 1,621. In 1968–1969, his third year with the team and the last year of the Celtics' dynasty, he averaged 19.7 points per game.

Red Auerbach once said, "Bailey Howell has been a Celtic all his life. It just took him a lot longer to get the uniform." He probably would have retired a Celtic also, but in 1969–1970 his production dropped off considerably, scoring 500 fewer points (and playing almost 500 fewer minutes) than the previous year, and the club exposed him to the expansion draft. The Buffalo Braves picked him up and then immediately traded him to Philadelphia, where he played his final year.

Without Bailey Howell, the Celtics probably would not have won their final two titles in the 1960s. Not the coolest Celtic ever, he proved himself one of the finest, earning selection to the Basketball Hall of Fame in 1997. In Howell's case, sometimes nice guys finish first.

 **Race**

Racial issues are as inextricably linked with the Boston Celtics as they are for the city of Boston itself. Boston had long prided itself as a beacon of tolerance and a force for positive change. William Lloyd Garrison famously founded the abolitionist paper the *Liberator* with the stirring, "I am in earnest—I will not equivocate—I will not excuse—I will not retreat a single inch—and I will be heard!" Garrison's intransigence nearly cost him his life. The city embraced Frederick Douglass, and West Roxbury's Robert Gould Shaw led the African American 54th regiment in its assault on Fort Wagner, costing him and many of his men their lives.

Despite this proud history, Boston after the end of the World War II began to change, as the city transitioned from having a relatively small African American population to a much more significant one, in neighborhoods once almost exclusively populated by Irish and Jewish citizens. The Boston School Committee instituted a misguided policy, segregating its school populations, with the African American students receiving a separate and unequal education, restricted to largely crumbling schools in the inner city.

The Boston Red Sox of that period exemplified the segregation efforts, passing up Willie Mays and Jackie Robinson, only desegregating its major league roster after every other franchise had, after Robinson had retired.

In contrast, Walter Brown and Red Auerbach led the desegregation efforts in the NBA, drafting the first African American player, Chuck Cooper, in 1950. Consistent with this policy, the team fielded the first starting lineup of all African American players and the first black coach, Bill Russell. While some NBA franchises kept an inordinate number of white players on their rosters, particularly reserves, when Bill Russell, for example, took a breather, fellow African American centers Wayne Embry or John Thompson replaced him on the floor.

Unfortunately, Boston and its suburbs stood on the brink of folly as many of the African American players on the team experienced ugly racial incidents once they drove away from the Boston Garden postgame (and sometimes endured racist taunts even while playing). Few resided in Boston after they retired.

By the mid-1970s, after federal judge Arthur Garrity ordered forced busing to desegregate the Boston public schools, the city exploded. Racism oozed in the streets, and the city stood embarrassed throughout the world with grainy images of buses leaving South Boston, as violent as those of Bull Connor in Alabama a decade earlier. In the minds of many black people, and white people, Boston was the most racist city in America.

After 1980, when Larry Bird first came to Boston, race relations receded from the front pages of the dailies. The team got much better—and much whiter—as Boston increasingly became the setting of very popular television shows like *Cheers* (which come to think of it, had an all-white cast and, seemingly, clientele) and *St. Elsewhere*. Bostonians largely basked in the economic "Massachusetts Miracle," which helped propel Governor Michael Dukakis to the Democratic nomination for president in 1988.

By 1986 the Celtics had eight white players and four black players in a league that statistically was three-quarters African American. It was also the finest team in the NBA. As the city of Boston began coping with racial issues and many of the most incendiary bigots moved from the city to virtually all-white suburbs, the Boston Celtics, once the paradigm of racial tolerance, ironically looked like an organization that promoted white supremacy.

It appeared as if the club had consciously, or at least subconsciously, infused the team with white players, and increasingly, that became the perception of many fans and other clubs' players. The perception lasted beyond the early 1990s, after such stars as Larry Bird and Kevin McHale retired, and the team became almost exclusively African American. By that time, few people cared, inside the city or throughout the rest of the NBA, as the Celtics, through mismanagement, became a laughingstock.

When the Celtics finally won their first championship in 22 years, all but two players were African American, and while the issues of race have not disappeared, no one could accuse the Celtics of being racist. Regretfully, issues of race remain, and while the new Garden welcomes many more black fans than the old Garden, it still sports a more heavily Caucasian fandom than many other NBA arenas.

36 Celtics on the Diamond and the Gridiron

Celtics guard and later general manager Danny Ainge once played for the Toronto Blue Jays, a fact readily known even to the casual fan. Not Hall of Famously, mind you, for in his three major league seasons, from 1979 to 1981, he accumulated a lifetime batting average of .220, playing a bit in the outfield and all infield positions with the exception of first base. Unlike most signed baseball prospects, he did make the majors and had his own bubble-gum card. For Boston Red Sox followers, he did not hurt their team too much, so in these ways his career can be measured a success. Although not nearly as successful or as colorful as early Celtic Gene Conley.

One of the most versatile, if not most talented, athletes in the 20th century, Gene Conley wove stories about himself in baseball and in basketball. His baseball career started in 1952 and ended in 1963, spent mostly with the Braves. He won 91 games and earned selection to three All-Star Games. But at 6'8" he also served as a useful backup in the frontcourt of the Celtics and later the Knicks.

In his first, brief incarnation with the Celtics in 1952–1953, many fans mistook him for center Ed Macauley, so naturally Conley signed a number of autographs in Easy Ed's name. In one of the more hilarious instances of identity theft, he subbed for Macauley in a northern New England radio show, convincing the host he was Macauley himself.

Any chance Conley had of maintaining his status as a two-sport star temporarily disappeared when the Boston Braves moved to Milwaukee. There are various cloak-and-dagger accounts of how this decision came down, but from then until 1958, Conley only played baseball.

Chiefly, his notoriety arises from an incident which occurred one hot summer's day in 1962, as a Red Sox, when he and teammate Pumpsie Green left the team bus in a traffic jam for a couple of beers. When they returned, the bus had left, and Conley disappeared for a few days, during which time he notably tried to book a flight to Israel despite the absence of a passport on his person. He did return to his mates, chastened and fined a bit, but team owner Tom Yawkey, quite a partier himself in his youth, largely let him off the hook.

Just before Conley embarked on his professional career, Chuck Connors, who played with the Celtics in their first year, also came to bat once for the Brooklyn Dodgers in 1949, going hitless. Connors got a better shot in 1951 with the Chicago Cubs, where he hit .239 in slightly more than 200 at-bats. Not a truly gifted baseball or basketball player, Connors did not receive his big break until he went to Hollywood and starred in *The Rifleman* in the late 1950s and early '60s.

Certainly the best basketball player of the bunch was Hall of Famer Bill Sharman, whose accurate shooting complemented Bob Cousy's ball-handling in those great Celtics backcourts in the early dynasty years. In baseball terms, though, Sharman resembled more aptly Moonlight Graham. Brought up by the Brooklyn Dodgers in the fall of 1951, it developed into an inauspicious time for a rookie to come up to the show, as Brooklyn staged one of the great collapses in pennant-race history, culminating in Bobby Thomson's "Shot Heard 'Round the World" home run to win the final playoff game for the New York Giants. During that fall stretch, Sharman did not play and did not bat, although he did get ejected from a game with the entire Dodgers bench, a rare feat.

Even though they never played a regular-season game in the NFL, John Havlicek and K.C. Jones tried out for the Cleveland Browns and Los Angeles Rams, respectively. Chosen in the seventh round of the 1962 draft by Cleveland, Havlicek survived until the

Is the Ball Supposed to Be Round?

In 1946–1947 the Celtics, making no effort to hide their desperation to find anyone with a minimal amount of athleticism, signed up two local football players, Don Eliason and Hal Crisler, who in the fall played for the Boston Yanks. Eliason played in one game, and Crisler lasted for four, but neither produced, and the experiment ended. Finding Boston almost as barren a landscape as Walter Brown was finding it for basketball, the Yanks folded after the 1948 season.

final cut, a huge relief to Red Auerbach. In the one exhibition game in which he played, Hondo recalled the one play that may have sealed his destiny: "I looked across the line, and there, facing me, was Big Daddy Lipscomb....Well, at the snap, I kind of blasted straight ahead, or at least that's what I intended to do, except that Big Daddy started grabbing everyone in sight, including me, throwing us around until he got to the runner. I ended up at the bottom of the pile. I wasn't sure if he'd knocked off just my helmet or my whole head."

The Rams gave K.C. a tryout in 1958 as a defensive back, where he played some exhibition games before injuring his leg and convincing himself that basketball was the preferable contact sport. Neither Havlicek nor Jones played college football, and yet their athleticism warranted an extended look by these pro teams.

The days of two-sport stars have probably ended, despite the examples of Bo Jackson, Deion Sanders, and Michael Jordan leaving their primary sports for baseball, and particularly in Boston, it is difficult to see teams any more open to this concept than they were when Gene Conley climbed the mound at Fenway and played on the parquet.

37 Garnett

After 12 years in the NBA, forward Kevin Garnett was a member of an unenviable and unofficial group of superstars who'd never won a title, a shame since he'd led his Minnesota Timberwolves to the playoffs each year from 1997 to 2004. His team always got knocked out of the playoffs early with the exception of 2004, when they lost in the Western Conference Finals. After that critical juncture, they did not become a perennial contender but rather fell off the map competitively.

For three more years Garnett played magnificently for the franchise, but once they stopped winning, he became a victim of a youth movement. At that point, Timberwolves GM Kevin McHale, apparently on orders from ownership, executed the deal whereby the Celtics traded a batch of players and draft choices to Minnesota for KG, setting the table for Boston's return to a title.

It is not hard to see why. On one hand, Kevin Garnett is one of the greatest defenders in NBA history. He blocks shots, can steal, and is simply one of the greatest defensive rebounders who ever played, among the top 10 players ever in that category. Elected to 10 All-Defensive Teams by the conclusion of the 2009 season, he has always played with a rare intensity, like Dave Cowens, contesting everything. He also possesses a unique way to directly communicate his feelings to opponents during hotly contested moments.

On offense, the 13-time All-Star and one-time Most Valuable Player (2003–2004) once led the league in points scored, and in his final nine years in Minnesota always averaged over 20 points a game. On four occasions, his offensive rebounding prowess has

Celtics forward Kevin Garnett goes up for a dunk against the Portland Trail Blazers during a game on January 22, 2010, after having been sidelined with an injured right knee since December 28, 2009. Photo courtesy of AP Images

placed him in the top 10 in that category, and he also is an adept playmaker, assisting in his teammates' scoring. And yet again, his devotion to winning, reflected in his often being among the leaders in minutes played, sets him apart.

Laudable as it is, the extensive minutes that Garnett has devoted to the NBA might be having a deleterious effect on his career, as evidenced by his knee injury that kept him out of the latter part of the 2008–2009 season and which may have slowed him down for much of the 2009–2010 season. He may recover fully, to lead his new team to future titles, or 2008 may prove as mercurial as 1986 was for Bird and McHale: an exhilarating moment before a team-wide decline. If he regains his health, the Celtics might wish to place an order for the club's 18th championship banner.

38 Attend a Banner-Raising or Number-Retiring Ceremony

Believe it or not, it might be easier to attend one of these ceremonies in the future than it has been to buy a ticket and see these types of ceremonies in the past. While the team has raised 17 banners to the rafters and retired 21 numbers (in Johnny Most's case, a microphone, and in Jim Loscutoff's instance, the nickname "Loscy"), early on these affairs were fairly humdrum.

Initially the gala event was Bob Cousy Day in 1963, when Celts fans cheered for their retiring star, with dignitaries speaking, highlighted by Cooz's own extremely emotional speech, something that every current or past fan should listen to. John Havlicek's last game merited a similarly lavish appreciation of the departing star, but these types of events largely fell out of favor because many players either did not know in advance when their career would end or did not want to make a fuss over it, preferring to leave quietly.

The retiring of numbers early did not possess nearly the gamut of emotions surrounding Cousy's Day. Indeed, Bob Cousy and Ed Macauley each had their number retired on the same day in October 1963, with rocking chairs set out for them on the parquet to use during their retirement years. Bill Russell famously wanted his number raised before a game and only received proper acclaim later when he and the city of Boston had reconciled, with an appreciative crowd showering him with respect and adoration, almost a renewal of vows between the former superstar and fandom. Jo Jo White had his number retired, but the honor again merited only a slight mention in the *Globe* the next day.

By the time Larry Bird, Kevin McHale, and Robert Parish had their numbers retired, the event took on a bittersweet, nostalgic pitch, as the Celtics had become an also-ran in the league, so the event took on a celebratory air for glories past. At Bird's fête, Magic Johnson showed up wearing a Celtics uniform, which thrilled the crowd, and again harked back to the glory days of the 1980s.

Sometimes a number being retired takes on a somber tone, as was the case when Reggie Lewis' number was posthumously retired. It did serve to provide perspective for the late star's fans, who had for too long read awful stories of his medical condition, his death, and the litigation that arose thereafter. It also helped heal wounds when the club raised Cedric Maxwell's number to the rafters, a cleansing of some of the ill feelings that accompanied Max's departure from the team prior to the 1985–1986 season and festered for so long after.

Subsequently, it appeared that the retirement of players' numbers had largely run its course, but when Paul Pierce retires, how do you not close out his number also? If the Celtics continue to add banners, other numbers will undoubtedly rise with them.

Not all banner-raisings are created equal. For instance, few equate Don Nelson or Satch Sanders with Larry Bird or Bill Russell. Likewise, when Macauley and Cousy had their numbers retired on

The Celtics did not honor their stars adequately until Bob Cousy retired. Since then, the franchise has become increasingly adept at staging events for their departing luminaries.

the same day, at least the Cooz had on a previous occasion received the crowd's undivided adulation, but Easy Ed had to share his big day with the more famous and beloved guard. But therein lies the essence of the Celtic mystique, the banners hanging from the ceiling are all equal and were only achieved through team effort. So if a role player's number hangs on the same flag as a squad of Hall of Famers, it is because the titles matter most, and the superstars and lesser luminaries each contributed to the success of the Celtics.

One final caveat regarding the raising of a banner or a retirement of a number: get your tickets early, and if the tickets are sold out, have an awareness and appreciation for Boston and Commonwealth of Massachusetts scalping laws before you purchase a ticket on the street.

"I Love Walter!"

Walter is Walter McCarty, Celtics forward from 1997 through the middle of the 2005 season, when the club swapped him for a second-round draft choice. A star high school basketball player from Evansville, Indiana, he played college ball at Kentucky under then-coach Rick Pitino, helping his team to their 1996 NCAA championship. Chosen by the New York Knicks in the first round (19th overall), he rejoined Pitino the next year in his former coach's later incarnation as president and head coach of the Boston Celtics.

While Pitino definitely liked Walter, Celtics television commentator Tommy Heinsohn felt even more strongly about the quality of the young man's competitiveness and contributions to the team. Seemingly each time McCarty came off the bench to drill a three or make a tough rebound or steal the ball, Heinsohn bellowed out, "I love Walter!" Walter McCarty outlasted Pitino with the Celtics, surviving as a jack of all trades whose best years scoring were his first and last full ones with the team, although he mainly served as a backup and never averaged more than 9.6 points a game for a season.

Shortly after he was traded from Boston, he retired from the game but later reunited with Rick Pitino as an assistant coach at Louisville. Poor Walter McCarty never had the luck to play on a championship team as a professional. For many years he basically served as one of the few bright spots on a miserable Celtics team, but he always worked hard and provided effective play off the bench. Had he played during the Celtics' first dynasty, no doubt the team would have retired his number (0). Given the fact that he displayed such professionalism during a generally ugly and forgotten stretch of team history, they still can.

40 Howie McHugh

Despite operating the Boston Celtics on a very tight budget, Walter Brown's early teams stood perpetually on the verge of financial collapse, prepared to join the defunct BAA and NBA teams that folded before them. Besides Brown and whoever warmed up the coaching chair before Red Auerbach's hiring, the club possessed a staff that could be counted on one hand with fingers unused, but public relations director Howie McHugh served with distinction from the inception of the franchise in 1946 until just before his death in 1983. A hockey man like Brown, Howie McHugh had played goalie at Dartmouth and had to quickly learn the lexicon and the flow of basketball and then translate it to the masses.

With so few employees, the actual naming of the club came down to a convocation of Brown and McHugh, with Howie suggesting a bunch of names, such as the "Whirlwinds" (the old Boston barnstorming group of the 1920s), none of which inspired the imagination. At that point, Brown proposed naming his team the "Celtics" after the original Celtics, with a nod to Boston's teeming Irish-Catholic population. His PR man protested, but Brown owned the team, so he prevailed, with McHugh thereafter spreading the gospel of the Celtic Mystique.

McHugh also played a noteworthy role in the Celtics' first home game when Chuck "the Rifleman" Connors busted the glass

Although he played hockey in college, PR man Howie McHugh helped popularize the Boston Celtics, living long enough to see Larry Bird accomplish the rest.

backboard at the old Boston Arena. McHugh had to rush to the Boston Garden to retrieve a substitute backboard. Unfortunately, some rodeo bulls got in the way, but McHugh prevailed and brought the backboard back to the Arena, and the Celtics began their first game in Boston.

Indeed, in many ways McHugh discovered Connors as an actor, and while the Rifleman had a wretched shooting percentage during games, Howie perceived the young man's talents in putting on a show in front of crowds and employed him liberally in speaking engagements throughout the area to promote the team.

McHugh liked to have fun with the English language in his press releases, and his quips helped augment many a sports article in Boston, almost until the time he passed. Franchises folded frequently during the early days of the NBA (and its predecessor incarnation), but Howie McHugh deserves much of the credit for popularizing the team and keeping it alive, living long enough to see it become the preeminent club in league history.

41 DJ

Nothing in his past suggested that Dennis Johnson, "DJ" to his adoring fans in Boston and in his previous professional stops, fit the classic Celtics mold when on June 27, 1983, the Phoenix Suns traded him and draft picks to the Celtics for backup Rick Robey and picks. In Seattle and Phoenix, the freckle-faced guard clashed with his coaches, and while he excelled, winning the 1978–1979 Finals MVP award, he accumulated baggage.

Despite his excellence on the court, particularly on the defensive end, Johnson earned a reputation as a clubhouse lawyer, more specifically a gravedigger for coaches. That explains in large part why the Celtics obtained him relatively cheaply in their deal with Phoenix. And yet, to his credit, Johnson rose from the ashes in his new home.

Red Auerbach did not see a troublemaker, just someone who wanted to win, and DJ rewarded him with seven years of excellence as the team's point guard. Nine times in his career he earned selection to either the first or second NBA All-Defensive Team, and yet until his last year, he averaged at least 10 points a game in each of his years in Boston, topping off with a 15.7 average in 1984–1985.

Far from being a troublemaker on the team, he made Larry Bird a better player (Bird always maintained that DJ was the greatest teammate he ever had) and welcomed every opportunity to shut down the opponent's most potent scoring threats. He was a big-time player in a franchise that increasingly aspired to win titles every year. Only 10 men in NBA history scored at least 15,000 points and recorded 5,000 assists before Johnson accomplished the feat.

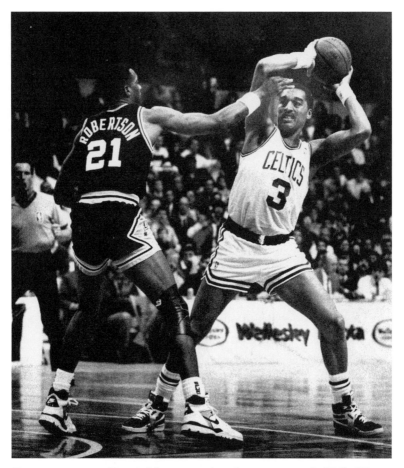

For too many years, Dennis Johnson was denied entrance into the Hall of Fame, an honor that was bestowed upon him posthumously. Celtics fans knew what they had, and Larry Bird considered Johnson his finest teammate.

Through the 1987 Finals, DJ played on championship-contending teams, helping to lead the Celtics past the Pistons that year when he ran down the paint and caught Larry Bird's pass, after Bird famously intercepted Isiah Thomas's inbound pass in the fifth game of the Eastern Conference Finals. It was DJ's signature moment, and yet after the Celtics lost in the Finals to the Lakers that year, his career began to decline, a rather natural declension for a basketball player in his thirties. From playing nearly 3,000 minutes in 1986–1987 (plus playoff minutes), he logged about 300 fewer minutes the next year and repeated this proportional decline the next two years, until he played only about 2,000 minutes in his last season at age 35 in 1989–1990. He retired a Celtic, and a grateful front office retired his No. 3 in 1991. He later served as a Celtics assistant coach for five seasons.

The failure of the Hall of Fame to select defensive stalwart Satch Sanders has justifiably received criticism, and more so than any other professional sport, defense has never been accorded a proper place when reviewing a basketball player's body of work. The non-selection of Dennis Johnson for so many years was even more difficult to discern, given not only his excellence on defense but his scoring touch, particularly before he came to Boston and accepted his role as a point guard with an extremely gifted scoring center and set of forwards.

Johnson posthumously and rightfully earned induction into the Hall in April 2010. Sadly, he died in early 2007 while coaching the Austin Toros, the Celtics' Development League entrant, never to enjoy this belated appreciation of his talents.

42 Ambassadors of Love

Particularly during the cold war, the United States had a weapon in its arsenal more influential than an unused megaton nuclear bomb—the Boston Celtics. The State Department sponsored trips abroad to spread the gospel of basketball, with the Celts the most obvious choice for the key ambassadorial role, primarily during their dynasty years. With relatively low salaries for players, the State Department in essence could provide team members with vacations to exotic locales abroad, while the club exemplified the American Way—leadership by example.

Ironically, the African American athletes often received better treatment abroad than they did in exhibition games in certain areas of their own country. What did not change was the closeness of the team members and their coach, oftentimes lending a foreign twist to the pranks they pulled on each other. Sometimes the good-natured ribbing took on an even more ominous turn. For example, there was the time that Red Auerbach convinced some Polish coaches to pose as Communist state police agents. The faux agents persuaded Tommy Heinsohn to leave his room for interrogation, scaring the Celtics forward to no end, until he finally determined that Red had plotted the whole venture. Allegedly, he got back at his coach with an exploding cigar.

The junkets were not restricted to iron curtain countries, as the team flew to Burma as late as 1970. The tours did provide a glimpse of first-class basketball and inspired players in the host countries to

Red Auerbach and John Havlicek spread the Gospel of Basketball in Burma in one of the team's overseas good will junkets. The young Burmese man at the far right is wearing longer basketball pants way before they became fashionable.

take up the sport or improve existing programs. The Olympic Dream Team probably did the rest, but by then international basketball had grown considerably, aided in great part by the Celtics' goodwill trips abroad.

43 View "Celtic Pride" and Then...View Celtic Pride

Released in 1996, the film *Celtic Pride* starred Daniel Stern, Dan Aykroyd, and Damon Wayans in a comedy imaginatively set after the sixth game of the NBA Finals, with the series tied between the Celts and the Jazz. It came out at a fortuitous time, as the team's mystique had suffered for several years in mind-numbing and seemingly endless mediocrity, culminating in the real-life club enduring a record of 15–67 just after the film's release.

The plot centers around two friends who take umbrage at the Jazz's star Lewis Scott (Damon Wayans) celebrating after that sixth game, so they kidnap him before Game 7 of the Finals. The Scott character breaks free and runs onto the court just before the beginning of the deciding game, and rather than ruin the ending, suffice it to say that it is a fun watch for Celtics fans. As added bonuses, it contains cameos of Larry Bird, Bill Walton, and Bob Cousy, not to mention some interior shots of the old Garden.

Once you see *Celtic Pride*, you must view archival footage of the great players and coaches who developed the concept of Celtic pride, or mystique. The Internet will lead you to many of the most famous plays and games in sports history, but you are at the whim and caprice of poor production and even shoddier editing. There are also several good collections one might view, sanctioned by the appropriate entities, which possess a much higher quality. For old fans, it is a must to revisit the games and plays of the past, and for fans too young to have ever seen these games, it is even more vital to see how the Celtics prospered through all the rule changes and attitudinal shifts in the sport.

Celtic pride did not commence when Ray Allen and Kevin Garnett joined the team, and when the team wins, they have no need of overzealous rooters kidnapping the opposing team's superstar.

44 Pose with the Red Auerbach Statue

It's hokey, it's corny, it's something the most obvious tourist would never contemplate doing. All that may be true, but you still have to have your picture taken with the bronzed statue of Red Auerbach, immortalized in Boston's Quincy Market. Even Red Auerbach himself, oftentimes a curmudgeon, did it.

The statue was unveiled on September 20, 1985, to celebrate Red's 68th birthday, depicting him sitting on a bench with his victory cigar already lit up, celebrating another Celtics win. After he died, appreciative fans adorned the area with flowers and other mementoes in a collective mourning for their beloved coach.

Just a few steps away, Converse Shoes dedicated a space to Larry Bird, complete with a plaque outlining his accomplishments and a pair of replica bronzed shoes. You cannot step into the shoes, but you certainly can compare your foot size with that of Larry Legend. Unfortunately, most folks will not be able to measure up as Bird played in size 13½ sneakers. But, then again, outside of Michael Jordan, how many people can measure up favorably with this beloved great?

Another set of bronzed shoes, much smaller than those worn by Bird, lie nearby. The replicas of the running shoes honor local legend Bill Rodgers, "Boston Billy," the victor in four Boston Marathon races.

For those unfamiliar with Boston, Quincy Market is the ancient commercial area of the city, anchored by Faneuil Hall and containing many shops, offices, and restaurants. For the truly adventurous, try to find the location of Chelsea's restaurant in this area, a now defunct establishment. Its passing would little be noted except that, in May 1985, Larry Bird, teammate Quinn Buckner, and friend Mike Harris were patronizing the establishment when an altercation occurred, involving at least Bird and Harris against a fellow patron. The fight supposedly spilled out into the street, with Harris ending up as an emergency-room patient at Massachusetts General Hospital. An allegation was made that Bird struck the other individual in the mêlée.

The alleged victim of Bird's ire lawyered up, and the matter eventually faded away, but Bird will never speak about the incident and perhaps he cannot. Speculation arose that Bird's badly damaged right thumb, which may have accounted for his uncharacteristically poor shooting against Philadelphia in the Eastern Conference Finals, was aggravated in the scuffle at Chelsea's. According to *Boston Globe* columnist Dan Shaughnessy, Bird denied it, contending he hit the guy with his left fist.

In the event you are unable to find the old Chelsea's location through detective work, it is located near State Street and Merchant's Row, and an astute fan or seasoned bar habitué can pinpoint exactly where the old watering hole once sat. Beware though, if you see a very tall man with blond hair and an accent peculiar to French Lick, Indiana, looking at you with disapproval, you might wish to keep on walking past and stop asking questions.

45 Visit the Boston Beer Works

Situated at 112 Canal Street, outside of Boston Garden, the Boston Beer Works is a terrific place to eat, a restaurant that transcends the simple sports-bar label. Certainly you can order nachos and burgers, which incidentally exceed most competitors' pub fare, but also choose the raspberry mako shark or a sesame ginger stir fry.

Given the name of the restaurant, the owners do not take their beer lightly, but do not expect to order a can or a bottle of a national brand, because the Beer Works is literally a working brewery which only serves its own blends. If it is not busy, the management will show you how they do it, but even during dinner time or after a game, some of the giant metal containers are visible. They brew 60 different varieties of beer annually, with up to 16 different variations on draught at any time.

The brewmasters even have the luxury of taking their time with some of their creations, utilizing wooden barrels to produce a single brand of beer, sometimes taking up to one year to develop it from scratch to a stage suitable for a diner. If you visit after they have produced an 11 percent ABV bourbon stout (after four months of production), ask for it and prepare to enter a realm of beer enjoyment experienced by few sublunary souls.

So the place has great food and drink, but does it have televisions to watch the Celtics? Yes, in fact, the Boston Beer Works has 21 televisions, and upstairs you have your choice of 15 pool tables if you need some exercise before or after lunch or dinner. While the Boston Beer Works seats 557 patrons (off-season, they also seat customers on the sidewalk, café style), get there early, because 20 minutes before game time might not get you in, plus there is too much to enjoy at the restaurant itself to rush around.

Even if you do not stop by the Garden for more than a game or two a year, the Boston Beer Works also has restaurants located outside of Fenway Park and in outlying Salem, Lowell, and Hingham. They also retail their Boston Red, BlBueebeery Ale, and Fenway Pale Ale, which hopefully your local potent potable proprietor carries.

46 Bird's First Banner, 1981

From 1976 to 1979 the Celtics declined as a team to the extent that, instead of vying for the championship, they settled for a 29–53 record in 1978–1979. They ran through three coaches in three years, seemingly turning Boston into a coaching graveyard, but in the midst of the frustration, the club had gambled on drafting Larry Bird a year early.

And won.

The inmates having run Boston Garden in the years after the 1976 championship with rotating owners, coaches, and players—some woefully unmotivated souls—the club hired a former Marine drill sergeant, Bill Fitch, as their new coach.

Fitch began pruning the bad apples right away, and then quite discriminately figured out which veterans wanted to win and helped to motivate them toward a championship. In his first year, Fitch reversed the club's fortunes dramatically, winning 32 more games than the previous edition had. Bird played with Cowens and, ever too briefly, "Pistol" Pete Maravich, while Cedric Maxwell developed into a star, and Nate "Tiny" Archibald guided the team down the court. In the backcourt, Archibald was joined by other talented guards M.L. Carr, Gerald Henderson, and Chris Ford. Most important, Fitch had surrounded himself with players who competed.

Unfortunately, the first year that Fitch coached in Boston ended in the third round of the playoffs, as Julius Erving, Darryl Dawkins, and Bobby Jones of the Philadelphia 76ers defeated them in five games.

In 1980–1981 the Boston Celtics put it all together for their 14th championship after Robert Parish joined the team at center and forward Kevin McHale became the team's sixth man, both becoming Celtics as a result of the famous trade with Golden State for Joe Barry Carroll. After Cowens' retirement, Parish played exceptionally well, spelled by Rick Robey, while McHale backed up Bird and Maxwell at the forward position. As before, the team had four talented guards in Archibald, Carr, Henderson, and Ford.

During the regular season, they compiled a 62–20 record, but their one more win since the previous year did not adequately tell how much more powerful the team had become in the meantime. In the Eastern Conference semifinals, they swept the Chicago Bulls, facing the 76ers again in the Conference Finals.

The 76ers returned their strong frontcourt from the previous campaign, but point guard Maurice Cheeks had improved considerably, and the club had drafted a future star at shooting guard, Andrew Toney. A similar result as the previous season seemed assured as the Celtics quickly went down 3–1 in the series. Having dug themselves deep, the Celts did not crawl out of their predicament easily. But crawl out they did—winning the fifth game by two points.

Traveling to Philadelphia for Game 6, Robert Parish needed to establish a presence, which he did, scoring 21 points and retrieving 10 rebounds. Dr. J tried to guard Bird, failing in the attempt, as the 76ers squandered a 17-point lead at home. Again, Boston won by two, causing Philly's Andrew Toney to lament, "I can't believe they're a better team than we are. Two of three we lost, we should have won." Retorted Larry Bird, "Too many people give up in this world. We didn't."

Forcing a Game 7 at the Garden, the Celts arrived at Logan Airport well past midnight, but this did not deter approximately 1,500 screaming fans greeting them there. The team needed all of this support because, with 5:24 left in the last game, they trailed Philly 89–82. At that point the Celtics' D dominated, and the 76ers scored only one more point the rest of the contest, as Boston edged them out 91–90 to advance to the Finals against the Houston Rockets. Naturally, Bird won it after rebounding a missed Dawkins shot and driving the ball the length of the court for the win, while on defense Cedric Maxwell shut down Julius Erving.

Houston relied on center Moses Malone and some still reasonably effective veterans such as Rudy Tomjanovich, Calvin Murphy, and Bill Paultz. Swingman guard/forward Robert Reid experienced his finest year in the NBA that season. Having dispatched Philadelphia, Boston seemingly had a much easier assignment before it in the Finals.

Unfortunately, Houston came to play, and in the first game, only a monster game by Larry Bird saved his team from defeat. His 18 points, 21 boards, and nine assists led the Celts to a narrow 98–95 Game 1 victory. On one play, Bird acrobatically lunged toward the basket after missing a 22-foot shot, grabbed the ball with his right hand, flipped it in the middle of the air to his left hand, and tossed the shot in. Red Auerbach crowed that it was "the greatest play I've ever seen."

Moses Malone once said, "We never had a jinx against the Celtics. We just never won any games against them." In Game 2, the Rockets played a glacially slow game, finally winning 92–90 to square the series. In the next tiff, the Celtics sped it up, scoring 41 fast-break points to win 94–71, giving Bird the opportunity to rub it in, asserting, "With Moses out there, they'd have trouble getting back on the break." All boasting aside, the Rockets won the fourth game by having Robert Reid shut down Bird and having Mike Dunleavy score 28 points for them.

That proved to be high tide for the Rockets, as they simply did not have the talent or the speed to match up against Boston. The Celts won the final two games and their first title since the Bicentennial. Bird and Auerbach smoked cigars after the clinching game, Cedric Maxwell won the MVP award for the Finals, and the team flew back to Logan Airport, greeted by 2,500 fans. And on the day of the celebratory parade, in front of thousands of fans, Larry Bird told the world what he really thought of Moses Malone.

47 Second-Greatest Celtics Team

The 1985–1986 Boston Celtics team was arguably the greatest ever assembled. They compiled a 40–1 record at home en route to a regular-season record of 67–15. In the playoffs, they swept Michael Jordan and the Bulls, walked past the Hawks (4–1), then swept the Bucks on the way to the Finals, where they dispatched the Rockets in six games. The Celtics lost no home playoff games.

The '86 team fielded five future Hall of Famers—Larry Bird, Robert Parish, Kevin McHale, Bill Walton, and Dennis Johnson— a flush by most reasonable estimations, but Danny Ainge also played very well at guard, and this team had valuable subs like guard Jerry Sichting and former All-Star Scott Wedman. Except Walton, the players all operated at or near the zenith of their powers and, more important, played well together as a team. For instance, Larry Bird attempted and made his breathtaking no-look passes to teammates not because he had eyes at the back of his head as

Johnny Most claimed, but because he'd played so long and so well with the same core of players that he knew their moves.

Almost by consensus, the '86 team is acknowledged as the greatest Celtics edition ever, which then begs the much more controversial question, what was the second-greatest Boston squad?

Subjectively speaking, look no further than the 1961–1962 Boston Celtics. It is a peculiar choice, and in most Internet lists or even more reliable lists proffered by sportswriters, this team often does not even make the top five, but at least one mind will not change on this issue.

Chauvinism suggests that the second-greatest Celts team should have Red Auerbach as its coach, not to mention the estimable Walter Brown as its owner. Led by Bill Russell and a host of other future Hall of Famers, namely forwards Tommy Heinsohn, guards Sam Jones, K.C. Jones, Bob Cousy, and sixth man Frank Ramsey, the '62 team reeled off a 60–20 record and then defeated a very competitive Philadelphia team in seven games to face and defeat the L.A. Lakers in the Finals, again in seven. Add Satch Sanders and Jim Loscutoff at forwards and such valuable subs as Gary Phillips and Gene Guarilia, and it is not difficult to see why the 1961–1962 club dominated their opponents.

In defense of the '62 team as the second-greatest ever, it has Auerbach as the coach, with him coaching most of his early dynastic stars in their prime. By 1962–1963 the club picked up Havlicek, but Ramsey's game had declined dramatically from the previous year, Cousy was in his last year, and Heinsohn played almost 400 minutes fewer than in '62 and never regained his health until he retired as a 30-year-old at the end of the 1965 playoffs.

The '62 team might have an advantage over the '86 Celts because there were fewer teams and thus a higher concentration of talent, particularly since drafting of international players had not caught on that much, even by the late 1980s. Or did the earlier Celtics incarnation feast on weaker opponents, franchises led by

Should've Been

Neither the 1986 nor the 1962 champions won the most games in franchise history. That honor belongs to the 1972–1973 club, led by Dave Cowens, John Havlicek, and Jo Jo White, that compiled a 68–14 record. In addition to this troika, the team boasted some other very good players, such as Paul Westphal, Don Chaney, Paul Silas, Don Nelson, and Satch Sanders. This excellent team did not win a title and in fact did not even compete in the Finals, as it lost a seven-game series with the Knicks due largely to an injury to Havlicek.

owners who largely still followed the unspoken rule that a team should keep the number of African American players to a minimum, even as Walter Brown and Red Auerbach did not sub-scribe to such nonsense? Ultimately, the 1962 players pale in juxtaposition to the '86 squad, but the gap is not that wide, and the 1962 team certainly has historically not received its due as arguably the second-finest in franchise history.

One thing that all Celtics fans can agree to is that the earlier team incarnation had much better luck than Larry's Legends, a point punctuated by the fact that in the 1962 draft the club selected John Havlicek, and in 1986 they picked Len Bias.

48 Visit Matthews Arena

It was not even held at the Boston Garden. No, the now legendary Boston Celtics staged their first home game at the Boston Arena after being displaced by a rodeo show. Only 4,329 fans managed to show up, many of these dignitaries or folks who otherwise received comped tickets just to help fill up the place. Some of them might have even arrived to cheer on the various competitors for the first game on the card, a game of hoops between the Pere Marquette Knights of Columbus and the North Cambridge K of C.

For history buffs, North Cambridge won.

Then the Celtics and their opponents, the Chicago Stags, ran onto the floor and started their warmups. It was November 5, 1946, and none of the Celtics on that roster made a name for themselves with the exception of their center, Kevin "Chuck" Connors, later the star of *The Rifleman*, a long-running TV show in the late 1950s and early '60s. Goofing off, Connors threw a ball that broke the glass of the backboard.

With no spare backboards in the Arena, a posse was dispatched to the Boston Garden to obtain one, thus delaying the start of the game for an hour. During the interim, the teams staged an enervating foul-shooting contest won by the Celtics. Bored, many of the attendees left the Arena, depriving the home team of much of its original advantage.

Across town at his headquarters at 18 Tremont Street, a young John Fitzgerald Kennedy monitored the results of the final election for the U.S. House of Representatives' 11th district seat. He had previously bested nine other rivals in the Democratic primary, compiling a remarkable 40 percent of the vote. But it was a nail-biter in the general election, as the Democrat party in Massachusetts was taking a beating by the still-formidable state Republican party. Politics being the favorite Kennedy blood sport, no one ducked out of 18 Tremont Street to take in the basketball game, or the rodeo, for that matter.

Back at the Arena, eventually a proper backboard was reinstalled in the west end, but it did no good for the home team, which lost its first home game by two points. In time, the Stags disbanded, and the old Garden no longer exists. Little known, the parquet floor that became synonymous with the Boston Garden was actually the one used that evening at the Boston Arena, moved later as professional basketball in the city finally took hold.

Jack Kennedy ended up having a better evening, defeating his Republican challenger in the face of poor statewide party results, as two great Celtic dynasties began that same night in Boston, the Kennedys and the basketball club.

The Boston Arena is now known as the Matthews Arena, and it still houses basketball and hockey games as the home venue for Northeastern University. First built in 1910, it sustained two fires and has undergone a number of renovations, and yet still retains its Victorian charm. Nearby, old dead-ball baseball legends such as Hugh Duffy and Tommy McCarthy played, and on campus you will find a statue of the winningest Red Sox pitcher of them all (tied with Roger Clemens), Cy Young.

Reggie Lewis played his college basketball here, and after his tragic, untimely death, a memorial service was held here for his many grieving friends, family members, admirers, and fans.

The old Boston Garden no longer exists, but if you wish to see where the Celtics first started playing on their parquet floor, schedule a trip to Northeastern.

49 Dance with Gino

In the old days, Red Auerbach heralded a Celtics victory before time ran out by pulling out a cigar and lighting it, to the delight of fans and the utter displeasure of opponents. In the new millennium, the team now curiously plays back an old *American Bandstand* clip highlighted by a bearded man with a Gino (in honor of Canadian disco singer Gino Vannelli) T-shirt dancing happily away. The fans then join in the fun.

As a result of an investigation conducted by the *Wall Street Journal*, no less, the identity of the dancer apparently was the late Joseph R. Massoni of Rialto, California, who sadly died of pneumonia in 1990.

Supposedly, the Gino shirt was not even his, but borrowed from a friend for the show.

If the memories of some long-suffering fans are reliable, "Gino" did not always make an appearance to herald an apparent victory, but rather played at other times, since a victory rarely occurred in the pre-Garnett Garden days. Back then, the poor marketing department of the Celtics tried everything to inject life into a moribund franchise with little success, but Gino survived through thick and thin, and if you let down your hair and dance just right during a Celtics home game, you might even become immortalized yourself on the Jumbotron. Like Gino himself.

At Fenway Park, Red Sox Nation serenades the players with "Sweet Caroline," but at the Garden, the fans rock to *American Bandstand* and its most enduring guest dancer.

Walter Brown

Celtics owner Walter Brown did not even particularly like basketball, referring to it for years as "bounce-ball." However, if he did not initially cotton to the sport, as president of the Boston Garden (in addition to the Bruins in hockey), he welcomed an empty sports arena even less. Anticipating robust postwar profits in sports and recreation, he met with a number of magnates in the summer of 1946 and helped to found the Basketball Association of America, the precursor of the National Basketball Association.

Now that he has been dead for more than 45 years, when most folks reflect back on Walter Brown, they tend to view him as a good-natured, calcified figure, sort of like George Washington, a man who sort of once lived. The hazy image belies the very fiery individual who accomplished so much for Boston sport in his 59 years. Basically, he was a big-hearted Irish man, sensitive, and most open to articulating his hurt.

Although he preferred hockey, he found out it did not take long to develop a feel for bounce-ball, stating on one occasion, "Once I got into pro basketball, I found out there were a lot of other people in the game who knew nothing about it."

Prone to losing his temper, even Brown admitted, "When you're the kind of guy I am, who boils over easily and is sorry later, you'd damn well better have more luck than sense." For years he scheduled luncheons at the Hotel Lenox in Boston's Back Bay, at which time he invited players and members of the press for his own version of "Festivus," where he publicly berated his players for their perceived faults. Of course he always apologized and indulged his players, overpaying them every bit as much as crosstown Red Sox owner Tom Yawkey did his charges.

Traditionally, he would send a contract down to a player with the amount of salary left blank, and often a player like Frank Ramsey would send it back with the instruction to Walter to write in a figure that he thought was fair.

Unlike Yawkey, Brown proved a social progressive, not resisting integrating his roster but rather embracing the introduction of the first African American player in the NBA, Chuck Cooper. In this spirit, the Celtics were also the first to field an all-black starting five and the first African American coach, Bill Russell. Indeed, after Walter Brown died, one local scribe wondered what success the Red Sox might have encountered had Brown owned them and desegregated the club much earlier.

Brown brought Boston alive at night after the commuters largely left the North Station area of town. The Celtics and the Bruins had their fans, as did aficionados of the circuses and concerts staged there. Almost everyone treasured the old Boston Garden, faults and all, particularly as it got older, and fans remembered the

Beloved team founder Walter Brown enjoys a rare moment of relaxation, an anomaly for such an engaged and engaging man.

venue as the site of an event shared with Mom, Dad, brothers, sisters, and friends. If one rooted for the Celtics, even in the late 1950s and 1960s when the Celtics seemingly won title after title with ease, they hardly ever sold out their 13,909 seats, so few had to resort to sitting in the hopelessly obstructed seats that littered the areas behind poles and under mezzanines.

Having established his Celtics, Walter Brown watched his team founder for its first several years, nearly driving him into bankruptcy as he struggled to keep the team alive as other franchises folded around him. Walter Brown needed stars, but first he had to hire a good coach, and he picked the finest one out there in Arnold "Red" Auerbach in 1950.

Auerbach and Brown were equally cursed with short tempers, and their relationship easily might have disintegrated under the stress of keeping the franchise alive and developing a championship-caliber club. Oddly, they got along quite well and respected each other immensely. They innately sensed the good in each other, and Brown implicitly trusted his coach to deliver his team to excellence and relieve the financial pressures that plagued the Celtics as the league gained a fan base.

Walter Brown died in 1964, succeeded by a platoon of owners since, but in Boston, he is still the Owner, the man who gave the city a basketball dynasty, and his symbolic No. 1 has long since been retired by the team.

51 The Celtics Fan

The Boston Celtics fan is a most misunderstood animal, often viewed from afar as a most ungrateful sort. After all, how could the old Boston Garden not sell out consistently during the prolonged excellence of the Russell era? During the dynasty's later years, when Bobby Orr's Bruins came from nowhere to own the town, that hockey ticket became so hard to obtain that impatient fans often had to wait to receive it as an inheritance from a dead loved one.

In defense of the Celtics fan, the enthusiasm for basketball itself grew enormously in popularity during the 1980s, so to suggest a lack of loyalty in Boston presupposes that it was wildly successful everywhere else in America's professional arenas. When the NCAA tournament became a huge national event and the pro game grew increasingly exciting with the advent of the three-point shot and the infusion of international players (and the elimination of prejudice against African American athletes), basketball prospered, as other sports like boxing declined.

Unfortunately, as the sport grew, the Celtics enjoyed an exciting era with the coming of Larry Bird and his teammates, which had the consequence of not only selling out the old Garden, but depriving longtime followers access to good tickets. Fair-weather customers strolled into the Garden and bought expensive tickets and cheered for Scott Wedman, in the mistaken belief he was Larry Bird. Many old fans only got in by buying obstructed-view seats, although these true fans could tell when Larry had the ball, even if they only could see his shoes.

The team declined by the mid-'90s, with the fad-following customers the first to leave, heading out to buy pink Red Sox hats, as they and their progeny began to haunt Friendly Fenway. And as trying as it often became to watch some of the more hapless versions of the Celtics, men and women, once young, took their children to the North Station area to learn to love the team as they had, and always would.

The true fan welcomed false prophets like David Gavitt and Rick Pitino because they never ceased to believe. They tuned in to Tommy Heinsohn as they had once set the dial on their transistor radios to listen to Johnny Most, because they never wanted to cease to believe.

Loving the Celtics is more pure than it has ever been, since folks now buy tickets because they want to see their team, not jump on a bandwagon. When a championship comes, like it did in 2008, great, but seeing each game or watching it on television is the goal. Obtaining a season ticket or a bloc-of-tickets package is huge; having to relinquish it is heartbreak.

But the Celtics will never leave, and in living rooms and sports bars across New England, the game is on. The Celtics fan has grown more mature and grounded than ever, with the team in sickness and in health, through good times and bad, and when a banner is raised to the rafters of the Garden, it simply reinforces the feeling that sometimes heaven and earth unite.

52 Get Bill Russell's Autograph

Ah, the Holy Grail. Despite his athletic talent and high intelligence, Bill Russell unfortunately is defined by his quirks and the manner in which he, as a very sensitive person, reacted to situations that he encountered in his life. One prime example of this was his refusal for decades to sign autographs, a practice that an ESPN writer traces back to 1964, although it does not appear he enjoyed signing for people much before that date, either.

It made many of his teammates cringe. Bob Cousy, for one, absolutely hated seeing it happen, and it impelled him to do the opposite when a fan approached him. It bothered Cousy so much that he openly commented about it, even writing about it over 20 years after he and Russell had last served on the same Celtics roster together. An FBI file contained this entry about Russell, describing him as "an arrogant Negro who won't sign autographs for white children."

To be fair, it doesn't appear he signed a whole lot of autographs for black kids, either. This practice even extended to teammates like Tommy Heinsohn, who simply wanted to do a favor for someone else. Russell sometimes tried to explain why he did not sign, but such attempts only made him come off as the kind of guy who even Ebenezer Scrooge would call a curmudgeon.

Perhaps it had something to do with his Jesuit college education, one of the chief tenets of which is to think and speak and act in a consistent manner. This may or may not have played a part in

Russell's practice. If it did, then he should have spent a moment reading Emerson and known that consistency is the hobgoblin of little minds. In any event, he deviated sharply from his cherished practice in 1992, when he decided to sign his autograph for money, becoming a memorabilia show draw.

Did Russell do it for the money? After all, since he failed to sign for so long, his signature rightly or wrongly held a lot of value through simple supply and demand. Or had Russell mellowed in all these years, as he saw that Boston was not as racist as he once thought, or that he meant a lot to people, even those for whom he did not sign? Only Bill Russell could spark a philosophical debate about autograph-signing.

Perhaps Russell has recognized the folly of his refusal to sign (for free, at least), seeing this practice as a simple justification for acting rudely. In that event, maybe one day you will be lucky enough to see Russell at an event or speaking somewhere and approach him and ask for an autograph. And it is hoped most profoundly that he leans down, grabs the Sharpie, and signs for you.

53 When Boston Was Not a Basketball Town

Springfield, Massachusetts, is only 90 miles away from the capital city of Boston, although many people believe Springfield is the capital. Boston, of course, has long been the center of basketball in New England due to the excellence displayed by so many Celtics squads, but it did not start out that way.

Trivia buffs know that James Naismith founded basketball in 1891 at the Springfield YMCA, attempting to provide the young men there with a wholesome indoor sporting activity to bridge their otherwise cold hibernatory New England nights between the close of football and the dawning of a new baseball season. Like George Washington cutting down the cherry tree or Abner Doubleday inventing baseball around Cooperstown, New York, it is a treasured part of our folklore. Best yet, with basketball, the story is true, right down to the peach-basket hoops.

And yet for all of the proximity of Boston to Springfield, and presumably vice versa, the new sport of basketball did not seem to catch on very well in the Commonwealth's capital. Midwesterners embraced it, and even folks who lived down in the southern states and were not cooped up by the cold each winter adapted to it quite well. So fast did the sport grow that by 1904 it wended its way into the Olympics as a demonstration sport.

Professional basketball teams flourished all over America, particularly after World War I. On the West Side of New York, tough Hell's Kitchen men formed the nucleus of the Celtics, an incredible barnstorming team that spent 10 postwar years playing games all over the country, winning at their height 90 percent of them. Back in Boston, the city meekly let at least two professional teams die on the vine, the Whirlwinds in the mid-1920s and the Trojans a decade later. It was not just basketball, either; the Boston Redskins did not inspire much loyalty until team owner George Preston Marshall moved them out to Washington.

The Boston Whirlwinds came and left the city…sort of like a whirlwind. They had just come off a barnstorming tour in towns in Massachusetts, Rhode Island, Maine, and New Hampshire when, on January 23, 1923, they met their supreme test in playing at home against the legendary original Celtics. They lost to the Celtics on that occasion in a high-scoring affair, 29–20, before 4,000 fans, although the Whirlwinds did rebound later that season against a New England Oil team.

By December 1924 the lineup of the Whirlwinds changed completely, with at least two players being locals, "Fiddle" Morey of

Roxbury and Charlie Mernot of the city's West End. Shortly after, the Whirlwinds apparently disbanded.

Concerning the Trojans, they participated in the American Basketball League in 1934 and 1935, with mixed results. The team played at the old Boston Arena, arrayed with such stars as "Husto," who "played with the Celtics, and Bender, a Jewish boy, [who] was one of the greatest courtsmen ever turned out of Columbia University." The team was captained by Russ Saunders, "the high-priced big shot of the local five."

Players came and went, with the club at one juncture attempting to entice local professional football star Cliff Battles of the Boston Redskins to sign up, a ploy that the early Boston Celtics later briefly pulled off with some of the Boston Yanks' football players. At one point, they canceled all scheduled league games for a week to accommodate barnstorming trips to play teams in Worcester and Bridgeport, Connecticut.

By March 1935 the club barely took up a paragraph in the sports pages, with what little fan base they had left faced with the stark realization on St. Patrick's Day that the Jersey team had beaten them "to push the Trojans deeper into the cellar." A few days later the club got trounced in New York and then disappeared, as most fans began to worry about the Bruins, suburban high school tourneys, and the upcoming spring for the Red Sox.

Although the Trojans swooned, the American Basketball League survived the defunct Boston franchise by 20 years, but by then, of course, the Celtics had begun to take root. Until then, Boston's sports fandom devoted themselves to cheering on Eddie Shore and the Boston Bruins, together with local high school varsity teams.

Even though the Trojans did not thrive, one of their players, Lou Bender, fared much better, later becoming a very successful attorney, dying less than six months before his 100th birthday.

No, Boston was a Bruins and Red Sox town, with little love for basketball. It would be nice to say that the Whirlwinds and Trojans are fondly remembered by basketball lovers throughout New England, but in truth they are as forgotten as the name of Sam Adams' imaginary friend. The phrase "Banned in Boston" originally meant the tendency of the city fathers to keep out any hint of risqué entertainment within their jurisdiction, as earnestly as if Cotton Mather still oversaw the public morals, but it meant so much more when in 1925 the city cut basketball in the public high schools.

Racial undertones did not dictate the public taste, either, as the Bruins and Whirlwinds/Trojans each wheeled out all-white rosters. At that time, basketball was a slow, lumbering sport encumbered by a lack of shot clock and three-point shooting opportunities (think how ugly a dunking competition back then would have been), while hockey had exciting and fast players. Plus, back then people loved to see a good fight.

If you wanted to watch or play basketball, better to head to Worcester, New England's second-largest city and the home of Holy Cross College, where collegians like Bob Cousy ran circles around their opponents in the years just after the end of World War II. Anywhere but Boston.

54 Bicentennial Banner

Red-headed Dave Cowens starred on the Celtics' 1975–1976 club along with Jo Jo White, forward Don Nelson, John Havlicek, Paul Silas, and Charlie Scott. Since it always seemed Red Auerbach tried to trade Silas for Scott or vice versa, it was refreshing to actually see the two talented players on the same roster, and it did lead to success for head coach Tommy Heinsohn.

Unfortunately, the Celtics during the off-season had traded their talented young guard, Paul Westphal, to the Phoenix Suns for Scott, a trade that worked out well for both organizations in the short run, and for Phoenix for a number of years thereafter. Too well, as events transpired.

For the fifth year in a row, Tommy Heinsohn led his men to an Atlantic Division title, with a 54–28 mark. With the exception of guards Jo Jo White and Kevin Stacom, the remainder of the roster consisted of swingmen, probably constituting some obscure NBA statistic. Historically, in Boston this versatility did not reflect mediocrity but strength, as Coach Heinsohn could call on individual players to assume roles designed to exploit an opponent's weakness.

As they had done in the 1974 playoffs, the Celtics played the Buffalo Braves first. Jack Ramsay coached the Braves again, but this time Bob McAdoo dominated this club, which placed second in the Atlantic Division with a 46–36 record. The Braves' center/forward, John Shumate, regained his health for the playoffs, so the Celtics faced what Tommy Heinsohn called a "tough, tough series."

Philosophically, the Celtics had decided that pressing hard during the regular season had done them no good, as exhibited by their 1972–1973 and 1974–1975 editions, which overran most opponents during the regular season, then faded in the postseason. To address this trend, Heinsohn loosened his grip on his players in the spring of 1976, as the club lost four of its last five games before the playoffs began. Dave Cowens had sat out these games with bone spurs in his right heel and continued to recuperate in the 10-day interim before the team played its first playoff game. Waxed Heinsohn, "We've worked very hard during the layoff. I just hope that we're not sloppy and can do the fast break and the other things we do well."

In the first playoff game, Don Nelson came off the bench with two quick field goals to cut into a lead that the Braves had established, after which the Celtics began to take the game over. Tempers erupted as Havlicek almost got into a fight with John Shumate, with "Shu," a former Notre Dame Fighting Irish star adopting a Joe Louis stance. Havlicek let it pass as his team won. Unfortunately, Hondo injured himself in practice after the first game, ending up on crutches and unable to play the next game. Don Nelson saved the day in the second game by sinking four free throws late, as the Celts won 101–96.

With Havlicek having to sit out the next two games, Ernie DiGregorio lit up the boards as the Braves evened the series. Fortunately, Charlie Scott had a hot hand in the last two games of the series to lead his team to the next round.

In the Eastern Conference Finals, tough coach Bill Fitch led the Cleveland Cavaliers, a team stocked with no superstars, but rather a number of good players such as Austin Carr, Bingo Smith, Campy Russell, Jim Chones, Dick Snyder, and an aging Nate Thurmond at center. The Celtics had to worry most about the health of John Havlicek, not fully recovered from his recent injury sustained in a team practice.

Nonetheless, the Celtics won their first two games, as they ran their fast break and smothering defense quite advantageously. In the second game, the Cavs threatened until Nate Thurmond fouled out, with Cowens eating Thurmond's replacement alive. Seemingly poised to put away an inferior opponent and sweep the series, Boston instead lost its next two games to knot the series at two games apiece.

Into the fray came John Havlicek for the fifth game, "trot[ting] out in uniform onto the Boston Garden's parquet floor just as warmups had almost ended." Hondo actually did not participate in the game until only 5:03 remained in regulation, but he sank two critical free throws with 11 seconds left to help lift his team to the victory and a one-game lead in the series. Afterward, the modest Havlicek, commenting on the crowd cheering wildly when he came onto the court, admitted, "I hate that. I'd like to weave my way in

By the mid-1970s, nothing seemed to come easily to the Celtics, and yet with an undersized team, they still managed to win two more titles.

without anybody noticing, just sneak in and join the others." As if he could.

Havlicek played a bit more, 23 minutes, in the sixth game as 21,564 Cavs fans turned out to see their team lose the game and the series. Cowens came up big with 21 points and 18 boards, as did guard Jo Jo White, with 29 points. Cleveland coach Fitch conceded, "You won't find them making many mental errors," as the Celts advanced for their series in the Finals against an unlikely Phoenix Suns team.

In the regular season, John McLeod's Suns had limped to a 42–40 record, not surprising for a team with few stars, dependent mostly on former Celt Paul Westphal, Rookie of the Year Alvan

Adams, and surprise contributions from role players. Yet the Suns came alive in the playoffs, most recently shocking a much stronger defending NBA-champion Warriors team led by Rick Barry, Phil Smith, and Jamaal Wilkes. Still, as expected, the Celtics defeated the Suns in the first two games, after which talk of a sweep emerged in the streets and newspaper pages of Boston.

Phoenix quieted such talk with two wins of their own, evening the series and setting the stage for the fifth game at the Garden. Hailed widely as the Greatest Game Ever, it took the Celtics three overtimes to finally win, a testament to the remarkable play and stamina of their guard, Jo Jo White. Boston then traveled to Phoenix, but the Suns had already given their last measure, and the Celtics flew back to Logan Airport as champions.

The Celtics had just won their 13th title, but Karma reared up soon thereafter, not only for the Celtics but also for the Boston Bruins. Basking in the glow of victory, Paul Silas jokingly mused, "I just remembered something. My contract's up this year, isn't it? Hmmmmm." And the Celtics' Boston Garden mates, the Bruins, just lost their superstar defenseman Bobby Orr to the Chicago Black Hawks. Auerbach had the chance that summer to avoid the Bruins' brand of public relations disaster by signing his star player, but chose to play hardball and lost Silas. In Boston, in the bicentennial year of 1976, it had suddenly become a place to refrain from embracing.

55 "Bad News" Barnes

In Celtics lore, the team contained a wealth of Bad News Barneses. The first was Jim Barnes, a native of Tuckerman, Arkansas, and Stillwater, Oklahoma. After Walter Brown died, a businessman named Marvin Kratter became the owner, hoping that he might sell a few more beers, no doubt for one of his other concerns, Knickerbocker Beer. Toward the end of his stewardship of the team in 1968, he brought in a backup forward/center named Jim Barnes, a graduate of Texas Western College (later renamed UTEP). He had previously played for the Knicks, Bullets, Lakers, and Bulls, in a largely disappointing career that petered away shortly after he left Boston in 1970.

Although there are no statues of Jim Barnes in Quincy Market or outside of the Boston Garden, he did leave an impression during his brief tenure here. As coaches, Red Auerbach and Bill Russell had few unbendable rules, mainly because they chose professional players for their rosters. They did expect players to arrive at the locker room two hours before the game began and, certainly, to show up to hear the remarks of the coach before the game started.

One snowy day, Jim Barnes failed in both pursuits, coming into the dressing room in the middle of the pregame talk, wearing sandals, no socks, and the lightest of clothing to brave the harsh weather outside. Oblivious to the situation, Barnes walked up to Kratter and greeted him by pointing a finger into the owner's stomach and saying, "Hey, Big Money, what's happening, man?" Kratter sold the team shortly thereafter.

Another time, Barnes started at center, and rather than try to get his hand on the opening tip-off, he punched the opposing center right in the face. Referee Earl Strom called him for a technical right away, but back then a single T did not disqualify a player, usually it took two to toss someone. But one word—pertaining to a person having an Oedipal relationship with his own mother—always merited such a strict penalty. Barnes, normally a very peaceful fellow, leveled that one ugly word at Earl Strom, who promptly threw him out of the game.

"Thanks, Earl," said Jim Barnes, "I had a date tonight."

The second Bad News Barnes hailed from the streets of Providence, Rhode Island. As the sequel to Jim Barnes, Marvin proved the rare exception to the rule that the original is always better. For starters, Marvin was a much better ballplayer than Jim, having starred at Providence College and then earned Rookie of the Year honors with the Spirits of St. Louis of the American Basketball Association. In his first two years of professional ball, Marvin scored an average of 24.0 and then 24.1 points per game, while also establishing himself as one of the league leaders in rebounds, steals, and blocked shots.

Marvin Barnes possessed some of the most wide-ranging talent in basketball history and ideally would have racked up monster career statistics to bear this out, but early on he exhibited peculiar behavior, once disappearing with his agent for a spell during his first pro season. In the NBA, Detroit and Buffalo took him on briefly, and when the Braves moved west to become the Clippers, Boston obtained him in a trade before the 1978–1979 season. The Celtics dumped, among others, malcontent Sidney Wicks to obtain Barnes, Tiny Archibald, and two draft choices. Once in his new surroundings, Archibald's career entered a renaissance phase while Red Auerbach parlayed one of the draft choices to bring Danny Ainge into the fold.

Had Barnes gotten his life together, he might have been remembered as being part of one of the greatest trades in league history and had his number raised to the rafters of the Garden. He did not, playing sparingly that year, before the team waived him and he officially received his last rites as a player the next year with the Clippers. During one game with the Celts, he recalled the following experience:

> I remember this one game, I was sitting at the end of the bench.
> I had a towel over my head and I was snorting coke and my
> nose was bleeding. Don Chaney and Nate Archibald moved all
> the way up to the front, and I had four or five seats between me
> and the next player. I was snorting coke, and it was tearing my

membranes up. Snorting it and blowing my nose. It was like my brains were coming out in the towel, and I couldn't stop snorting it, anyway. It was terrible, man. I was addicted.

After he shot himself out of town in the NBA, he did time in jail and had no home for spells, but has largely straightened out his life, mentoring young men back in Providence to avoid the lure of drugs. In other words, "Do as I say, not as I did." The intentions are undoubtedly sincere, but no guarantees of good behavior ever attach to Marvin Barnes.

56 Cherished Rituals

Most athletes prepare for a game or a match in a fairly consistent manner; it is only when elements of superstition or compulsiveness seep in, then the pregame activities become much more interesting.

Not that he wanted it this way, but Bill Russell, for instance, used to throw up before virtually every basketball game he played as a professional. It is a tribute to him as a player that this did not seemingly weaken him at all, but rather made it easier to adjust to the pressure of the upcoming game.

Before the tipoff of a game, Kevin Garnett walks up to the Celtics' broadcasters with white rosin in his hands and, in a form of benediction, showers them over the heads with the powder. He also head butts the padding around the shaft of basketball backboard.

While the fans witness Garnett's pregame activities, the antics pale in comparison to the extensive preparation of Ray Allen. Allen gets to the gym or the arena early and takes a plethora of shots, a habit extending back to childhood. On occasion, Allen might suggest that a teammate sit in a new seat.

St. Christopher

Walter Brown used to carry a St. Christopher Medal with him at every Celtics game, and after he died in 1964, his widow gave it to Red Auerbach. Auerbach, in turn, kept it with him during the entire 1964–1965 championship season.

Celtics fans are no better, shifting in seats or standing stock still during a run by the team. Any of these rituals practiced by players and fans alike are harmless, and in the case of the Boston Celtics, they seem to work.

57 Fight Night at the Garden

Back when most sports fans in America actually cared about professional boxing, the Garden sponsored numerous prize fights, mostly in front of thousands of guys with suits, overcoats, and fedoras. Back then, folks dressed for sporting events in their finest finery. Some of the greatest fights occurred in the Garden when the Bruins came to town, with celebrated pugilists such as Eddie Shore and Terry O'Reilly sending many an opponent home crying.

But in hockey, fights are supposed to occur—in fact, they are encouraged. In basketball, considered a non-contact sport, fights ideally should never occur. But occasionally a corker breaks out, and as the late Johnny Most would point out, it was always the other team's fault.

Red Auerbach recognized that his team needed some fighters, so he purchased Bob Brannum from the Sheboygan Red Skins in 1950, and later brought in Jim Loscutoff to protect some of the starters. Even with such stalwarts as Brannum and Loscy out there, the Celtics' stars of the 1950s still had to fight their share, and no one fought better than gentlemanly Bill Sharman.

Perhaps the most notorious fight in team history occurred on April 1, 1962, when the Celtics faced Wilt Chamberlain and the Philadelphia Warriors in the fifth game of their playoff series. Wilt got angry because Sam Jones was running circles around him, so he hit Jones on the chin and then started grabbing for his arms, with Jones convinced the much taller man "was trying to break them." The players all the while were swearing at each other. Sam then fell and went to the sideline and picked up a stool to ward Wilt away, thus commencing, you guessed it, "April Stool's Day."

Quipped Clif Keane of the *Globe*, "It was then that Wilt looked like a lion, after having impersonated a lamb in the court all afternoon." Jones explained his choice of the chair for shield (or as a weapon) afterward, stating, "If I'm goin' to fight him, I'm not going to fight fair."

Having kept Wilt at bay, the scene shifted to the Warriors' Guy Rodgers, who took a swing at the Celts' Carl Braun. Blood gushed out of Braun's mouth as enraged Garden fans started punching Rodgers until the police intervened. Into the fray jumped the Celts' "Jungle Jim" Loscutoff who saw red, charging after Rodgers. Loscutoff fell once and overshot his victim on the second try, as Rodgers grabbed a stool of his own to keep Loscy at bay. Fans, players, and police all milled around the parquet.

Once order was restored, the third act of the tragedy commenced when Tommy Heinsohn went after the Warriors' Ted Luckenbill, earning Heinsohn an ejection. In all, the NBA commissioner fined Jones, Loscutoff, and Heinsohn for the Celtics and Rodgers and Luckenbill for the Warriors. Admitted Loscy afterward, "I don't know what I'd have done to [Rodgers]. But if I ever got my hands on him, I might have broken him in two." Little noted at the time, Boston won the game.

The old days were fading, however, and while the Celtics have engaged in some good punch-ups since (Parish vs. Laimbeer, Sichting vs. Sampson, McHale v. Rambis), the old insane days have probably ended, largely because the players make too much money to risk it over a game of "hit the other guy over the head with a stool."

But rest assured, as any player who had gone baseline once too often has learned, basketball is a contact sport, and while the new Boston Garden does not hold itself out as a prize-fighting venue, fight nights at the Garden have not ceased forever.

58 Celtics Mascots

Given the Celtics' name, anointing the leprechaun as the mascot took little imagination, but unlike the Notre Dame Fighting Irish leprechaun who roamed the sideline in South Bend for decades, Boston largely kept its mascot on patches and pennants.

That changed in 2002, when the club introduced "Lucky," its real-life leprechaun, capable of awe-inspiring gymnastic feats—particularly on trampolines, where Lucky soared into the air and performed dunks only dreamt about by Bill Russell or Robert Parish. The man who donned the gold-and-green shamrock vest and bow tie, Damon Lee Blust, disappeared in late January 2009, due to an unspecified dispute with the team.

High above courtside, the late Red Auerbach undoubtedly lit a cigar when he heard the news and, after glancing briefly at the Boston Celtic Dancers, smiled and said, "One down, one to go." The cigar did not stay lit for long, though, as a new Lucky is now gracing the parquet, with another performer taking on the role.

Red Auerbach famously desegregated before any other NBA club and placed the first African American starting five on the court, but in other aspects he proved less ecumenical, most famously claiming the team would never allow cheerleaders onto the floor. Perhaps out of respect for Red, the team owners honored this demand as long as he lived, but have since added cheerleaders to the repertoire, the last NBA team to do so.

A brief mention should be made of an unofficial mascot of the team, Busty Heart, the scion of a well-off suburban Boston family, who once attended prep school at Dana Hall. In her later incarnation, she was noticed in the 1986 playoffs by Johnny Most, among others, as the Celts' announcer commented, "There is a blonde with very large assets dancing in the stands. She looks like Morganna but much larger." She distracted the Atlanta Hawks to no end.

Busty became a huge, if temporary, sensation, stretching through the 1986 Finals and even bedeviling Jack Nicholson the next year before she disappeared from the hardwood courts. She is still entertaining millions, recently auditioning on *America's Got Talent* in an act that must be seen to be believed.

'Toine

An extraordinarily galvanizing figure in Celtics history, Antoine Walker burst into Boston in the 1996–1997 season as, hopefully, the team's next great power forward, and he did make the All-Rookie first-team that year, averaging 17.5 points per game. Thus began the peculiar career of the 6'7" forward, a three-time NBA All-Star and one of the most reviled players the Celtics ever fielded.

His athletic pedigree was particularly strong, prepping at Chicago powerhouse Mt. Carmel High and apprenticing in a starring role with Kentucky, starting on their 1996 NCAA national championship team under Rick Pitino. Probably, he should have stayed in school another year or two, but the NBA draft beckoned,

If ever a man came to Boston in the wrong era, it was Antoine Walker. Had he played under Red Auerbach with no three-point temptation, 'Toine may have made the Hall of Fame, or at least received a kick in the pants from Red every time the player wiggled after making a basket.

and he knew he would be selected in a very high position, so he declared.

Boston, by this time, had tired of their center, Eric Montross, so the club packaged him and a first-round draft choice to Dallas for two first-round choices, one in 1996 and the other in 1997. The Celtics chose Walker with the sixth pick in the '96 draft, selecting his former Kentucky teammate Ron Mercer with the next year's pick.

In the 1997–1998 season the Celtics had a team with some very strong young players, including Walker, Mercer, and Chauncey Billups, but unfortunately their notoriously impatient head coach, Rick Pitino, began to trade away many of his most promising players soon thereafter. Billups left later that year in the Kenny Anderson trade, and the club ended with a poor 36–46 record. A lingering feeling developed that Walker and Mercer did not play for their old coach with the same vigor as they had in college, but in any event, in his second year as a professional, 'Toine averaged 22.4 points per game. This was the first of five times in his career that he averaged more than 20 points per game.

The next year, the NBA lockout rocked basketball, and one Pitino confidant believes this issue proved a watershed event for the coach, as he saw some of his younger players, Walker in particular, come back not in the best of shape. This defense of Pitino ignores the fact that he traded Mercer, but kept Walker aboard, a curious personnel decision to make concerning a player in which one has supposedly lost faith.

Regardless, Pitino and Walker did not replicate their college success, and Pitino quit the team in 2001. Before he left, he drafted Paul Pierce from Kansas, and Pierce and Walker became a very effective scoring tandem for the team. Boston reached the Eastern Conference Finals, losing the series to New Jersey 4–2 at the end of the 2001–2002 campaign, a monumental achievement in light of the club's recent record of frustration and the talent outflow caused by Pitino.

New coach Jim O'Brien accomplished quite a bit in the wake of Pitino's abrupt departure, and although the Celts did not improve the next season, they did win the first round of the play-offs. By this point, the talented Walker had his fans but also his bitter detractors; the latter group did not like to see him send up so many three-point shots, and most did not like the way he wiggled after scoring a basket. Early in his career, Walker had rebounded well, but increasingly he became an indiscriminate gunner, astoundingly leading the NBA in 2001–2002 both in field goals attempted and three-point shots attempted. Although he averaged 22.1 points per game that year and led the NBA in minutes played, he did not get near the leader board in field-goal percentage or three-point percentage.

While fellow forward Paul Pierce played an intense game, to some Walker looked oblivious to the game around him except when sending shots up to the basket. The criticism was unfair. After all, Walker placed near the top of the league each year in minutes played—the club did not have the second coming of Sidney Wicks or Curtis Rowe. Increasingly, though, Walker took too many shots, particularly from three-point range, when his ability to place the basket through the net did not warrant this.

Coach Jim O'Brien had seen enough, and the club dealt Walker and Tony Delk to the Dallas Mavericks in October 2003 for Raef LaFrentz, Chris Mills, Jiri Welsch, and a draft choice (later used to pick Delonte West). It was the typical "change of scenery" swap, in which the two teams hoped that in a different climate, Walker and LaFrentz might prosper, neither of which occurred. In fact, the Celts worsened noticeably, causing O'Brien's departure from the team as its head coach in midseason, as another wave of rebuilding began in Boston.

Strangely, Walker came back to the Celtics during the 2004–2005 season, and his second act did not work out, as the club lost in the first round of the playoffs in Doc Rivers' first year as head coach. During the off-season, Walker became part of a massive five-team trade, the end result being that the Celtics ended up with little of value in return. Walker played another three years, but irreversible decline had set in, and by the end of 2008 he was finished.

Embarrassingly, Walker later got picked up for alleged drunk driving and then was arrested in a casino, as the millions of dollars he had earned as a player had disappeared.

Quietly controversial to the end, even his detractors largely felt saddened by Walker's plight, and while a return to the NBA is highly unlikely, it is hoped that 'Toine can stabilize his personal life. Had he played in the 1960s, Red Auerbach and Bill Russell probably could have straightened out his game, and with no three-point play, he would have not had the irresistible temptation to bomb shots from all over the floor. But he played for Boston during a largely dry spell, and should be remembered along with Paul Pierce as one of the few talented players on the team during that period.

60 The Curse of Len Bias

Until the Boston Red Sox won their first World Series in 86 years, a popular excuse had long floated around attributing this long period of futility to the Curse of the Bambino. In other words, once then–Sox owner Harry Frazee sent Babe Ruth to the Yankees, Fate stepped in to ensure the club did not win thereafter. It was nonsense, of course, the Sox failed for so long because Frazee continued to send future Hall of Famers and other stars to New York for nothing in return. And when Tom Yawkey took over the team, he refused to desegregate his team until 1959, letting Jackie Robinson and Willie Mays slip through his fingers.

This did not stop the plethora of "curses" that subsequently spread across America to explain why teams did not win. After the Celtics stopped winning championships after 1985–1986, it became only a matter of time until the Curse of Len Bias emerged.

The Celtics had chosen Len Bias as their first draft choice directly after earning their 16th title in 1986, and Bias died shortly after. The curse for Len Bias was crack cocaine, a drug that proved lethal when he used it after returning home from his meet-and-greet in Boston after the draft.

The Celtics did not fall precipitously without Bias, as the Sox did without Ruth, and had Bill Walton not been injured, the team might have beaten the Lakers in the Finals in 1987, rather than losing 4–2. The curse lay in Cleveland picking Brad Daugherty with the first choice, because Bias was the obvious second pick. Had Cleveland drafted Bias and Boston settled for Daugherty, they would have had a very talented 7′ center at their disposal to step in for Parish in the absence of Walton. The estimable Daugherty, who later played on five All-Star teams, was the prototypical Celtic; Bias was not.

Assuming that Cleveland had picked Bias with the first choice and Boston passed on Bias, where were the Celtics' next best alternatives? Had they chosen Chris Washburn, William Bedford, Roy Tarpley, Kenny Walker, Pearl Washington, or Walter ("Truth") Berry, they would have struck out badly and had their salary cap hampered. There were some very nice other players out there, such as Chuck Person, Ron Harper, Mark Price, Dell Curry, and Jeff Hornacek, but none of these players would have suitably replaced the Celts' superstars.

The Celtics did not win a championship again until 2008 because of a number of poor personnel decisions, not just the Bias pick. They made the choice to hang onto their stars for too long, and then made a number of mistakes thereafter, not conducive to ensuring a new period of dominance or even true competitiveness

No Such Luck

Stung by Bias' death, the Celtics lobbied the NBA for some type of compensatory relief, which the league denied. Had the commissioner granted the Celtics the second pick in the 1987 draft, it is fascinating to speculate whom the team would have chosen: eventual second selection Armen Gilliam, or would they have "gambled" on Scottie Pippen, Kevin Johnson, or Reggie Miller?

for a title every five years or so. Their only hope of remaining among the elite teams in the 1990s lay in choosing Len Bias and hoping he was the clean-cut, born-again Christian who played basketball better than anyone coming out in the '86 draft. Instead, they chose Len Bias with all of his attendant human frailties, fatal flaw and all. That is not a curse, it is just a tragedy.

61 Attend a Celtics Road Game

A generation ago, traveling across America and seeing new baseball parks became suddenly popular, a fad that has not translated to the hardwood courts. It is not difficult to see why, since most vacations take place during the summers, and when a family does take off during a winter break, normally the destination is to a warmer clime, not necessarily to the homes of the Minnesota Timberwolves or Toronto Raptors.

On occasion, work or school might transplant a native Celtics fan away from the Hub, and if you cannot love your team at the Garden, love them where you are. It is easy to root for the home team, but the true fan will never get the full aroma of the Celtics' great rivalries unless and until he or she travels to a venue where the home fans absolutely hate the Celtics, from Honey Russell all the way through Kevin Garnett. The current Madison Square Garden is the fourth incarnation of the venue, but since it opened in 1968, just as the Celtics-Knicks rivalry began to intensify, it can claim some of the best moments between the clubs. At one time, the MSG would have resembled one of Dante's rings of hell for a citizen of Celtic Nation, but after Pat Ewing retired, the Knicks have not claimed quite the same cachet; and yet this is still where Bill Russell faced off against Willis Reed.

The Palace of Auburn Hills opened in 1988, foreshadowing the richest period of the Pistons' history. Between Detroit and Boston, there festers a rich tradition of the teams hating each other, what with Robert Parish nearly chopping down Bill Laimbeer like a tree in one memorable playoff game. Compared to some of the more aggressive Pistons, Isiah Thomas and Dennis Rodman came off as some of the more benign players on those teams, made all the more insufferable because the rise of Detroit coincided with the long decline of Boston. The rivalry is long-standing, and the mutual animosity is intense. The Motor City is the place to go for at least one game.

Philadelphia has never quite recovered from the disappointment of seeing Wilt Chamberlain lead the 76ers to only one championship as the Celtics came into town and dominated. It quieted down for a spell after Wilt left but intensified in the Bird years, particularly when Larry Legend chided an over-the-hill Doctor J, leading to a physical standoff between the two. The Sixers have played at the Wells Fargo Center since 1996, formerly making their home at the legendary Spectrum. As intense as the Celts-Sixers rivalry has been at times, it can never approximate the pure hatred between the Boston Bruins and the Broad Street Bullies at the old Spectrum, but it has come very close at times. The Spectrum housed its last event in 2009 and will be razed soon, so you might want to check out the exterior before the wrecking ball hits it.

The Lakers play in downtown L.A., but for more than 30 years they called The Forum in Inglewood their home, back when a young Paul Pierce tried to sneak into games. At a Celts-Lakers game, you might see more stars than on Rodeo Drive, and if you cannot get tickets for a game while you are out there, do not fret. The Staples Center also serves as the home for the Los Angeles Clippers, so you might get to see your favorite team after all, starting up a whole new rivalry.

62 K.C.

One of Bill Russell's oft-told tales concerns his freshman roommate at the University of San Francisco, guard K.C. Jones. The taciturn K.C. supposedly did not speak at all to Russell for the first month except to shake him in the morning, imploring him to "wake up, Russ" and to say good night to him. Jones did become more loquacious with time, but he maintained a dignified reserve through his playing and coaching career, a trait that served him well in the presence of veteran ballplayers.

Due to military commitments, Jones did not join the Celtics until the 1958–1959 season, coming off the bench when starting guards Bob Cousy or Bill Sharman tired. Coach Red Auerbach brought him along slowly, analyzing the young guard as "an All-American who couldn't shoot…[his defense] was of a gambling kind." K.C. Jones himself held no illusions that he was the second coming of Sam Jones, admitting, "I'm not a good shooter…and I try to make up for it with ball-handling and defense."

One example illustrates his value to his team: on one play, he dove headfirst after a ball destined to go out of bounds. Russell recovered it and heaved it to Sam Jones, who made the easy basket. Nowhere in that play does K.C. Jones' contribution show up statistically, except he tried his whole career to outplay the opponent and otherwise make up for any deficiencies in his game. He succeeded,

One of the more reserved players in Celtics history, K.C. Jones displays plenty of intensity in this scoring attempt. His laid-back demeanor proved a perfect antidote much later to the methods of Celts coach Bill Fitch, as Jones took over the helm and guided a veteran team to two NBA titles.

as evidenced by Auerbach admitting, "From the day he reported...he did everything I asked him. He went in and dogged his man."

Recognized as one of the premier defensive guards of his era, he played within himself during his nine-year career, with his points-per-game average topping off at 9.2 in 1961–1962. He retired after

> ### A Winner All the Way
> Although primarily known in his post-playing career as the head coach of the Celtics, K.C. Jones only coached five years in Boston, spending at least parts of six other seasons coaching other clubs. After a poor first experience coaching the San Diego Conquistadors in the ABA in 1972–1973, he never coached a team thereafter that finished under .500. His winning percentage as a head coach in the NBA was a phenomenal .674, even higher than that of Red Auerbach.

the 1966–1967 season. A popular teammate, he had a beautiful singing voice and, on good authority, did very accurate impressions of Bob Cousy and Bill Russell.

His career with the Celtics did not end there, as he later served as an assistant coach under Bill Fitch. And when it appeared that the stern taskmaster had gone as far as possible with the team after the Bucks swept the Celtics in the 1983 playoffs, then–general manager Auerbach hired K.C. as the head coach. In that role, he guided the team to championships in 1984 and 1986, leaving after the 1987–1988 season.

Elected into the Hall of Fame in 1989, his No. 25 was retired by the Celtics in 1967, a rapid and fitting response from the team. One last note: "K.C." is not a nickname or shorthand, as his birth certificate simply reads, "K.C. Jones."

Organist John Kiley

Go to a Celtics game today, and besides the game itself, a cornucopia of lasers and lights, loud booming sounds, and images on the Jumbotron will amuse you. But for almost 30 years, through 1983, you needed only the players and team organist John Kiley. Kiley did not share his talents with basketball fans alone, as he played organ for the Bruins, Red Sox, and Boston Braves.

Kiley got his start by visiting silent-picture theaters in Roxbury and Dorchester—then two of the most Irish neighborhoods in Boston—at age 15. Soon, his talents took him throughout the city, and while video killed the radio star and the silent-film star, Kiley continued to flourish when he became the music director at a Boston radio station.

Kiley had the knack for pulling a tune out for any occasion, most notably playing *Ode to Joy* after Carlton Fisk's home run to win the sixth game of the World Series for the Red Sox in 1975.

Tastes change, and the Jumbotrons across America at times contain some interesting content to help create or perpetuate new traditions. Much of the sweetness of the game experience disappeared, however, with the advent of these Goliaths, as they replaced spontaneous and oftentimes witty improvisations by talented musicians like John Kiley.

64 Watch the Game at the Fours

It's different now, but in its heyday, the old Boston Garden abutted Causeway Street, an avenue darkened and obscured even on a sunny day by the ugly MBTA trolley tracks that arose overhead. The trains made noise and kicked up dust, and few but the firm of heart hung around there much. You parked your car or got off the train for a game or event, and only lingered if the local shot-and-beer joints or the X-rated movie house enticed.

In 1976 into the breach came Tim Colton with the Fours, then known as the Four B's. The place served good food and provided a safe atmosphere for fans and players alike to come in and have a beer and a meal. In 1986, after brother Peter Colton had joined up, the

Fours expanded, opening up a second floor and another bar, with an elevator to accommodate the guests. Boston had a great sports bar, and the North Station area around the Garden had a mecca for fans.

Of course, the old Garden and the trolley tracks both have disappeared, and only a couple of old bars remain. But the Fours not only remains, it thrives, being voted one of the 25 greatest sports bars in America. Many, if not most, sports establishments serve up good beer and great atmosphere, but the food is not quite up to the level of what Fido or old Shep would eat.

The Fours serves up delicious food, burgers, and sandwiches, yes, and some of the greatest steak tips in creation. As proof, a large and loyal lunch crowd fills up the seats each day, a relative rarity for sports bars. The atmosphere and the beer are excellent also.

The two floors over the years have accumulated some very valuable items, and for Celtics fans, the three jerseys of Larry Bird, Kevin McHale, and Robert Parish are a must. Ask Peter Colton why Parish's jersey is white and the other two stars' are green, and he has a great story. One night, an unwelcome guest came in and took Parish's green jersey (and a jersey once worn by hockey's Ray Bourque), leaving the other two still on the wall. Later, Robert Parish's agent came into the Fours and wanted to know why McHale and Bird had a jersey up, but none worn by his client. Colton told him about the loss, and after a number or days passed, one of Parish's white jerseys came in the mail.

You can also sit in the downstairs bar where Bird and McHale once sat with their friends. On one end of the bar is a framed announcement of Bird's first signing with the team, signed by Larry Legend himself. David Wesley and Red Auerbach used to stop by quite often, too, signing placemats for the customers. Nowadays, most Celtics train in the suburbs and do not patronize the Fours as often as before, but former Celt Rick Weitzman comes by frequently, and LeBron James paid a visit during a Cavs stopover.

65 Spider

In the old Boston Garden, the "Bull Gang" crew had to turn a hockey rink into a basketball arena, or some other type of stage, in order to keep the attractions running in and out of the venue, and the workers who had these jobs tended to retain them for decades. The most famous of all was Rudolph "Spider" Edwards, who broomed the floor of the parquet at Celtics games for 30 years, often cleaning the floor during timeouts also.

A Philly native, Spider came to Boston because he loved the Celtics and the old Boston Braves baseball team; the Braves, of course, left town, but Spider stayed and started working at the Garden in 1964. In time, he became as recognizable as many of the players, and certainly more accessible, with generations of fans often passing him on the street or in a store and hailing him like an old friend.

Even Larry Bird noticed. Once at a draft-day celebration at the World Trade Center, Spider sat at a table patiently drawing out his draft picks when Bird walked by him and then stopped. Bird then walked back and said hello and apologized for not greeting him the first time he passed.

Spider did clear up one misconception about why he ran his broom over the floor: "People think it's because the players' sweat, but that's not the main reason. Most of all, it's the dust that keeps coming up from the subfloor. All that pounding. All that dust. You have to keep after it."

By 1997, with the old Garden gone, Spider became expendable, a character from a time that seemed long past. With him went one of the many charming people who had once graced the old Garden and who should have had a place in the new arena.

Somebody Cleaned Up

In September 1996 an auction of old Garden artifacts was held in Boston, and one of the items auctioned off was Spider's old broom. The winning bid was $1,600!

Red Claws

In the formative years of the NBA, owner Walter Brown saw many other franchises start up and die. Seeking at all costs to avoid the same fate for the Celtics, he sent them on glorified barnstorming tours throughout New England, picking up games with most takers. Some of the trips brought the team to the deepest regions of Maine, a practice that later prosperity halted.

In 2009 the Celtics heralded a return of sorts to the state by announcing the formation of a Development League affiliate in Portland, named the Maine Red Claws. The club is also affiliated with the Charlotte Bobcats, with each team eligible to place two first- or second-round draft picks apiece, with the remaining spots filled by free agents. Celtics rookies Bill Walker and Lester Hudson spent time as Red Claws during the initial season, called up by the NBA team as needed.

Formerly the Celts sent their prospects to Utah, a logistical hurdle, but now the club can call up its players as replacements and have the player brought down to Boston in about an hour and a half, prepared to play in the evening. That is assuming the team is at home when the emergency arises, because travel for the Red Claws is arduous. In their Eastern Conference alone, their neighboring rivals are Iowa; Sioux Falls, South Dakota; Fort Wayne,

Indiana; Erie, Ohio; and Springfield, Massachusetts. Then they have to play nine West Coast clubs.

The joint arrangement with the Bobcats aside, the Red Claws possess strong ties to the Celtics, with Jon Jennings, its president and general manager, a former assistant coach during the Bird era. Head coach Austin Ainge is the son of Celtics GM Danny Ainge. The club might also possess one of the greatest basketball logos of all time, a red lobster holding a basketball in its claw, ready for a slam dunk. Even Kevin Garnett might think twice before going baseline with that thing.

Like the big-league club, the Maine affiliate also has dancers, the Lady Red Claws. Undoubtedly, the Celtics have more talent than their affiliate, but the Lady Red Claws can clearly hold their own with their big-league competition.

67 Celtics' Scoring Record Set

A master in the low post, Kevin McHale had more moves to the basket than the number of variations of the Boston accent. He even had a move that resembled a waiter in a restaurant tripping on the rug and dropping a tray full of plates, which sounds awkward, but it almost always worked.

He utilized all the moves in his arsenal on March 3, 1985, in a game against the Detroit Pistons, when he shattered the Celtics' single-game scoring record with 56 points, erasing Larry Bird's 53 in a regular-season game against the Indiana Pacers set in 1983 and John Havlicek's playoff-record of 54 against the Hawks in 1973.

The Pistons in that era thrived on a tough image, so leave it to the good-natured but wily McHale to run circles around them. McHale himself seemed shocked afterward, recounting that he had never scored 56 points in his life, with the possible exception of a memorable game in his childhood, when he deadpanned, "Yup, I must have been playing in that playground from 1:00 o'clock in the afternoon to 5:00 or 6:00 o'clock at night."

Good-natured kidding followed him into the team dressing room, where M.L. Carr joked that he just might someday break the record, while Larry Bird opined that "it might wait 'til the next game" for him to reset the record.

Bird may have been joking, but he literally set the record straight less than 10 days later, when he potted 60 points in a game played in New Orleans against the Atlanta Hawks. Boasted Bird, "When I'm shooting the ball like that, nobody's going to stop me."

It was a heady time for Bird and Boston: *Cheers* was a hit show, and millions became television buddies with Sam and Diane and Norm and Cliff, in a bar where everybody knew your name. Unemployment was low, and housing prices kept rising, fueled by loans from such venerable (and soon all defunct) banks such as Bank of Boston, Bank of New England, BayBank, and Shawmut. Not only had the local Celtics rebounded, but the Red Sox, Bruins, and Patriots all verged on prosperity. No longer did the pall of forced busing in the schools or the ghosts of Curtis Rowe and Sidney Wicks haunt the Hub.

This was the time when Larry Bird walked into three-point shooting competitions as part of the annual All-Star festivities and called the contest in his favor before he took a shot. In 1985 he appeared on the cover of *Time* magazine, in addition to the usual suspects—the sports magazines and sports sections of the newspapers.

Because Bird basically believed the record belonged to him, a common misconception subsequently arose that he somehow selfishly yanked the record away from poor Kevin McHale, his own teammate. Not so, in fact, when McHale netted his 56, Bird generously helped him with timely passes and let Kevin have some shots he normally reserved for himself. Similarly, when Bird came back with his own scoring run, McHale helped him get there.

One day the Celtics all got old, the banks failed, Diane Chambers relocated to the West Coast, and housing prices plunged in Massachusetts. But for a while, Larry Bird reigned supreme, and for an ever briefer nine-day spell, so did the incomparable Kevin McHale.

68 Kentucky Colonel

In basketball franchises characterized more by Fantasy League–type players procured than by actual championships earned, being a starter is key. Traditionally, the Celtics' sixth man has not been looked upon as someone not good enough to start, but rather as the player who comes in and throws the opposition onto its heels. There have been many great ones—John Havlicek, Bill Walton, Kevin McHale, Rasheed Wallace—but forward/guard Frank Ramsey kicked off the tradition.

At 6′3″ Ramsey played as a swingman, extremely hard to imagine today when his height might barely qualify him to play guard. Hailing from Kentucky, Ramsey signed up with Auerbach in time to play 64 games in the 1954–1955 season. His versatility and willingness to play the role assigned him cost him thousands of points in his career, and he never averaged more than 16.5 in a season.

With Frank Deford, Ramsey once cowrote an article titled "Smart Moves by a Master of Deception," in which the player largely devoted his comments to how to draw phantom fouls, inside basketball at its best or worst, depending on one's perspective. Heavily illustrated, the piece is simply terrific, sort of the equivalent of learning how a magician performs his or her tricks. So good, in fact, that if the book you are currently reading permitted 101 things to see and do, reading this article would have made the cut.

To preface the article, there is a wonderful quote about Ramsey from Bill Russell, to wit that on one occasion Frank came into the game and drew a foul so quickly that he "was still so cold he had to warm up before shooting his free throw." It's easy to see why. Ramsey had a ploy that he used when his man was driving successfully past him; knowing he would be beat, Ramsey held his feet and shifted his body toward the opposing player and then flopped, appearing as if he was the wronged party.

Most coaches would have gone apoplectic seeing a player so openly expose his secrets to the entire league and its referees, and yet Red Auerbach loved this kind of stuff because it appealed to his street-smart desire to get inside the opponent's head.

Nicknamed the "Kentucky Colonel," Ramsey actually coached the Kentucky Colonels pro basketball team. Inducted into the Hall of Fame in 1982, his No. 23 was retired by the Celtics, and he has remained in touch with many former teammates.

Always known as a fighter, one opponent that at least temporarily got the upper hand on him was a tornado that ran through his home in Madisonville, Kentucky, in 2005, leaving nothing but a brick fireplace in a home he built. He lost most of his memorabilia, and his truck and car even flew more than 50 yards away. The tornado never got close to the wily Ramsey himself.

John Y., the Anti-Brown

When Celtics founder Walter Brown died, the city of Boston mourned, deservedly so, as he had nurtured the team and kept it alive largely with money he did not have, and then helped lead it to a dynasty. Then came a Brown of a different breed, John Y., who took over a share of the team ownership in 1978, and in brief and inglorious order desecrated this legacy on his one-way ego trip.

Brown made his fortune buying out Colonel Sanders and transforming Kentucky Fried Chicken into a huge national fast-food chain. He later bought the Buffalo Braves basketball team, which prompted him to engage in one of the strangest transactions in sports history. Bored with Buffalo, he engaged in a bizarre franchise swap with then–Celts owner Irv Levin, whereby Levin obtained the Buffalo Braves (which he promptly moved to San Diego to become the Clippers), and Brown came to Boston.

Heretofore, the Celtics had a decent run of luck with Kentuckians, principally with their sixth-man extraordinaire, Frank Ramsey, the Kentucky Colonel from Madisonville. But Brown was not content to serve as a colonel; he had to run the whole show, even though he had no idea what he was doing. Even worse, his wife, former beauty queen and NFL sideline reporter Phyllis George, had become fascinated with Bob McAdoo, so without consulting Auerbach, Brown swapped center/forward Tom Barker and three first-round choices to the rival Knicks for McAdoo on February 12, 1979.

By then, McAdoo had long lost his ability to blast through a season with 2,000 points guaranteed, and while he might have served as a decent backup as he later did with the Lakers, he no longer deserved star treatment. More important to Celtics fans, Red never would have made this trade on his own. Publicly he supported the transaction, maintaining, "I think people will accept the trade after they understand our thinking." He supposedly had to convince player/coach Dave Cowens to accept the new player, but neither GM nor coach had any enthusiasm for this development.

Not content to ignore his general manager, Brown also belittled him in the presence of others. He classlessly excoriated Auerbach after one loss, sarcastically braying, "Here comes our great leader now. Say something intelligent, great leader."

Auerbach held his cool on that occasion, but after McAdoo came aboard, Auerbach began maneuvering to either leave or somehow extract Brown from the franchise. Reportedly, Auerbach flirted with taking the GM job at the Knicks, a move that even Brown knew would explode into a public-relations fiasco. Auerbach had laid down the gauntlet, essentially telling Brown that Boston was not big enough for the both of them, and that within two weeks, either Brown would have to leave town or Auerbach would transfer his allegiance to New York.

Belying his self-styled riverboat-gambler image, John Y. Brown folded, and in late March 1979 he began to muse about a future outside of Boston. Having just returned from a guest appearance at the Camp David accords between Israel and Egypt, he assessed his own intractable situation with Auerbach and began to openly speculate about his own potential in politics. Laconically, Brown attempted to excuse his own sorry tenure as owner, saying, "I may well sell out of the basketball team in Boston because I don't have that much interest in it."

Seeing that John Y. had caved, Auerbach largely kept quiet, but Dave Cowens openly exulted at the potential shift, gloating, "That's the best news I've heard all year. Go ahead [quote me]! What do I care if he's leaving." Luckily, the team already had a part-owner in Harry Mangurian, who soon thereafter relieved Brown of his burden. For his part, Auerbach swiftly righted the ship; he signed M.L. Carr off the Pistons' roster and then made a deal for compensation with that team by basically expanding it so that he dumped McAdoo and picked up two first-round picks from Detroit.

Long after Brown left town, Red Auerbach parlayed one of those picks into a deal that brought Kevin McHale and Robert Parish to the team, at which time they began raising the banners to the top of the Garden again. Brown became governor of Kentucky, and Red remained a Celtic.

 **Satch**

Most adolescents who came of age in the 1960s and early '70s did not belong to the cool group in school, but if you rooted for the Celtics in that period because they had Thomas "Satch" Sanders on their roster, you almost felt as if you belonged. Bill Russell always tells the story of President Kennedy meeting the Celtics at the White House, and when it came time for Sanders to greet the president, all he could say was, "Take it easy, baby." The nickname "Satch" came from star pitcher Satchel Paige, and Sanders always seemed to carry that jazz vibe during his entire 13-year career in Boston.

He did not start off as the epitome of cool. Indeed, in his first Celtics practice as a rookie, he came onto the court decked out in glasses and kneepads. Seeing this, Red Auerbach almost lost his Chinese lunch and called the young man over to him, asking him a series of rhetorical questions about his appearance and then instructing him on how he should dress on the court. He counseled Sanders that glasses conveyed weakness and offered to buy him contact lenses and then told him to lose the kneepads. As insurance, Red asked one of the veterans to steal the kneepads if he ever saw them again.

Sanders probably should have kept the kneepads and a strong pair of glasses (or even better, goggles), because Auerbach told Sanders from the outset that his role on the team was not to shoot the ball, but rather to play defense and grab rebounds. Once the coach felt satisfied that Satch understood his assignment, he then required him to post up against the opposing team's prime scoring forward. From the very outset then, the young All-American from NYU, the eighth man chosen in the 1960 draft, knew he had to subordinate many scoring opportunities, deferring to teammates like Tommy Heinsohn, Sam Jones, and John Havlicek.

Quiet and unassuming, Sanders was very popular with teammates and fans alike, although opposing players often resented his sometimes clutching ways. Sanders stuck himself to the opposing star and, by the mid-'60s, had firmly established himself as one of the league leaders in fouls. As a starting forward, he often failed to finish many games after being tossed by the referees.

Most of his scoring was off of rebounds or fairly straightforward (and lightly defended) shots. He topped out in his highest points-per-game average at 12.6 and never scored 1,000 points a season, and yet with Satch starting, the club won eight championships. He was vastly underrated, too; although he was one of the leading defenders in the NBA, particularly early in his career, he only won one second All-Defensive Team selection, that in 1968–1969. The Celtics, though, always appreciated him, retiring his No. 16 in 1973, his final season as a player.

After his career ended, he did stay in basketball, coaching at Harvard, where he caught the eye of Red Auerbach again, this time for a different reason. After his Harvard men blew a big lead in the second half, Red heard Satch not yell at them but basically let them off the hook for their performance. Strangely, his gentle nature may have provided him with the opportunity to become head coach of the Celtics in 1978, after Auerbach fired then–head coach Tommy Heinsohn in the middle of the season.

Feeling perhaps that the teams needed an antidote to the fiery Heinsohn, Satch got the job, together with all of the headaches of a team filled mostly with either injured players or selfish players, and his tenure did not last long. The next season, after the Celts opened up at 2–12, Satch lost his job when Dave Cowens became player/coach. Fortunately, perhaps Satch's greatest contributions to the sport of professional basketball remained.

Perceiving the lack of guidance for many NBA players and the failure of many of them to successfully transition into post-playing careers or take healthy advantage of the opportunities that present themselves, Satch was the natural choice to become vice president of the NBA's Player Programs department in 1987. In view of his many contributions to the game, Thomas "Satch" Sanders was awarded the league's John W. Bunn Award for Lifetime Achievement by the Basketball Hall of Fame.

71 Hall of Famers

Every person associated with the Celtics who has had his name, number, or microphone retired—with the exception of Reggie Lewis, Jim Loscutoff, Jo Jo White, Satch Sanders, Don Nelson, and Cedric Maxwell—have earned selection into the Basketball Hall of Fame, and their character and achievements have been recounted several times in this tome, as expected. However, several other Hall of Famers have either played with the team or otherwise been associated with the club who have not had numbers retired.

Early coaches Honey Russell and Doggie Julian made the Hall of Fame despite each coaching the team for only two years apiece, four losing seasons in total. Russell starred in the old American Basketball League and coached at Seton Hall, while Julian coached Holy Cross into a national title and wrote the influential book *Bread and Butter Basketball*.

Some entrants to the Hall made it despite what they did to the team. Dave Gavitt, for instance, virtually founded the Big East Conference in college basketball, but his years as an administrator were marked by a marked decline in the team's standing. A little-known fact about Gavitt is that he was chosen to coach the 1980 U.S. basketball team in the Olympics, only to lose his chance due to the boycott following the Soviet invasion of Afghanistan.

Others, like Dominique Wilkins, Dave Bing, Bill Walton, and Pete Maravich played very well against Boston during their long careers with opposing teams. Wilkins did not do much for the Celtics, but Dave Bing still managed to score more than 1,000 points late in his career, in his one year with a very poor team. In contrast, Bill Walton won the Sixth Man Award for an excellent 1986 team, and although he did come back for some games the next year, in essence, he too only had a year with the Celtics. Pete Maravich played briefly with the team, during Larry Bird's rookie season, and it is fascinating to think what they would have been like together for a whole career. Would they have sparked each other to incredible scoring and assist heights with no-look passes? Or would Bird have told Maravich early on to stop hogging the shots?

Nate "Tiny" Archibald played a handful of seasons in Boston and is probably thought of as a Celtic by most fans, although he put up titanic scoring numbers with the Cincinnati Royals and Kansas City–Omaha/Kansas City Kings. Big men Arnie Risen, Wayne Embry, and Clyde Lovellette had successful stints as reserves late in their careers with the team. While some may argue whether Andy Phillip put up Hall of Fame numbers, he too sits in the Hall after playing with the team the final two years of his career.

One of the most intriguing selections, Bob Houbregs, suited up for the Celtics from November 28, 1954, all the way through December 8, 1954, at which point the team released him. The second player chosen in the 1953 draft, the Celtics chose the center/forward in the dispersal draft after the first incarnation of the Bullets folded. He lasted five years in the pros, until he ran into a "basket support" and hurt his back. He later served as a general manager of the Seattle Supersonics.

Good Draft to Let In
After Bob Houbregs was selected as the second player in the NBA Draft in 1953, the Celtics drafted future Hall of Famers Frank Ramsey and Cliff Hagan, together with another good player, Lou Tsioropoulos, a product of nearby Lynn Classical High and later the University of Kentucky.

Former Celtics public relations man Bill Mokray made the Hall due to his extensive contributions as a historian of the game, as did announcer Curt Gowdy and *Globe* columnist and author Bob Ryan.

Finally, while he did not see much action at center briefly backing up Bill Russell, John Thompson brought the Georgetown Hoyas to national prominence and led that team to a championship.

72 22-Year Title Drought

Having won their 16th championship after defeating the Houston Rockets in the 1986 Finals, the Celtics appeared poised to build on their already very strong foundation, leave the Rockets, Lakers, and all other franchises in their wake, and embark on a run of new banners lofting up to the top of the Garden.

The annual draft on June 17 promised to only add to the already formidable Celtics arsenal and provide them with enough youthful talent to transition into a new era of dominance, after the Big Three of Larry Bird, Kevin McHale, and Robert Parish retired. Due to their trade of Gerald Henderson to the Supersonics in 1984, the team held the second pick of the first round, with speculation centering on the team either picking up center Brad Daugherty or forward Len Bias, depending on whom the Cleveland Cavaliers, holding the first pick, ended up choosing.

Seemingly, the team could not go wrong. If Cleveland chose Len Bias, the most coveted player in the draft, the Celtics then still had Daugherty, the gentlemanly 7' center from North Carolina. If the opposite occurred, then Bias, the extraordinarily talented forward from Maryland, fell to Boston. Bias could spell Larry Bird and might even exceed his feats one day, he held so much potential.

In the draft, Cleveland ultimately picked Daugherty, with Bias coming to Boston as hoped, with Red Auerbach proclaiming, "After five seconds of deliberation and with no intrigue, the Boston Celtics take Len Bias of the University of Maryland." The choice seemed preordained as Bias had worked at Auerbach's basketball camp and seemed like a nice young man, starring for the Terrapins coached by Red's friend Lefty Driesell. Plus, Bias was "born-again," and probably more pious than Danny Ainge and Greg Kite, the two Mormons on the Celtics. Auerbach crowed, "Bias is the player we wanted. Everybody in the league wanted him."

Everybody in the league except for the Cleveland Cavaliers, it seemed. On draft day they seemed destined for consideration as all-time chumps in the wake of another Auerbach coup. Never mind the ugly rumors circulating around Washington at the time concerning Bias' alleged dangerous drug use—after all, the player was born-again. Bias came up to Boston, looked great in a Celtics hat, said all of the right things, then flew back home to celebrate with his friends.

Two days later all of Boston received the shocking news that Len Bias had died, the victim of cocaine poisoning. The keystone for future greatness had suddenly crumbled cruelly to dust; and on a crass level, the NBA never compensated the club for its loss in any way, even with a draft pick the next year. Celtics-haters rejoiced in the tragedy—maybe now the windows at the Garden might open up to let out the smell of cigar smoke, the aroma of accumulated institutional arrogance along Causeway Street in Boston. Lost in all of the practical considerations, another young life had been snuffed out by crack cocaine, one of the most lethal and unforgiving drugs known to man.

For the Celtics, the bad news continued during the 1986–1987 year as Bill Walton only played in 10 games due to injuries. As the NBA's Sixth Man Award winner during the championship year, the future Hall of Famer Walton had thrived, giving Robert Parish some rest and helping to rededicate the team to excellence, as he preached keeping the team off beer that year.

The Celtics' record dropped to 59–23 during the 1986–1987 regular season, although they still made the Finals, where they ultimately lost to the Lakers 4–2. Had Bias not succumbed and had Walton remained healthy, it is difficult to see the team failing to run the table that year, as starters Bird, Parish, McHale, Dennis Johnson, and Danny Ainge played remarkably well in this most difficult season.

The next year the team did not even reach the Finals, losing to the hated Pistons 4–2 in the third round of the playoffs. The five starters continued to play well, and Jim Paxson provided some relief off the bench, as did promising newcomer Reggie Lewis, a draft-day steal out of nearby Northeastern University. But other players did not prove so resilient, including once-great center Artis Gilmore, who on some nights looked like a statue that at any point might demolecularize on the parquet, leaving nothing but dust and a green uniform around him.

Resigning as coach before the 1988–1989 season, K.C. Jones turned over an aging team to his successor, Jimmy Rodgers, a fact that became starkly evident when Larry Bird only played in six games that season, enduring surgery. The club went 42–40 and got swept in the first round of the playoffs. Bird returned the next year, and the club did much better, but again lost in the first round of the playoffs, spelling the end of the brief run of Jimmy Rodgers as coach. In May 1990 the team let go of Rodgers and went hunting for a new chief of basketball operations, eventually choosing Dave

Gavitt, a former basketball coach at Providence and one of the people most responsible for the formation of the Big East Conference. Gavitt in turn tabbed Chris Ford as the team's new coach.

Ford had some success in 1990–1991 and the next year, but the team did not go far into the playoffs. In Ford's third year as coach, Larry Bird had retired, and Reggie Lewis collapsed in the first game of the playoffs against the Hornets. Tragically, Lewis died that summer. The team imploded the next two years and hired M.L. Carr to coach in 1995–1996, but the team continued to struggle. In 1996–1997 under Carr, the team went 15–67, their worst record ever, as critics speculated that the club tanked it in order to have the best opportunity of drafting Tim Duncan that summer.

The reverses and tragedies sustained by the club promised to disappear with the hiring of Rick Pitino as coach and president in May 1997.

73 Fellowship of the Miserable

Hugely successful as a college coach with Boston University, Providence, and Kentucky, Pitino had a reputation as someone who could rebuild a team into prominence, a trait that the New England Patriots had seen in Bill Parcells before they hired him. Pitino wrote a book titled *Success Is a Choice.*

Pitino came to Boston and had a great press conference, with Celtics banners lowered so as to appear behind him, citing Bob Cousy, and emotionally adding that indeed the Cooz would live to see another banner raised. He continued to say the right things, adding, "I'm thankful to be here. I'm honored. I can't wait to get started. I wish practice started tomorrow." As Pitino beamed and choked up at all the right times, GM Jan Volk walked the plank, M.L. Carr received a newly created job with the team, Red Auerbach apparently officially became a figurehead, and an exit was painted out of the front office for Larry Bird. It was Rick Pitino's team now.

Few dissenting voices spoke up, and whatever slight negativity surrounded the hire centered around the coach's previous, abbreviated, but not unsuccessful coaching stint with the New York Knicks. But this was the Celtics, and Pitino as the man of the hour appeared to provide the answer to every question, the balm to every wound. Said retired great John Havlicek, "If you had your choice of anyone in the country, in the world, to coach this team, who would you want? Rick Pitino is the man.... So as far as I'm concerned, the Celtics have hit the lottery." It seemed that way. After all, Pitino loved the city, having turned around the Boston University program, and had just come off an NCAA championship in 1996 at Kentucky.

Pitino seemingly also had walked into a great situation as the Celtics, by dint of their horrible record from the previous season (the team could only go up) and an old trade (Eric Montross to Dallas) had two very high picks coming their way. If the team scored in the lottery, it had the potential to end up with the first pick and the rights to Wake Forest Center Tim Duncan.

It did not work out as planned. In the 1997 NBA Draft, M.L. Carr, representing Boston, watched in utter despondency as the club ended up with the No. 3 and No. 6 choices in the draft. No longer could they dream of rebuilding the franchise around the great Tim Duncan, and as the post-draft hangover set in, Pitino only saw his inherited group of largely mediocre players with huge and seemingly insuperable contracts under the salary cap. Heartbroken, he used the picks he did have to select point guard Chauncey Billups from Colorado and Ron Mercer, a protégé of Pitino's from Kentucky. In the ensuing season, the team won 21 games more than the previous season, largely on the back of looming star Antoine Walker.

The improvement was ephemeral, as it is not clear that the Celtics wanted to win any games the season before, as the front office salivated over Tim Duncan or, at worst, Keith Van Horn. Pitino did do the right thing in renouncing several crummy contracts, but he then went and overpaid Travis Knight at center, locking him up for seven years. As it became clear later, as a shrewd trader or talent evaluator Rick Pitino was no Red Auerbach.

Thin-skinned Rick Pitino had known very little adversity and much success in his coaching career, but early on in his Celtics tenure he lashed out at the callers to the very popular local sports talk shows, referring to them as "the fellowship of the miserable." The platoons of "first-time callers, longtime listeners" constituted some of the most fervent sports fans in a very enthusiastic environment for local franchises, and Pitino unwisely attacked them, because in order to satisfy them he had to start putting banners up on the ceiling again. Failing that, he had just alienated a very vocal segment of the populace.

Patience never having been a Pitino virtue, he engineered one of the team's worst trades ever on February 18, 1998, when he swapped point guard Billups, guard Dee Brown, forward John Thomas, and center Roy Rogers to the Raptors for point guard Kenny Anderson, forward Popeye Jones, and center Zan Tabak. Billups of course developed into one of the greatest point guards in NBA history, playing long after Anderson retired.

Although the Celtic mystique had lacked its luster for several years, Rick Pitino and the brain trust made one extremely good decision when they drafted Paul Pierce from the University of Kansas with the 10th pick of the 1998 draft. The cynical may point out that the poor judgment of the general managers of the nine clubs that drafted before Boston created this opportunity, however, that does not override the fact that in this instance, Pitino got it right. Even at the time it was doubtful that Pierce would drop as far as he did, but some teams made their choices on perceived needs (the Denver Nuggets drafted Pierce's college teammate Raef LaFrentz based on their wish to obtain a big man) or a misplaced belief that they already possessed a small forward and did not need Pierce.

The Celtics were still almost a decade from competing for a title, but in Paul Pierce, they obtained the first element that would someday return them to the promised land. Unfortunately, in the lockout season of 1998–1999, the team only went 19–31, and in March Pitino blundered into another trade, this time with Cleveland, acquiring center Vitaly Potapenko for Andrew DeClercq and first-round draft choice. The surrendered draft pick translated into the Cavs selecting Andre Miller, with future star Shawn Marion available at that pick.

Potapenko repaid his coach for this bold move on September 20, 1999, by allegedly engaging in a heated discussion with his fiancée, at which time the police arrested the center for disorderly conduct. Even though the charges eventually went nowhere, Potapenko endured the spectacle of the local television cameras showing him going into his arraignment in East Boston District Court, another black eye for the once proud franchise. Panic had set in with Rick Pitino.

The 1999–2000 season demonstrated the short-sightedness of the Pitino regime, as the team placed fifth in the Atlantic Division with a 35–47 record despite the scoring contributions of Pierce and Antoine Walker. Perpetuating his propensity for uttering memorably self-defeating quotes, Pitino frustratingly stated after a close loss to the Raptors on March 1, 2000:

Larry Bird is not walking through that door, fans. Kevin McHale is not walking through that door, and Robert Parish is not walking through that door. And if you expect them to walk through that door, they're going to be gray and old.

What we are is young, exciting, hard-working, and we're going to improve. People don't realize that, and as soon as they realize those three guys are not coming through that door, the better this town will be for all of us, because there are young guys in that [locker] room playing their asses off. I wish we had $90 million under the salary cap. I wish we could buy the world. We can't; the only thing we can do is work hard, and all the negativity that's in this town sucks. I've been around when Jim Rice was booed. I've been around when Yastrzemski was booed. And it stinks. It makes the greatest town, greatest city in the world, lousy. The only thing that will turn this around is being upbeat and positive like we are in that locker room…and if you think I'm going to succumb to negativity, you're wrong. You've got the wrong guy leading this team.

The head coach did everything but start quoting Richard Nixon about not having Rick Pitino to kick around anymore. Citizens of New England might not be able to name all of the presidents or identify all of the state capitals, yet even two decades after Pitino's meltdown, they could quote whole sections of his speech verbatim. Clearly Pitino was in way over his head, and yet it was never Pitino's fault for the poor performance of his charges on the court: the fans were negative, the lottery selection did not hand him Tim Duncan on a red carpet, the players he largely selected let him down. Less appreciated by Pitino was the fact that at one point he lost most of his self-confidence. He did not have all the answers, and his charisma had taken him further than justified.

During the off-season, Pitino started leaving hints that unless he turned around the team, he meant to leave it. The next year replicated the frustration, as the team started the season at 12–22, at which point Pitino resigned on January 8, 2001. After getting drubbed by the Miami Heat, he stayed down in Florida and worked out his exit with team owner Gaston, a fitting end to a failed experiment. Co-captains Pierce and Walker continued to star for new coach Jim O'Brien, and Pierce scored more than 2,000 points for the club, the first time anyone had performed that feat since Larry Bird over a decade earlier. Antoine Walker led in three-point shots taken and three-point shots made, but had begun to wear out his welcome as fans got on him for taking so many shots behind the line and for looking as if he did not care. In a rare case of simpatico between the Celtics' core fans and their late coach, everyone seemed to hate Antoine Walker's game.

It is unfortunate Rick Pitino did not work out as the Celtics' coach, as he dearly loved the city and the history of its basketball club, an affection that fans were more than willing to reciprocate, having seen their beloved team struggle for so long. One vignette, not known by many people, sums up Rick Pitino: at the Fours sports bar across from the Boston Garden, when players still dropped by quite often, they generally craved their space, but Rick Pitino graciously talked with whomever approached him, often at great length discussing basketball or whatever topic presented itself. He wanted his experience in Boston to work out, the fans did, too, but unfortunately, he did not get the job done.

74 Danny Ainge

Irish eyes were not smiling in the 1981 NCAA tournament when, with seven seconds left, Brigham Young's guard, Danny Ainge, dribbled the length of the floor to score the winning basket to defeat Digger Phelps' strong Notre Dame squad. It was Ainge against Kelly Tripucka, Orlando Woolridge, Tracy Jackson, John Paxson, and Joe Kleine, and that day Danny slew Goliath. This from a redheaded guard born on St. Patrick's Day!

Of course, like Bill Sharman, Ainge's biggest professional quandary involved choosing between professional baseball and basketball. Red Auerbach always seemed to believe in the end that basketball trumped the other sports, drafting Ainge for the Celtics in June 1981 while he was still playing for the Blue Jays. Unlike Sharman, Ainge received a fair chance in the majors, playing parts of three years with the Toronto Blue Jays, but by the end of three big-league seasons, it appeared Ainge did not possess the tools to exceed a .220 batting average. In any event, by 1981 he had demonstrated his talent in basketball, so he became a Celtic.

Boobirds at the Garden greeted his early years with the team, as he simply did not seem to fit in. He played behind Gerald Henderson, with talented guards M.L. Carr and (later) Dennis Johnson taking up valuable playing time. In an early team practice, he could not hit any of his shots. At the end of 1984, though, Red Auerbach decided that Ainge could start and disposed of the estimable Henderson. Along with Johnson, Ainge became one of the guards associated with the golden age of the team in the 1980s, as he developed a knack for hitting three-point shots.

Ainge certainly distinguished himself on the great 1985–1986 championship team, but as the team slowly fell out of competition for future titles, he became one of the few stars who might bring back a decent return in a trade as rebuilding began. In 1988 he made his first and only All-Star appearance, but by February 1989, the Celts traded him along with Brad Lohaus ("the next Larry Bird") to Sacramento for Joe Kleine and Ed Pinckney. The trade helped both teams without making either appreciably better, as Boston continued to slip.

He played another six and a half years in the NBA, with his first full year in Sacramento being his best scoring campaign at 17.9 points per game. He continued to play well and aggressively in the community-property state franchises of Sacramento, Portland, and Phoenix, until his retirement in September 1995. For three-plus years he coached the Phoenix Suns and later did some sports commentating, but his Celtics career had not yet ended yet.

Local ownership, led by Wyc Grousbeck and Steve Pagliuca bought out Paul Gaston, and on May 9, 2003, Danny Ainge took over as the team's general manager, inheriting several problems and a recent legacy of mishaps and tragedies. But Ainge was tough and smart, and by now Celtics fans no longer pined for a savior or a quick fix. In contrast to the jubilee that greeted Rick Pitino's arrival in Boston, Ainge came across as optimistically subdued, stating, "It's not going to stop me from being honest. I can't sugarcoat what's not there." Larry, Kevin, and Robert did not come through the door that day, but a realistic Danny Ainge did, and now the Celtics had a chance again.

Unlike Rick Pitino's first draft, when the club obtained the picks that brought in very good players but came away disappointed, Ainge lowered the scope of expectations and, after some dealing, came away with picks that translated into guard Marcus Banks and high school center Kendrick Perkins. Banks never starred for the team, but Perkins over time became the low-post presence that Pitino always wanted and never got.

Vin Baker was one of the first issues Ainge had to face as the new GM, and the troubled center seemed to have changed in the fall of 2003, contributing to his team. But by winter he had relapsed, and the team suspended him. Mercifully, the Celtics eventually granted Baker his outright release on February 18, 2004, after which the Knicks, Rockets, and Clippers took brief chances on him, until his career finally ended, simply another tragedy dogging the team after 1986.

Coaches shuttled in and out, with Jim O'Brien, temporarily replaced by John Carroll. On April 29, 2004, Ainge tabbed Doc Rivers as the club's new head coach, and he promptly led them to first place in the Atlantic Division, although they did not advance past the first round of the playoffs. The team had drafted well going into that campaign, having obtained Al Jefferson, Delonte West, and Tony Allen. Unfortunately, the team skidded badly in 2005–2006, finishing the season with only 33 victories.

Although the Celtics had acquired some talented young players and still had Pierce, its fortunes receded, and many feared a return to the Pitino days, where excuses were made for not winning and victory proved enduringly elusive. Pierce got hurt, and the team had no superstars left, although young players like Rajon Rondo at point guard and Al Jefferson at forward played well. The team lagged, and Doc Rivers looked as if he were merely replicating the M.L. Carr playbook by losing enough to get a lottery pick, as speculated by most of the fans as the team sank to a 24–58 record. Danny Ainge then went about rolling the dice.

Starting with the 2007 draft, he added talented stars Ray Allen and Kevin Garnett to give Paul Pierce some long-awaited assistance, and then rounded off the bench. With the improvement of young players Rajon Rondo and Kendrick Perkins, Danny Ainge had crafted together a championship roster for the first time since he suited up as a guard for the team back in 1986.

75 Visit the Sports Museum

If you are in town to take in a game, you cannot miss the New England Sports Museum, literally and figuratively. Not only is it an exciting attraction, but it is housed in the same Garden where the Celtics and Bruins play all of their games. One caveat: you must plan ahead, setting up a visit, group tour, or other event in advance by consulting their website.

Founded in 1977, it started off in Soldiers Field Road, a modest museum at the time that, due to donations of time, money, and memorabilia, has now become a half-mile long walk through the rich history of Boston sports. Not only are the Celtics and the other professional teams highlighted, but careful attention is also paid to the local programs at the area universities and such traditional events as the Boston Marathon, Beanpot hockey tournament, and the Boston Neighborhood Basketball League summer seasons.

For Celtics fans, you will not want to miss the Paul Pierce and Ray Allen exhibits, a mural of the '08 team, and a piece of the old Garden parquet signed by Celts stars and other luminaries such as Red Auerbach. They have a recreation of the Armand LaMontagne statue of Larry Bird and another LaMontagne life-size work, this one of Ted Williams holding a giant fish. The first floor of the museum, of course, is the Garden itself.

Another Celtics connection: at one point Hall of Fame center Dave Cowens served as the chairman, and he continues to support the museum through fund-raising efforts and service on the board of trustees. The guiding hand throughout its history has been Richard A. Johnson, its curator, who not only has carefully collected and preserved the local sports history but has spearheaded community efforts such as the Stand Strong program for at-risk youths and the Will McDonough writing contest. In all, more than 7,000 area youth are served through the programs of the New England Sports Museum.

As an adjunct, the museum also sponsors speakers from hallowed New England teams of the past, often in the Fours restaurant nearby, recently hosting an event from three of the original Patriots and also a Bruins roundtable.

The highlight of each season occurs at the museum fund-raiser known as "The Tradition" event, when the Garden is opened up for a reception and then a fête honoring the greatest legends of New England sports. Generally, a Tradition award goes to retired hockey, basketball, baseball, and football players, but also to such diverse other figures as figure skaters and jockeys. Each honoree is introduced—Bobby Knight once gave a rousing speech for John Havlicek—and after the star receives his or her plaque, they are interviewed by the emcees. Some twice-told tales are related as well as some first-time admissions, and old film is often shown of the star. It is a touching event and a credit not only to the guests and dignitaries but to the host, the Sports Museum.

76 The Celtic Dancers

Traditionally, dedicated Boston sports fans exhibit a marked adversity to change, keeping their sports teams and arenas like museums, or at least in shape befitting an attraction on the Freedom Trail. For example, many of the streets and walkways contain only brick, and one of the newer homes in the city is the Paul Revere house in the North End of town.

Most prominently, this trait has led to resistance to alterations to the Red Sox's Fenway Park, where many traditionalists are sickened if any advertisements appear along the outfield, particularly on the sacred Green Monster in left field, oblivious to the fact that these walls were heavily festooned with such crass appeals to commerce in the 1930s and 1940s.

This same Luddite tendency led to a fierce, albeit unsuccessful effort to keep the old Boston Garden from being razed. At least, when the new Garden opened (although it was not known as such right away), the banners and retired numbers still hung from the rafters, and the team played on a parquet floor. But with lasers and a Jumbotron, a lot of modern entertainment has seeped into the show.

Red Auerbach in particular resisted having any cheerleaders or dancers on the floor, eschewing the example of the Laker Girls and their most famous alumna, Paula Abdul. Red died in 2006, the year that the Celtics formed the Celtic Dancers, a group of young women who dance and entertain the crowds. They seem popular, and the world has not ended for Celtic fans, or if it has, it emanates from a loss at home by the ballclub, and not any of the routines displayed by the Celtics dancers. Tryouts take place each year in New York, Los Angeles, and Boston, and the chosen few generally practice a few times a week in addition to performing at the home games.

Those resistant to change often muse that Red Auerbach must be rolling in his grave at the thought of the introduction of the Celtic Dancers. Wherever Red is now, he most likely does not care, but if he is rolling, perhaps he is simply keeping beat with the hip-hop choreography.

 Jo Jo White

Just around the time that Easy Ed Macauley began his intercollegiate career at St. Louis University, another future Celtics legend, Joseph Henry White, was born in that Missouri city. Celtics fans know him as Jo Jo.

Unlike Easy Ed, who always gravitated to his hometown, Jo Jo's path took him away, at first to the University of Kansas and then to Mexico City in 1968 as a member of the U.S. gold medal basketball team. In the 1969 draft, Red Auerbach picked him with the ninth selection, a most wise choice since no one chosen before Jo Jo amounted to much in the NBA, except for the first choice overall, a fellow from UCLA then known as Lew Alcindor.

Supposedly, White fell so low in the draft because of real concerns many NBA franchises had that White might have to enter a draft of another sort, that for selective service during the Vietnam War. At the strong urging of Bill Russell, Auerbach chose White, and soon Jo Jo found himself in the Marine reserves, safe from a call-up for active military service due to President Johnson's reticence to activate reserve forces.

As many feared, the Celtics' dynasty ended the year before White suited up for Boston, as the club had just won its 11ᵗʰ title but had lost Bill Russell and Sam Jones to retirement. The ensuing 1969–1970 season satisfied no one, but the team's new guard showed promise. After the season, Auerbach drafted Dave Cowens, so the Celtics began to improve with this infusion of youthful talent and threaten to win championships again.

By his third year, White averaged 23.1 points per game and had started a string of six consecutive seasons where he played more than 3,200 minutes. These game minutes placed him in the top 10 league-wide in this category for five seasons during this span, contributing to his reputation as an iron man. During this same period, he also placed in the top 10 for assists and, between 1971 and 1977, played in every All-Star Game. Most important from the Celtics' standpoint, he played a significant role in bringing two championships to Boston, one in 1974 and the other in 1976.

In the 1976 championship year, White distinguished himself as the finest player in arguably the greatest basketball game ever, as his 33 points and tireless play for 60 full minutes led his team to a victory in triple overtime over the Phoenix Suns in the fifth game of the Finals. After the Celtics sewed up the banner after the Game 6, White was selected as Finals MVP.

Decline set in for the Celtics the next year, although White continued to thrive, playing a career-high 3,333 minutes, averaging 19.6 points per game, and contributing to his team with his assists and floor leadership. But the next year, 1977–1978, proved a most trying one for the team's iron man as he injured a heel, and injuries reduced him to 46 games that season. While the Celtics' front office in the early 1990s drew criticism for not trading away stars before they lost their value, in the late 1970s Red Auerbach had no compunction at pulling the trigger on an injured player. Midway through the next year, the club traded White to Golden State, and soon after, his career ended with a final stop in Kansas City.

The Celtics retired Jo Jo's No. 10, but he remains with the team, serving in the front office today, mentoring current Celtics to live life right. Just like Jo Jo White always has.

78 Dine at Ristorante Villa Francesca

Fine dining, either before or after a Celtics game, might be your preference, particularly if you just proposed during a 20-second timeout at the Garden. If so, stroll over to the adjoining North End of Boston to enjoy an intimate dinner at 150 Richmond Street at the Ristorante Villa Francesca.

When Kevin Garnett came to Boston, he talked about how the first thing he wanted to do was to dine at an Italian restaurant, and while there has never been a KG sighting at Villa Francesca, one of his superstar teammates on the Celtics has been there on more than one occasion. It is easy to see why. In each of their rooms, one is transported to Italy itself, with fine attention to detail from the ornate bar to the tasteful artwork. If you have never been to Boston but feel you have seen "Francesca" before, it may resemble a similarly well-conceived restaurant in Italy, or you might remember it from an old *Spenser for Hire* episode that was filmed in part in its interior.

Each stage of the meal is lovingly presented. The meat, seafood, and pasta dishes excel with Gamberoni Gondola (stuffed lobster) and Fettuccine Ai Carciofi standouts on a peerless menu. For desserts, there are a dozen Italian delicacies, best augmented with espresso, cappuccino, or a mocha.

If you still have time before the game, you may wish to take a walking tour through the North End, with Paul Revere's house and the Old North Church (one lantern if the Celtics win, two if they lose). If you think that you have run out of sightseeing, Quincy Market, Faneuil Hall, and the Old State House beckon, but leave some energy for the game. Plus, you want to get into the Garden early in case you are still hungry and want to be first in line for a hot dog or a pizza at the concession stands.

79 Rajon Rondo

Too often, attributing a huge upside to an athlete entering professional sports condemns the player to a career of frustration. Potential is nothing if not realized, and while every player theoretically can improve in the higher elevations and often does, it generally is too much to expect someone who was, for instance, a very good college player to become an exceptional professional athlete as the talent pool gets smaller and geometrically better in the pros.

Declaring for the 2006 NBA Draft after his sophomore year at Kentucky, Rajon Rondo caused few franchises to hear the siren call of upside when they considered his case. The Phoenix Suns chose him with the 21st pick in the first round, instantly packaging him with Brian Grant in exchange for the Celtics' first-round pick in 2007. The Celtics had a surfeit of point guards, so during his rookie year, Rondo saw limited time, averaging only 6.4 points per game.

During the off-season in 2007, the Celtics assembled the core of a championship team, adding Kevin Garnett and Ray Allen to the team to form the "Big Three" with long-suffering veteran Paul

Celtics point guard Rajon Rondo, wearing a Band-Aid on his chin from a cut he suffered earlier, looks to dish the ball during Game 7 of the 2010 NBA Finals against the L.A. Lakers in Los Angeles. Photo courtesy of AP Images

Pierce. Lost in the talk of the Big Three were the names of the center, Kendrick Perkins, and the point guard, the newly anointed Rajon Rondo. The team had tired of his competitors, particularly Sebastian Telfair, the patron saint of upside, as Rondo got the nod to lead the veterans down the floor.

Rondo rose to the challenge, making GM Danny Ainge's most significant decision the problem of who should substitute for the young point guard when he took a break during the games. The drop-off in controlling the ball down the floor in Rondo's absence necessitated bringing a backup point guard aboard, but no one doubted the second-year player's talent and his right to start. Sam Cassell came aboard and had some good scoring games and even better quotes for the press, but did not challenge for the starting job in any way.

Early in Rondo's career, he developed a keen knack for stealing the ball from opponents and also became a league leader in assists as he found the Big Three and other hot shooting teammates like Eddie House. In that sophomore year, the Celtics won the championship as his points-per-game average rose to 10.6.

Injuries, most notably to Kevin Garnett, prevented the Celtics from repeating in 2008–2009, and in the recriminations that began before season's end, Rondo's maturity was challenged by many, questioned even by some in the Celtics' front office. While he continued as one of the league leaders in assists and steals and had added almost two more points per game to his average, at times it looked like he did not care, and his work ethic paled in comparison to such veterans as Ray Allen.

Rather than ignoring the constructive criticism directed toward him, Rondo drew on it the next season to become one of the acknowledged greatest point guards in the league, earning his first selection to the All-Star Game, joining oft-honored teammate Paul Pierce. When Rondo did not see something he liked, he publicly called out his teammates, all the while adding another two points per game to his average. Increasingly, if he saw an open path to the net, he dribbled in through the paint and dared opponents to stop or at least foul him.

Rajon Rondo has become a team leader in the midst of veterans, has improved each season in the league, and has matured. Frighteningly for the other franchises in the league, it appears as if he still possesses considerable upside and intends to exploit it.

80 Curtis and Sidney

For many years, fans looked upon the three seasons spanning the fall of 1977 through the spring of 1979 as the ugliest period in Celtics history, redeemed only by the advent of Larry Bird in 1980. These three years have somewhat faded in the collective memories of most fans, because the later yawning gap between Bird's retirement and the team's finally winning its 17th championship lasted much longer and thus had many more hideous moments and odious characters to adorn its interregnum.

Mercifully, thousands of Celtics faithful either were too young to remember this time or were born thereafter, spared the vying forces of dissension and malaise that permeated the franchise. Still, the late '70s does possess its own charm, and for those fans who have a keen insight into that era, there exists a certain bond characteristic of any group of people who have plodded through an unpleasant experience together and survived.

The Celtics had barely won their 13th championship in the 1975–1976 season, but unlike the end of the Bill Russell era, they still had most of their stars returning for the next campaign and at least promised to compete with the rest of their conference. With a solid nucleus of Dave Cowens at center, Jo Jo White at guard, and a still very effective John Havlicek, few foresaw the rapid decline that did occur.

Bad trades marred any chance at sustained excellence. On October 20, 1976, in a three-way deal with Denver and Detroit, the Celtics lost forward Paul Silas and in return obtained Curtis Rowe. In Rowe, the Celtics picked up one of the most selfish players in their history, sacrificing the leadership, toughness, and rebounds Silas brought to the court. Most vexing, Rowe was a guy who seemingly only cared about individual statistics and yet habitually failed in this endeavor, rarely ranking as a top player in any category in the NBA.

Rowe, the man most deservedly associated with this grotesque period in Celtics history, epitomized the type of player the team never let on their roster during their glory years. An underachiever, Rowe famously once said, "Last time I checked, there weren't any Ws and Ls in my paycheck." He had made one All-Star appearance in his career, in which he scored a point, and seemingly rested on his perceived laurels thereafter. Like many of the players picked up by the club as the decade ended, Rowe was someone who looked good only to those people later fooled in Fantasy League drafts.

Red Auerbach has to accept the blame for picking up Rowe and his former UCLA teammate Sidney Wicks. Again, on paper, Wicks looked spectacular: Rookie of the Year in 1971–1972, he never averaged less than 19.1 points per game during his five years with the Portland Trail Blazers and made four All-Star teams. Word was that Auerbach thought the two might recreate some dynastic UCLA magic of their own, but quite the opposite transpired.

A tip-off to astute Celtics fans was the fact that Portland sold Wicks to Boston, requiring nary a star or draft pick in return. In the NBA, that constituted the closest thing to termination with extreme prejudice. In a termination of another type, center Dave Cowens retired eight games into the season for reasons still not completely clear, but in some part influenced by the loss of Silas and the importation of a non-winning attitude.

In the 1976–1977 season, as defending NBA champions, the team dipped to a 44–38 record, losing in the Eastern Conference semis to Philadelphia. Guard Jo Jo White had his usual iron-man season, playing 3,333 minutes and scoring more than 1,600 points, but Havlicek showed signs of age, and Charlie Scott missed a lot of games. Cowens did return to the team but only played 50 regular-season games.

In 1977–1978, the club flopped to 32–50, trading Charlie Scott for Don Chaney, Kermit Washington, and a draft pick right after Christmas. The club also brought in character player Dave Bing, but like Chaney, he had largely lost his effectiveness at this stage. On January 3, 1978, Tommy Heinsohn's luck finally ran out, as Red Auerbach drove out to the team's practice facilities at Lexington Christian high school to fire him. Auerbach struggled mightily with this decision, admitting that he did not sleep in the nights leading up to the termination.

"I had to tell Tommy," he recalled, "and it was killing me." Red kept delaying the inevitable, relating to the press later that "I couldn't tell Tommy before Christmas. Or even New Year's. What kind of guy would do that?… It was the most traumatic experience of my life."

Auerbach knew that the club's record had little to do with Heinsohn's style as Red himself "went to practice and practically pleaded with the players. But after I left, the situation would be the same." Advancing age and injuries slowed down the Celtics some-what, but the lackluster efforts of several other team members left a sense that, perhaps for all of his yelling and histrionics, the coach no longer had the means or the will to motivate his charges. Wishful thinking, as the then-fourth-winningest coach in NBA history left quietly, never to coach again, as a confused group of Celtics dealt with this sudden change.

As noted in the *Boston Globe* at the time, "The Celtics had changed…Paul Silas and Don Nelson were gone, to be replaced by Sidney Wicks and Curtis Rowe. Team decorum dropped consider-ably." Bob Ryan concurred in part and dissented in part, citing that Heinsohn was the "victim of unprofessional attitudes," while also pointing out that "Heinie coached the way Ralph Kramden would have, if given the chance."

Without Heinie to kick around any longer, another Celtics legend, Satch Sanders, by then the team's assistant coach, ascended to the team's head-coaching position. At the time it was hoped that the more low-key Sanders might prove the antidote to the excitable Heinsohn, and that he might communicate better with the more "modern basketball player."

The term "modern basketball player" carried a two-pronged meaning—one replete with racial overtones and one of a more economic connotation. Having endured centuries of slavery and then separate-and-unequal treatment thereafter, African Americans had more than sufficient reason for being upset with society, and it did appear a bit incongruous for a team increasingly rostered with black players to be yelled at by a white coach who not so long ago sported a crew cut. In a Boston still reeling from the effects of court-ordered busing, the racial angle escaped only the members of the local Flat Earth Society.

Accompanying these societal issues and shifts, basketball players began to earn very good salaries, not only with popularity gains in the professional game, but also with the presence of a competing American Basketball Association eager to lure NBA and college stars to their teams. Perhaps Satch Sanders could bridge gaps and restore the team to a happy, playoff-contending entity.

The hope proved fleeting, as little more than a week later, malcontent Sidney Wicks openly questioned if the next shoe would drop on him, musing, "I feel a trade is imminent.... I think it might be the best solution to the situation for all parties." Breaking a very long consecutive-game streak, Jo Jo White finally pulled up lame due to his aching left heel, and at about the same time, John Havlicek announced his retirement effective at season's end.

The team did play a bit better under Sanders than it had for his predecessor, as at times Sidney Wicks came to life and Dave Cowens seemed rejuvenated, while rookie Cedric Maxwell got some playing time. But Curtis Rowe got sidelined with a leg injury, and the team failed to even make the playoffs. In all fairness to Wicks and Rowe, Boston had exploded in the 1970s as federal judge Arthur Garrity ordered busing to remediate the racist practices of the school committee. In addition, wear and injuries had caught up to both players, yet they simply did not seem to care about winning basketball games.

The rebuilding began on August 4, 1978, when the Celtics traded Sidney Wicks, Kevin Kunnert, Kermit Washington, and Freeman Williams to the Clippers for Nate "Tiny" Archibald, Marvin Barnes, Billy Knight, and two draft picks, one of which ultimately translated into the selection of Danny Ainge. As an odd corollary, the team owners of the Buffalo Braves and Celtics also essentially traded franchises as ineffectual Irv Levin left Boston and blowhard John Y. Brown took over as owner. After a 2–12 start, the team jettisoned Satch Sanders as coach, promoting Dave Cowens as player/coach, hoping perhaps that it would prove as salutary to his career as it had for Bill Russell years earlier.

The team continued to plummet the next season under new owner John Y. Brown, most famous for marrying Phyllis George. George liked Bob McAdoo as a player, so on February 12, 1979, the club traded Tom Barker and three first-round picks for an over-the-hill McAdoo. McAdoo had scored well over 30 points a game in his second through fourth seasons (while playing an astounding number of minutes) and had as recently as 1977–1978 scored more than 2,000 points in a season, but he had little left except an enduring wish to put the ball through the hoop. The team finished well out of the playoffs again with a gruesome 29–53 record.

The carnage only ended with Brown leaving Boston. As part of a compensatory package in which the Celtics not only signed M.L. Carr but picked up draft choices from the Detroit Pistons, the team sloughed off Bob McAdoo.

Then in the fall of 1979, Larry Bird came to Boston, and the team hired former Marine drill instructor Bill Fitch as their coach.

On the first day of practice, Fitch saw Rowe jogging around and decided to cut him. Curtis Rowe never played another game in the NBA, as the Celtics reeled off three championships in the new decade.

 **Parquet**

The Celtics played their first home game ever on their now-famous parquet floor, yet the floor was located at the Boston Arena and did not permanently move over to the Garden until a bit later, once the new basketball franchise had asserted itself and sold enough tickets to justify establishing the Garden as its permanent home.

The Sports Museum at the new Garden contains a piece of the original parquet together with a brief history of the design as the Celtics' home-court floor. *Parquet* refers to intricate design in wood, taking advantage of alternating and sometimes crossing geometric shapes and lines. French King Louis XIV felt quite comfortable striding across the hardwood patterns gracing the floors at Versailles, although had he lived in 20th century Boston, he undoubtedly would have complained about the dead spots on the Garden floor. Incidentally, Red Auerbach inadvertently confirmed the existence of dead spots on his floor by insisting that Madison Square Garden had more of these areas than Boston's Garden did.

The Boston parquet floor experienced a rough creation, born out of shortages of some materials right after the end of World War II. Originally meant for hardwood floors at military barracks, the wood came from Tennessee to Boston for civilian use in 1946. Because of shortages, the East Boston Lumber Company had to construct the basketball floor from scraps, meaning that the parquet design originated out of necessity, not aesthetics. Without enough long pieces of wood at their disposal, the builders had to make panels out of what was available to them.

On one of his appearances on the 1980s hit show *Cheers*, Kevin McHale became obsessed by the question concerning how many bolts kept the floor in place, even attempting to calculate their number during a game. For trivia buffs, the Bull Gang at the Garden used 988 bolts (together with wood planks and screws) to hold together the 247 parquet panels.

Accounts differ if any pieces of the original parquet are still used for the floor at the New Garden, with some informed sources insisting that some old panels remain while others scoff at the suggestion. Along with the razing of the old Garden, many parts of the parquet panels were sold to the public, and today real or alleged parquet slices are auctioned off daily with the fervency of the marketing of slivers of the True Cross. Which means that there are probably more fake floor relics out there than the number of dead spots that once existed on the entire original parquet court.

82 Get on Max's Back in '84

For a young team coming off of a particularly ignoble era in club history, Bill Fitch was the perfect coach to restore Celtic pride and reinvigorate them into a championship club. But by the end of the playoffs in 1983, he no longer matched up with his team, an increasingly veteran group that inexplicably lost to an inferior Milwaukee Bucks team in the Eastern Conference Finals. By a sweep.

Enter K.C. Jones, the former standout defensive guard who had assisted Fitch. Jones understood that he had a club that largely knew how to win and did not need a firm hand to motivate them.

Jones trusted his players, and they returned the respect with a 62–20 record, a six-game improvement over the previous season.

Jones did not coach in a vacuum, having the luxury to call upon Robert Parish at center, Larry Bird and Cedric Maxwell at forwards, and guards Danny Ainge, Chris Ford, and M.L. Carr. Adding to this wealth, Kevin McHale came off the bench as the team's sixth man. And by virtue of an outstanding trade with the Phoenix Suns, Dennis Johnson came aboard as the point guard and defensive presence.

Not surprisingly, the club won the Atlantic Division and faced the Bullets in a best-of-five series in the opening round of the playoffs. The Bullets were a nasty team, none meaner than Jeff Ruland. Ruland had completed an outstanding season for Washington, leading the league in minutes played while averaging 22.2 points per game. Not able to match up well with Boston in most respects, the series became violent quickly as Washington fought hard, and the Celts returned fire. Cedric Maxwell said, "They're the most physical team in the league. They can be dirty and hit you with cheap shots. The longer the series goes, the worse it's gonna get as far as physical contact and animosity between each other."

The series lived down to its reputation, and after the Bullets stunned Boston in the third game to reduce the series lead to 2–1, Ruland crowed, "Go over and tell Maxwell and McHale that we can beat them." They could not, as the Celtics won the fourth and deciding game 99–96, causing Ruland to muse, "What do you do now? You go home, join the family, rest, beat the dog…" Next up for the Celtics: the Knicks and their star, Bernard King.

The Celtics should have walked through the Eastern Conference semifinals because, besides King, the Knicks consisted of some good players and useful role players, but did not stack up that well position by position. Almost as violent as the previous series with the Bullets, the Celtics took abuse from Knickerbockers and New York fans alike, as King and Bird each averaged close to 30 points a game. Each team won all of its home games, but since the Celts ended up in Boston Garden for Game 7, they prevailed.

In the Eastern Conference Finals, the Celtics faced the Bucks again, but while Milwaukee had a great coach in former Celt Don Nelson and some very talented players in Bob Lanier, Sidney Moncrief, and Marques Johnson, they nearly got swept, salvaging just one game in the seven-game series. Don Nelson admitted afterward that Boston had the better team, but also conceded that the Celtics had the better team last season, when Milwaukee prevailed. Dennis Johnson made a huge difference on defense, while Lanier measured Kevin McHale for particular praise.

Coached by Pat Riley, the Lakers certainly had their stars in Kareem Abdul-Jabbar, Magic Johnson, and James Worthy. But they also possessed a number of very good complementary players such as Michael Cooper, Byron Scott, Bob McAdoo, Kurt Rambis, and Jamaal Wilkes. While the Celtics had struggled a bit on their way to the Finals, particularly at Madison Square Garden, the Lakers cruised though Kansas City, Dallas, and Phoenix, losing only three games along the way. Time to beat L.A.!

In the first game of the Finals in Boston, the Lakers kept up this winning trend, stunning the faithful exiting onto Causeway Street. The second game, also at the Garden, looked grim very late in regulation as McHale missed two free throws with 20 seconds left and his team trailing by two points. Then, after L.A. inbounded, James Worthy made his famous crosscourt pass to a teammate, a heave still awaiting delivery to the proper party. Gerald Henderson stepped in to make his famous steal and subsequent layup to send the game into overtime. Eventually, the Celtics won in overtime, 124–121, with the teams flying to L.A. with the series knotted.

In the third game, L.A. blew the Celts out 137–104, as Jack Nicholson flipped his sunglasses to wink at Boston's fans in the West Coast. L.A. posted 47 points in the third quarter, as Robert

Parish took considerable heat, although Larry Bird thought his whole team needed heart transplants, calling his mates "sissies."

Tired of seeing the Lakers run fast breaks against them with impunity, in the fourth game Kevin McHale hammered Kurt Rambis on the way to a seemingly easy basket. It is still one of the most famous plays in NBA history, as the benches cleared, with McHale proclaiming, "It's a different ballgame now. You like to play the other way. Let's see if you like to play this way."

In that fourth game, Boston trailed by five points with less than a minute before coming back to force overtime. Cedric Maxwell claimed, "We wanted it so badly and did exactly what it took." M.L. Carr came up big in OT as the Celtics prevailed 129–125 to square the series at two games apiece.

The wondrous thing about this series is that each game etched out its own place in history, with the fifth game known for the Garden being 97 degrees inside. Kareem took oxygen on the bench while Larry Bird thrived, sinking 34 points and grabbing 17 rebounds. The Celtics won, of course, with Dennis Johnson noting, "Overall, this is probably the best game we ever played." Lakers coach Pat Riley added, "The man who made the difference was Bird. He made everything work. He was the catalyst, and that's what happens when great players come to the front."

The Lakers won the sixth game, as James Worthy came close to pounding Danny Ainge into the court. Worthy saved most of his disapprobation for Cedric Maxwell: "They've been verbally abusing us, and Maxwell made the choke sign. That's not professional." The Lakers locked it up with a 36–12 run, as the Celtics somewhat mysteriously failed to get the ball to Bird at the end.

Before the seventh and deciding game, Maxwell exhorted his teammates to get on his back, and he certainly delivered. Max did not believe that James Worthy could guard him and was magnanimous enough to inform the Lakers' forward of his opinion. The Lakers did close to within three very late in the game until the Celts went on a bit of a tear at the end to win 111–102. So uncertain had the outcome been until then that Red Auerbach did not light up a cigar until the game had ended.

83 Tiny

Drafted in the second round of the 1970 NBA Draft by the Cincinnati Royals, former New York playground legend Nate "Tiny" Archibald almost immediately helped the local fans forget, at least partially, Oscar Robertson, who had just departed for the Milwaukee Bucks. In his rookie season, Tiny averaged 16 points a game at guard and finished among the top 10 in the league in assists. Then, in his sophomore year, he tallied a massive 28.2 average as he topped 2,000 points, finishing third in the league in both scoring and assists.

In 1972–1973 the Cincinnati fans had to learn to let go of Tiny, too, as the club moved to Kansas City–Omaha, where he led the league with a torrid 34 points per game, becoming the only player to ever lead the NBA in both points and assists in a season. Parenthetically, Bob Cousy served as his head coach for the first three and a half years of his professional career, and while the Cooz may have preferred that Archibald concentrate more on playmaking, he had little choice. Archibald was by far the best player on the team.

Injuries limited him to only 35 games the next season, but he rebounded well in the next two seasons, at which point he averaged 26.5 and 24.8 points per game. With his stock in the league still high, Kansas City traded him to the Nets for two players and two first-round draft picks on September 10, 1976.

Archibald staggered a bit in New Jersey, playing in only 34 games, and yet the Nets swapped him to the Buffalo Braves for a

Unburdened with the necessity of trying to carry a team, Nate "Tiny" Archibald became a very effective team player once he became a Celtic.

player and two draft choices after the season, indicating the still high value placed on his stock as a player. He never played in Buffalo, again due to injuries, this time by blowing out an Achilles tendon, as the team thereafter ceased to exist (becoming the San Diego Clippers). As part of a complicated scenario involving franchise exchanges and all, he was dealt to the Celtics on August 4, 1978, along with a bunch of other players. The trade proved a boon for Boston, as they not only obtained Archibald and a draft choice (used for Danny Ainge), they also dumped the disappointing Sidney Wicks.

223

Starting as the point guard for the 1978–1979 Celtics, Archibald at first appeared to be merely a pain, feuding with player/coach Dave Cowens. In the beginning of the next year, he came into camp a bit rotund, but new coach Bill Fitch certainly changed his focus. At that point Archibald assisted in the rebuilding of the club by improving his attitude and accepting his status as more of a pure point guard and less of a scoring machine. The role fit him perfectly, as he never shot for an exorbitantly high average but always performed more than adequately as a playmaker, and with a talented supporting cast in Boston, he participated in his first and only championship in 1981.

Elected to the Hall of Fame in 1991, he remains in the NBA top 20 for career assists and assists per game.

84 Call Him Max

While Cedric Maxwell's mother, Bessy, played college basketball, his own career got off to an inauspicious start, or stop, as the case turned out to be: he was cut his junior year from his high school basketball team in Kinston, North Carolina, not the only superstar in the state to suffer this fate, as most fans know.

Nicknamed "Cornbread," no one in full possession of his sanity calls him that today. After watching a movie called *Cornbread, Earl, and Me*, a friend thought Maxwell looked like the lead character, and the media later picked up on it. That nickname, like his Celtics jersey number, has been long retired. Otherwise, he is pretty easygoing, continuing to work in Boston, a fixture on the radio.

He came to Boston during a particularly low point in franchise annals, and it was to young Cedric Maxwell that Curtis Rowe once notoriously said, "Last time I checked, there weren't any Ws and Ls in my paycheck." Max neither followed that advice nor attitude, and by his second year, he averaged 19 points per game and led the NBA in field-goal percentage. He duplicated the feat of highest shooting percentage the next year, 1979–1980, Larry Bird's first season.

By the next year, the Celtics had added Kevin McHale and Robert Parish to the frontcourt, and Maxwell never had to score as much as before. Bird, McHale, and Parish have come down in history as the era's Big Three, but McHale, for one, always considered Cedric Maxwell right up there with everyone else, forming more truly a Big Four. In 1981 the Celtics reversed their recent misfortunes and captured another title, with Maxwell named the Finals MVP.

Arguably, he probably should have won another Finals MVP in 1984, when the Celtics won their next title. In Game 7, Maxwell told his teammates, "Just hop on my back, and I'll take you on it," as he led them to victory (other versions of the same incident have him quoted as taking his team to the promised land). He drove the opponents crazy during this series with constant trash talk, but as a Lakers assistant coach conceded, "Give him credit. He was taking it to the hoop, and we were fouling him. He was able to deliver."

For Cedric Maxwell, fall came early that year. He had his knee scoped and did not respond as quickly as Red Auerbach wanted, causing a huge problem for the 1984–1985 edition of the team. His injury caused him to only play in 57 games and register an 11.1 points per game average, the lowest since his rookie campaign. By the end of that troubling year, the club deemed him expendable, trading him and a draft choice to the Clippers for Bill Walton. Max felt that his dedication was questioned and alleged disparate treatment, particularly since he did not hear much about Larry Bird lacking in anything when hurt. Red Auerbach did not take it well, basically proclaiming Max a persona non grata for several years after.

*Red Auerbach should have loved the dedication and intensity that Cedric
Maxwell brought to the floor each evening, but instead the two clashed. Long
having made peace with his past, Max is a popular broadcaster for the team.*

Maxwell's career is most unusual, a star who never played in
one All-Star Game or made an All-NBA team, even for defense. He
retired with only 10,465 points scored in all his years as a professional, a seeming typographical error given his prodigious talent,
but that is how the numbers added up. One way to measure his

greatness is to learn that of all the great Celtics players, Cedric Maxwell is second all-time in field-goal percentage.

Maxwell split the last three years of his career with the Clippers and the Rockets, but injuries had by then marred his career beyond redemption, and at the end of 1988, he retired, a very young man at age 32.

His exile from Causeway Street has long since ended, as he is now a very popular broadcaster and radio personality. The Celtics did the right thing on April 10, 2003, by informing Max that they intended to retire his number. He still has to listen to nonsense from time to time, as Larry Bird continues to rag on him for allegedly giving up in '85, but otherwise his legacy appears secure as a man who once told everyone he was going to carry his team. And did.

Sixth Man

Boston Celtics basketball did not begin with Bill Russell, since Red Auerbach had stockpiled talent for years. It did create a nice problem when Russell and Tommy Heinsohn joined the team, though, because it left Frank Ramsey with no place to play, or more accurately, out of the running for a starting position.

No problem, Auerbach created and enshrined in club culture the concept of the sixth man, the spark plug off the bench worthy of starting for any other franchise, and who lifted the team against the tired opposition who had no answer for the Celtics' onslaught of talent. Ramsey was an ideal sixth man because he not only accepted his role with equanimity, he proved very adept at jumping off the bench cold and immediately inserting himself into the flow of the game. Often he caused an opposing player to get called by the referees for a foul he did not commit.

John Havlicek accepted the sixth-man role with similar class, although in effect K.C. Jones and Sam Jones had already endured apprenticeships as sixth and seventh men at guards, waiting for Bill Sharman and Bob Cousy to tire in games, and later, retire from the game. Kevin McHale and Bill Walton also notably accepted the role, which by the time they played in Boston, had long become an honor. Such an honor that by 1983 the NBA had institutionalized the role league-wide, creating the annual Sixth Man Award, still given out each year.

86 Bill Walton

Before Bill Walton came to Boston as the team's sixth man in the fall of 1985, few fans in the city saw him as springing out of the Celtics' mold. He seemed too Left Coast, having played college ball at UCLA and pro ball with the Trail Blazers and Clippers. He hung out with the Grateful Dead and various left-wingers, and wore his hair really long with a scruffy beard. A Californian maybe, but no Bill Sharman.

Voted the league's MVP in 1978 and having led Portland to the title in 1976–1977, he never played anywhere near a full season of games, and his injuries kept him out entirely for a few years. Yet the Celtics traded Cedric Maxwell and a draft choice to the Clippers for him.

Fortuitously for the Celtics' front office, Walton was perfect. An Irish American himself, he grew up loving the Celtics and wanted to play in Boston very badly. Plus, he wanted to win a championship here.

Once given the opportunity, he demonstrated his leadership not only on the court but by entering into a pact with some teammates

Famous sixth men Bill Walton (left) and Kevin McHale enjoy a conversation, although McHale seems to be questioning what relevance the Grateful Dead have to the game of basketball.

Sixth Man Not Just for Celtics Anymore

Having created the sixth-man concept, Celtics players have not monopolized the award. McHale won it the second and third year after its inception, and Walton won it after its fourth year for his yeoman work during the 1985–1986 season. Since then, though, through the 2009–2010 season, no Celtics player has won the award.

to lay off beer during the year, figuring that with a title, the beer would inevitably flow. Always a very strong rebounder and shot-blocker, he also scored more than 600 points in his first year in Boston, spelling Robert Parish and occasionally one of the forwards. He won the Sixth Man Award that year, as he helped lead the team to its 16th banner.

This inspirational tale only lasted one year, though, and in 1986–1987 injuries kept him on the sideline almost the entire year, after which he retired. His career at an end, he did not lose the fans of Boston, returning to the city for various events and when work as a network analyst brought him to town. While other Celtics stars avoided the fans, at one playoff game he sat in regular seating as a visitor with a big stack of autographed photos of himself, which he handed out to each fan who approached him and requested one.

Though he has been inducted into the Basketball Hall of Fame, Walton's career is a tragedy in one way, considering how little he actually got to play the game. But he played it so well and with such passion, particularly during his swan song in Boston, that he is still so fondly remembered today. Fittingly, in his one full season in Boston, he played in 80 games, the most by far that he ever played in any one season in professional ball. With the possible exception of George Foreman, no athlete has so successfully and so positively recrafted his image as Bill Walton.

87 Visit the Basketball Hall of Fame

After you buy your ticket to the Naismith Memorial Basketball Hall of Fame in Springfield, Massachusetts, a staff member will take you up by elevator to the third floor of the museum, where the Ring of Fame is located. The Ring, as expected, is a circular area where the members are immortalized by a brief description of their accomplishments under glass along the perimeter. Often some of their memorabilia accompanies their biographies, such as Red Auerbach's cigar and a pair of Bill Russell's 1967 All-Star Game shorts.

As you might guess, the design of the museum is circular, so after you read about your favorite ballplayers, you can turn around and look over the railing at the two floors below. You are, in effect, at the rim of a basketball net.

On the second floor, the exhibits are eclectic, with displays not only concentrating on aspects of the NBA, but also college basketball, international basketball, women in basketball, and distinguished coaches and their programs. A must-see for any Celtics fan is the area dedicated to the Bob Cousy Award, where a film runs constantly of the Cooz in his Celtics heyday, running rings around his opponents and feeding his teammates on the fast break.

As a Celtics fan, on this floor you will also wish to view a replica of the life-size Larry Bird statue by Armand LaMontagne and have your picture taken with Larry Legend, if you are so inclined. There is also a separate exhibit for Paul Pierce with a pair of his shoes, warmups, Celtics and Kansas jerseys, and his famous headband. Befitting such a successful franchise, there is also a separate Celtics exhibit containing some of the history of the team together with tangible items, such as Robert Parish's shoes and the ball used during their first championship Finals game. Hanging up in that small booth area you will also have the chance to see the jerseys of Frank Ramsey, Dave Cowens, and Tommy Heinsohn, together with a No. 5 jersey. If you look hard enough on this floor you will also find jerseys for Sam Jones and John Havlicek, together with the aforementioned pair of Bill Russell's shorts.

On the first floor, there is a basketball court together with a number of old hoops and backboards off to the side, chronicling the history and development of the nets from the peach-basket era to the present day. Kids can shoot basketballs for as long as the museum is open, and the museum is available to host birthday parties and other events. Once you leave the museum, there is a terrific gift shop and a few places to eat.

The price of admission is not prohibitive, and the parking is good. The only problem is that, while signs to the museum work well to a point, it is easy to get lost in the last half mile or so of your journey, so get good directions. You will know you are close when you see a giant space needle with an orange basketball on top.

88 Loscy

Amid all of the retired numbers at the TD Garden's rafters, one name sticks out, that of "Loscy," one of the nicknames of former forward Jim Loscutoff. During his career he wore No. 18 but refused to have it taken out of circulation, permitting star center Dave Cowens to later use this number. So "Loscy" went up to confuse out-of-towners and distinguish the very popular forward.

Drafted as the third pick of the first round out of the University of Oregon, Jungle Jim Loscutoff never came close to leading the team or ranking among the top 10 league leaders in any category, save being the 10th-best rebounder in 1956–1957 and racking up the third-highest number of personal fouls a couple of years later. Both feats are remarkable in that he only played more than 2,000 minutes in one year as a professional. Ironically, he led his conference in scoring his senior year in college, but he never carried that part of his game into his professional career. It is at this point that clichés emerge to help define a player, and a copout for Loscutoff is to call him the "heart and soul" of the Celtics teams that he suited up for, for seven seasons.

The risk should be avoided. At the time Red Auerbach drafted him, the team needed a physical presence to assist Easy Ed Macauley under the boards. Having two excellent guards and a terrific offensive center had only brought the team to the playoffs, Auerbach yearned to cop championships, and he needed players who handled their roles well and subordinated their game to the team concept, hence the drafting and development of Jim Loscutoff.

Early in his career, he developed the reputation of being a bit of a hockey player in a basketball player's jersey, causing one anonymous opponent to muse, "If you undercut one of the Celtics, Jim would get you back. It may not be in that game, but eventually he would get you back. He would not forget. He held a grudge and would get you back hard." Historically, not enough emphasis has been attributed to the level of violence in early pro basketball, and the team needed a certain toughness. Celtics enforcer Bob Brannum had played his final game for the team at the end of the 1954–1955 season, and during Brannum's five years in the NBA,

Not as Tough as Brannum

At least one perceptive observer at the time believed that Loscy's reputation as a tough guy was a bit overblown. Coach Red Auerbach always insisted that Bob Brannum was a much tougher player.

Jim Loscutoff's nickname hangs from the Garden rafters, along with the retired numbers of other Celtics' legends. His No. 18 was later worn by Dave Cowens, a classy gesture by Loscy, who got to see his old number worn by someone who shared his will to win.

he finished in the top six players for total fouls for three seasons. Coincidentally or not, Brannum also sported No. 18, and Loscutoff definitely saw his role expanded to throwing a few elbows around. But once Bill Russell began playing with the club in 1956, the Celts had the finest physical presence in the post in the NBA.

Historically, when the Celtics fielded squads with veteran leaders, gifted and unselfish role players, and well-conditioned athletes, they prospered. But when they deviated from the formula, the entire franchise embarrassed itself. The team won because it had players like Loscutoff, who had no realistic chance of having a Hall of Fame career, but did have an opportunity to contribute to a juggernaut that produced championship trophies consistently. Reminiscent of Paul Silas with Dave Cowens, Loscy had Bill Russell's back.

Having accepted his role, Loscy sought to make the more talented players around him better, with rebounds, picks and, in some cases, protection. As Russell took over and the 24-second shot clock made the game more exciting, the perceived need for an enforcer became exaggerated, plus the club already had a much more accomplished pugilist in Bill Sharman. As a backup, Loscutoff stayed and flourished under the system set up by his coach. Then, during the summer, he had to get a job like many of his teammates. For at least one year, he served as a life guard.

Belying his reputation for rough-housing, Loscutoff iced the Celtics' first championship against the Hawks at the end of the 1956–1957 campaign. With time running down in the second overtime in Game 7 of the Finals, the Celtics inbounded and eventually passed to Loscy, who got fouled by Ed Macauley (at that point a Hawk), causing Easy Ed to foul out. Not the greatest marksman on the roster, Loscy sank both free throws to win the game for his team. Tommy Heinsohn topped all Celts that day with 37 points, but Loscy scored three, the final two points when it made all of the difference. Celtics 125, Hawks 123.

89 See a Championship Parade

Ideally, for Celtics fans, parades through the ancient streets of the city would constitute a yearly event, with the only variable concerning how quickly the Finals might happily conclude.

In June 2008, after the club defeated the Los Angeles Lakers, a rolling rally of 16 duck boats wended its way from the North Station area to Copley Square. The players waved and yelled to the crowd, all the while proudly displaying their trophy. The duck boats are popular converted WWII amphibious "DUKW" crafts that generally cart tourists around the streets of Boston and on the Charles River, used fairly extensively since the millennium to transport many of Boston's championship teams. They have become an efficient means of controlling the crowds, while keeping alive the festive elements treasured by players and fans alike.

The rolling rally is a relatively new concept, and during the team's salad days in the 1980s, the team jumped on flatbed trucks (followed by tourist trolleys housing employees, families, and the like) and ended up on City Hall Plaza, where massive crowds congregated. It is there, before a congested crowd that Larry Bird famously exclaimed, in response to a fan's sign, "Moses Malone does eat shit!" after the Celtics demolished the Houston Rockets in the 1981 series. The 1984 and 1986 celebrations followed suit but had become increasingly popular and even more condensed, and instead of Bird criticizing Malone, he dumped on Ralph Sampson.

Although Boston owned the NBA from the late 1950s through the next decade, no parades occurred until the spring of 1969. Previously, a fairly transparent and hastily conceived attempt at a public celebration occurred once when a few Celts were driven in open cars from Coolidge Corner to Exeter Street in Downtown Boston (approximately three miles) during the running of the annual Boston Marathon. Perhaps sensing the end of an era, after the 1969 Finals, the team (absent player/coach Russell) gathered in open cars for a motorcade from Boston Common to City Hall. At City Hall, Mayor Kevin White and about 3,000 fans met them at a bandstand, and John Havlicek introduced the players to the crowd. After the ceremony, the players signed autographs.

In 1976 the parade embarked from the Garden, then down Cambridge, Tremont, Boylston, and Washington Streets to City Hall, a relatively short trip, skirting some of the then-undesirable parts of downtown. At City Hall, Johnny Most introduced team members to the public, and Mayor White gave them each a gift, after which they attended a buffet lunch inside. Clearly, the types of celebrations and the modes of transportation have changed, but the parades will continue.

So, when the Celtics win their next championship, take the day off, come into town with as many friends and family as possible, wear as much green as you can, and wave pennants and giant green fingers in appreciation of your team's accomplishments. And for cigar fans, do not forget to light one up for the late Red Auerbach.

 **Nellie**

First the Chicago Zephyrs and then the Los Angeles Lakers gave up on Don Nelson, so after the young ballplayer's latest release, Red Auerbach gave the former two time All-American at Iowa a chance to play forward in Boston leading into the 1965–1966 season. "Nellie" not only made the team but became the team's sixth man, a role he perfected with his accurate shooting and enthusiasm for playing.

Unlike a previous sixth man, John Havlicek, Nellie never became a star, even though he did lead the league in field-goal percentage in 1974–1975. He played 11 years with the team, quietly making key shots, defending, and most important of all, playing key roles in bringing banners back to Boston in 1974 and 1976. In fact, in the playoffs in 1976, Bill Fitch (before he became the Celtics' head coach and Larry Bird's early mentor) asserted, "If I had [Nelson], I'd want him out on the floor in the last minute of every game in place of Wilkes or any other great young guys."

Notwithstanding his consistently solid play for the Celtics, Don Nelson is most fondly and immediately remembered for his timely shot in the seventh game of the NBA Finals in 1969 against the Lakers. Boston had led early, but the Lakers valiantly rallied, only to bench their center Wilt Chamberlain in the final 5:19 of regulation. It started when Chamberlain allegedly injured his knee going up for a rebound. Limping off the court, backup center Mel Counts (the very same player the Celtics had traded to obtain Bailey Howell years ago) came into the game, never to leave. Never mind that Jerry West had played with a pulled hamstring and scored 42 points in the game, Wilt came out during crunch time, with all the clichés flying about him.

Notorious for not wanting the ball when it mattered, Chamberlain uncharacteristically decided he wanted back in the game and motioned to his coach, Butch van Breda Kolff, to reinsert him in the lineup, a request that the coach refused to acknowledge, let alone honor.

Against this backdrop of a soap opera, Boston still hung on gamely to a 103–102 lead. Then Don Nelson took a jump shot from the foul line that hit the rear of the rim, bounced up and out, high into the air, apparently a clanger in the clutch...and then dropped in for the field goal. When asked about it later, Nelson admitted, "What can I say? It was a lucky shot—the luckiest shot of my life." The Celtics held, winning 108–106.

After this championship game, both Bill Russell and Sam Jones retired, so veterans like Nelson had to endure some rebuilding, but once the team added stars such as Dave Cowens and Jo Jo White, the team contended again. In total, Nellie played on four Celtics title teams (1968, 1969, 1974, and 1976) before retiring after the 1976 championship season. The team subsequently raised his No. 19 to the rafters of the Garden.

Retired as a player, Don Nelson almost immediately became the head coach and general manager of the Milwaukee Bucks, and he is now acknowledged as one of the greatest NBA head coaches in history, having also experienced success leading the Bucks, Mavericks, Warriors, and briefly, the Knicks. An innovator, he is credited with creating the "point forward," and although he has let up a bit, he continues to run his players pretty hard up and down the floor as he approaches his seventh decade. He has won three Coach of the Year awards and, except for two brief respites, has coached continuously since his retirement as a player.

Bostonians remember Don Nelson for his unselfish and steady play and for that one shot he took in the '69 Finals that should not have gone in, but did.

Bad Trades

Contrary to his wheeler-dealer image, during his coaching tenure, Red Auerbach actually executed very few player-for-player trades. After he brought the rights to Bill Russell, he kept a pretty pat hand on this type of transaction until almost 10 years later, when he traded Mel Counts for Bailey Howell. Freed of his coaching responsibilities, as general manager, Red did commit some faux pas, principally when he dumped solid players over money issues. On some occasions, a Celtics owner might make a trade behind Red's back, and certainly once Red began to act almost exclusively in a ceremonial capacity, other front-office personnel made their own moves, some good, some not so good. The following were the worst:

1. Inevitably, Rick Pitino's name comes up in any discussion concerning worst trades ever by the Celtics, and he made some stinkers, starting with dealing Chauncey Billups, Dee Brown, John Thomas, and Roy Rogers for Kenny Anderson, Popeye Jones, and Zan Tabak.

   To Pitino, Billups was like the child he never wanted, having seen the Celtics lose out on the first spot in the lottery the year Tim Duncan came out of Wake Forest. Patience not being a prominent Pitino virtue, he gave up on Billups way too early, while hoping that Anderson might prove a veteran presence capable of stabilizing the team and bringing them to greater glory.

   Anderson had actually played quite well in his first four seasons with the Nets, but even before he came to Boston, he had ceased to be a league leader in assists (a bit of a drawback for a point guard) and had begun to lose his scoring touch.

   Billups became a star after the trade, not only doling out assists and scoring field goals, but also developing a good three-point shot and establishing himself as one of the greatest free-throw shooters in NBA history, not to mention leading the Pistons to a highly improbable championship in 2004. He also made five All-Star teams after Anderson retired.

   As for 7' center Zan Tabak, he scored 59 points for the Celtics, and Popeye Jones scored 54, with Jones later packaged with Pitino's old protégé at Kentucky, Ron Mercer, in another deal.

2. Pitino executed another poor trade on March 11, 1999, when he unloaded Andrew DeClercq and a first-round draft choice to Cleveland for Vitaly Potapenko. DeClercq even-up for Potapenko might have made sense if Pitino wanted a low-post, physical presence more than a scorer, but sweetening the offer with a first-rounder was lunacy.

Cleveland used the pick to obtain Andre Miller, who had a nice NBA career, although they also could have used it on the next pick, the one the Suns used to bring Shawn Marion aboard. The deal made no sense.

3. Proving two wrongs do not make a right, the Celtics traded Kenny Anderson, Vitaly Potapenko, and Joe Forte to the Supersonics on July 22, 2002, for Vin Baker and Shammond Williams.

Anderson and Potapenko, of course, represented returns on unevenly bad trades ordered by former president and coach Rick Pitino. But, while they did not perform as the late unlamented coach had hoped, they did serve roles and played relatively hard.

Baker had starred early in his career, but had tailed off considerably with rumors of alcohol abuse whispered about as the likely culprit for the downturn in his play. With the Celtics, he was absolutely useless, ending his career with a 10-game suspension and ultimate release with extreme prejudice.

At least the Celtics got something in the end, eventually trading Williams in a package whereby they received in part, Mark Blount, who played some serviceable center for them.

4. The February 20, 2002, trade of Joe Johnson, Randy Brown, Milt Palacio, and a first-round pick to Phoenix for guard Tony Delk and forward Rodney Rogers may have constituted the worst transaction ever, made the more inscrutable as Rick Pitino had absolutely nothing to do with it. Otherwise, it had all the hallmarks of a Pitino clinker:

dump a promising young player, add in a bloated contract or two, and then gratuitously throw in a draft pick.

The trade in part seemed to represent a philosophy that, if the Celtics could not win a title, at least the team had to make it exciting for the fans. That certainly occurred as Delk and Rogers were good players, and the Celtics had even more talented people around them in Paul Pierce and Antoine Walker, but no title came that year. By the end of the 2002–2003 season, both Delk and Rogers had departed, while Johnson has provided the Suns and later the Hawks with a strong scoring touch on the way to four All-Star appearances and counting. The only thing not making this trade even worse is that the draft choice of the Suns, Casey Jacobsen, never had much of a career.

5. As mentioned in other sections of this book, John Y. Brown essentially traded his Buffalo Braves franchise for the Boston Celtics, and then gambled and lost by swapping three draft choices for Bob McAdoo, an epic bust. Brown is largely forgiven if not forgotten today, as he left town soon afterward, and Auerbach later traded McAdoo to the Pistons for two first round draft choices in 1980. Red parlayed one of those picks into a deal with Golden State that brought Robert Parish and Kevin McHale to Boston, so Celtics fans can laugh at it all now.

92 Bad Draft Coming into the Garden

Red Auerbach could do many things well, including utilizing draft rules to get the jump on the opposition, a talent that, for example, landed Larry Bird in Boston. He took some risks and was rewarded

The Good Old Draft Days
Not all drafts turned out poorly for the club, as the team stocked up with Frank Ramsey, Jim Loscutoff, Tommy Heinsohn, Bill Russell, Sam Jones, Satch Sanders, and John Havlicek from 1953 to 1962.

greatly. However, even the greatest Auerbach apologist has to admit that, in the NBA Drafts between 1963 and 1968, Red operated with somewhat less than the Midas touch.

Winning championships is not conducive to obtaining high draft choices, and since the Celtics dominated, in part this explains why new blood did not regenerate the franchise. In the late 1950s and early 1960s, young stars like John Havlicek and the Joneses had to wait to start as All-Star veterans stood in their path. After the selection of John Havlicek as the seventh player drafted in 1962 and up to the pick of Don Chaney in 1968, not one draft choice (in what was then much longer drafts than simple two-rounders) made a significant impact on the team. Unless one counted Mel Counts, whom Red Auerbach traded for Bailey Howell.

And yet the draft position of the Celtics does not excuse a lack of scouting during this period, as the team missed out on these lower draft picks: Gus Johnson in 1963; Willis Reed, Paul Silas, and Jerry Sloan in 1964; the Van Arsdale brothers and Keith Erickson in 1965; Archie Clark in 1966; and Phil Jackson and Bob Rule in 1967; all chosen by other clubs after Boston made its first pick. Other clubs had gotten better at drafting, particularly with the increasing popularity of college basketball, but Red Auerbach could not rely on a Bones McKinney locating a diamond in the rough for him any longer.

The lower-draft position did have a significant impact on the team during the 1980s, the wonderful years after Bird and friends joined the team. By then, the more astute fans, never mind pro scouts, had a pretty good handle on a player's relative worth, due mainly to almost nonstop programming of college basketball games. Yet, from 1987 to 1991, the club picked up a very good player in Reggie Lewis and three other talents in Brian Shaw, Dee Brown, and Rick Fox. They completely swerved off target only once in this span, albeit with their highest choice, with the selection of Michael Smith.

Good drafts did not guarantee success for the Celtics, either, as the team between 1996 and 1998 added to its roster Antoine Walker, Chauncey Billups, Ron Mercer, and Paul Pierce. Add 2001 pick Joe Johnson, and the team, had it held together, was probably a half-decent center away from becoming one of the dominant teams of the early millennium. Sadly, only Walker and Pierce contributed to the team for any length of time as the Celtics let the other three promising players loose for pitifully little value in return.

93 Honey and Doggie

Imagine how many championship banners might hang at the Garden had the Celtics just gotten off to a better start than they did. But the fact is they struggled their first four years, not compiling a winning season in any of them. In the first two years, under uninspiring coach Honey Russell, they foundered, although they did make the playoffs the second year. Apparently, they had delayed their compilation of the roster before their first year and did not catch up to the efforts of others franchises, as they fielded a team of largely mediocre players. Russell, a star player, principally in the 1920s and 1930s, experienced his greatest success as the coach at Seton Hall, both before and after his time in Boston.

In their third year, the Celtics hired Doggie Julian, the Holy Cross coach, believing he could replicate his collegiate successes and perhaps even fill the locker room with some of his former charges. Julian proved no more successful than Russell, as the team continued to lose an unhealthy amount of games. Doggie was dogged by the emergence of professional basketball's first superstar, George Mikan of the Minneapolis Lakers, and he had no one close enough in talent to challenge for the league title.

Seemingly, during those first formative years, there should be reams of funny Celtics stories, akin to the fables of the Amazin' Mets or some of the early editions of franchises in the American Football League or American Basketball Association. But, unfortunately, few exist. The club did have a player named Tony Lavelli, an accomplished accordion player who serenaded the home crowd during halftime.

A star basketball player at Yale, Lavelli, a cousin of Cleveland Browns Hall of Famer Dante Lavelli, played fairly well during his rookie season but then went to New York, where his career ended the next year. Other than that, the relative lack of athletic talent has left team history with a wasteland, an arid period during which the few fans left yearned for a savior.

Before the 1950–1951 season, Walter Brown hired Red Auerbach, and the team also picked up the rights to center Easy Ed Macauley and guard Bob Cousy, two future Hall of Famers, who immediately jumpstarted the club into the win column and the playoffs. Auerbach subsequently added guard Bill Sharman and

Doggie Style

Alvin "Doggie" Julian did little of value or of note during his two-year tenure with the Celtics, but he did lead Holy Cross to an NCAA title in 1947. After he left the pro ranks, he coached Dartmouth, leading them to three conference titles in the late 1950s. Like his predecessor, Honey Russell, he enjoyed his greatest success as a college coach. But he did beat Red Auerbach in one thing: he was enshrined in Basketball's Hall of Fame in 1968, a year before Red earned that honor.

forward Jim Loscutoff, and while the team flourished, it never did win a title until the 1956–1957 season with the rookie years of Tommy Heinsohn and Bill Russell.

Once Walter Brown and Red Auerbach had their players and system set up, they went on a run, but it took some time and considerable patience to assemble the first great Celtics team.

 **Silas**

Paul Silas had played eight years in the NBA before joining Boston for the 1972–1973 season, traded even-up to Phoenix for the rights to Charlie Scott. Silas had just executed his best offensive season, scoring 17.5 points per game, but in Boston he served more as a defensive presence, developing into an even more impressive rebounder and gaining league-wide recognition for his defense. He helped Dave Cowens play even better than before.

The Celtics in their dynastic days always had a place for a hard-nosed player like Silas, a 6′7″ forward who brought a bit of Satch Sanders with a scoring touch into each game he played. With Cowens, Jo Jo White, and John Havlicek, he helped lead the Celtics to two more titles in 1974 and 1976.

In 1974, after he watched Silas deny his men the backboards in the Finals, Bucks coach Larry Costello complimented the Celtics forward, whose "rebounding really hurt us. Our shooters couldn't handle him in the middle. He just muscled them." Celts teammate John Havlicek echoed the emotion: "There's no way either [Mickey] Davis or [Bob] Dandridge can handle Paul inside. He's an old center, you know."

In 1976 he again distinguished himself in the playoffs, perhaps most notably in the fifth game of the opening series against Buffalo,

Paul Silas and Dave Cowens were anything but twin towers during their time together, but they outhustled and outrebounded their loftier opponents. A long day's journey into night followed Silas' departure from Boston.

with the teams tied at two wins apiece. During a crucial run, the *Boston Globe* noted that Silas "didn't score a basket, but directly or indirectly, he had a hand in every point via his turnover-inducing defense or his rebounding." He certainly did rebound well in that game, copping 22 boards in all as Boston took a 3–2 lead in the series, eventually advancing to the Finals, where they defeated the Phoenix Suns.

After the Celtics won their second NBA crown in three years, a sticky problem arose in that Silas now had to sign a new contract. The negotiations did not go well, and Celts GM Red Auerbach drew a line in the sand, culminating in a deadlock in negotiations. At that point, Silas had painted himself out of Boston, a situation culminating in a three-team trade. Penny wise and pound foolish, the Celtics lost Silas and obtained Curtis Rowe, one of their worst performers ever. Dave Cowens took a leave of absence from the team shortly after the 1976–1977 season began, and even though he returned, the Celtics quickly turned into one of the uglier teams in the league and did not challenge for a title again until the introduction of Larry Bird.

Had Paul Silas stayed with the team, perhaps the Celtics would have placed another banner into the rafters after the 1976–1977 season. Instead, he distinguished himself in his last four years in the NBA, retiring in 1980 as one of the greatest rebounders in league history.

Reggie Lewis

Quiet, unassuming Reggie Lewis, did not get recruited by major colleges, despite playing on a virtual high school all-star squad along with Muggsy Bogues and Georgetown stars David Wingate and Reggie Williams. He opted to play for Boston's Northeastern University, not even the city's best college basketball program. Exploiting all opportunities before him, Lewis distinguished himself at Northeastern, enough so that the Celtics drafted him with their first-round pick in 1987, the 22nd selection overall.

He played little his first year, not surprising as the club still dominated most of the competition, but the 6'7" swingman saw dramatically more time beginning in the 1988–1989 season. From that point through the next four seasons, he averaged between 17 and 20.8 points per game, making the NBA All-Star team in 1992, and getting exposure on television for a shoe endorsement.

He quickly also became a favorite of fans in the neighborhoods of Boston, due to his charitable efforts. Although the Celtics had begun to fade as contenders, they still made the playoffs at the end of the 1993 season, and Reggie Lewis seemingly had a long and productive life ahead of him. He seemed to be getting stronger every year, having played 3,144 minutes that season, fifth best in the NBA.

Lewis had rallied his team to a very strong finish in the regular season just to make the playoffs, with the Charlotte Hornets slated as their opening-round opponent. Matters went badly almost from the start. During the first period, while jogging down the court, Lewis staggered forward and then fell to the parquet, without an immediate explanation for doing so. He came back in, finally leaving in the third period, when coach Chris Ford, in an agitated and obviously gravely concerned state, waved him out. The Celtics won that evening, on the way to losing their next three games and the series to the Hornets.

Ominously, after the game, Lewis stated, "Yeah, I was scared…I started having flashbacks to that Hank Gathers' thing." Hank Gathers, of course, had died three years earlier while playing a game for Loyola Marymount, a senseless tragedy affecting someone so athletic and young. To most Celtics fans, the comparison frightened and confused—could it really have been so bad?

The Celtics seemed to think so, as Lewis entered New England Baptist Hospital for a series of tests. Taking advantage of the plethora of highly trained physicians, the club assembled a dream team of 12 doctors to congregate and consider the results of the tests, after which a consensus concluded that Lewis suffered from serious heart abnormalities. Celtics forward Xavier McDaniel echoed everyone's concerns, stating, "Reggie's life is more important than a game for us. No one wants to see another Hank Gathers situation." Again, Lewis' condition had been compared to that of the late Hank Gathers. The Celtics would definitely not let Lewis play for the rest of the series with Charlotte, and it appeared his career itself had perhaps ended.

Underestimated as a high school and college basketball player, Reggie Lewis became a star with the Celtics. Had he and Len Bias played together, the club could have been a force well into the 1990s.

The situation got more peculiar right away, when on the evening of May 2, Reggie Lewis was whisked away from New England Baptist to Brigham and Women's Hospital nearby, switching hospitals presumably for a less-ominous second opinion. A little more than a week later, treating physician Dr. Gilbert Mudge strode

File Under "Small World"
As a footnote, the police officer who responded at the scene and tried to revive Reggie Lewis was James Crowley; years later, he was invited by President Barack Obama to the White House to help defuse the controversy surrounding his arrest of Harvard professor Henry Gates.

before a battery of reporters, opining that Lewis had a "normal athlete's heart with normal function," adding, "I am optimistic that under medical supervision, Mr. Reggie Lewis will be able to return to professional basketball without limitation."

Everyone was careful not to step on each others' toes, with Mudge citing the fact that he had more time to come to his conclusions, while Reggie Lewis left the hospital happy that he had an opportunity to return to his career. And that was the last most people heard until July 27, 1993, when fans in New England turned on their news broadcasts to learn that Reggie Lewis, while working out lightly by shooting baskets at Brandeis University, had gone into full cardiac arrest, dying that evening.

Without their captain, the Celtics lost 16 more games during the next regular season, not coming close to making the playoffs.

The whole city mourned and then the recriminations swiftly followed. Word leaked to the *Wall Street Journal* that Lewis had used cocaine, and Lewis' widow, Donna Harris-Lewis sued Dr. Mudge and others for medical malpractice. One jury came back hopelessly deadlocked, while a second jury vindicated Mudge, and finally, seven years after the death of Reggie Lewis, the legal process let him rest in peace.

Not so lucky was his widow, Donna Harris-Lewis, who many members of the press and public excoriated, as she too, eventually faded from public view with her two children, the legacy of the late, great Reggie Lewis. On March 22, 1995, the Celtics retired Reggie Lewis' number. Only he and Easy Ed Macauley had their numbers retired without winning at least one championship in Boston.

96 Ray Allen

Shooting guard Ray Allen excelled at the University of Connecticut and then saw little of New England professionally for the first 11 years of his career, as he starred for the Milwaukee Bucks and then the Seattle Supersonics. A gifted three-point shooter, he also owns the fifth-best career free-throw percentage in NBA history.

On draft night in 2007, Celtics GM Danny Ainge made his first major move toward securing Boston's 17th championship banner by dealing draft choice Jeff Green, along with Wally Szcerbiak, Delonte West, and a second-round draft choice to Seattle for Allen and Glen "Big Baby" Davis, a surprise move at that time because he seemingly traded away a promising rookie from Georgetown for, by NBA standards, an elder statesman. Later, the Celtics obtained Kevin Garnett, making the team an instant favorite for an NBA title.

Allen not only brought his shooting prowess to the team, but also his professional dedication. His work ethic to some might seem obsessive, generally getting to the court well before anyone else on the team, but no one can criticize the results. A nine-time All-Star, it is inevitable that Ray Allen will be largely remembered equally as a Buck, a Sonic, and a Celtic, but most New England fans know better. The storied Celtics franchise had not won a title in 22 years before Ray Allen joined the club, and his work ethic mirrored that of his great predecessors who established and cultivated the Celtic mystique.

By way of example, starting with his fourth year in the league, he always averaged more than 20 points a game until he joined the Celtics, at which point it dipped below that level. The slight dip in

Ray Allen reacts after hitting the game-winning three in a 111–109 double-overtime victory over Charlotte on April 1, 2009. Photo courtesy of AP Images

the average in no way reflected a decline in talent, but rather demonstrated Allen's dedication to the team concept, as Garnett, Pierce, Rondo, and others also needed to score. He also has continued to exhibit leadership by continuing to arrive at the arena

> ## He Still Got Game
> Though perhaps not as accomplished an actor on the court as the Celts' Frank Ramsey in drawing phantom fouls, Ray Allen more than held his own with Denzel Washington, costarring in Spike Lee's *He Got Game* as high school legend Jesus Shuttlesworth.

(almost always) first in whatever city he plays in, to practice his shooting.

Summing up, Sam Cassell once said of Ray Allen, "Ray? You get 20 points of scoring every day from him. If Ray Allen has six points at halftime, he will finish with 20."

97 Easy Ed

Virtually every article or book that mentions the Celtics' first star center, Ed Macauley, asserts that he got his nickname "Easy Ed" due to his fluid motion on the court, but say little else about the man other than what his statistics or All-Star selections reveal. Macauley himself disputes how he first received his moniker, maintaining that his college coach "said I would be captain one night, and all I had to do was lead us out of the dressing room then through a door. That's the only thing I had to do, and I did it. I pushed the door open, ran down the other end with the ball, and took a couple of shots. I turned around, and nobody was following me, and the reason they were not following me was because they were playing the national anthem. I was so nervous, I didn't even hear it."

Part of the problem for Ed Macauley lay in the fact that he stands virtually alone among players who have had their numbers retired by Boston (with Reggie Lewis the one exception) but who never played on a championship team. Indeed, the Celtics only began winning titles after his trade with Cliff Hagan to St. Louis for the rights to Bill Russell.

Another factor is that, except for his six years with the Celtics, his entire existence has been a St. Louis story, the tale of a local boy who left once, only to find he could return home again. Born in St. Louis on March 22, 1928, Ed Macauley attended St. Louis University High School, after which time his mother supposedly told him that he could attend any university that he wished, so long as it was a Catholic school and was situated in St. Louis. That made the choice simple for Easy Ed, as he enrolled in St. Louis University, where he starred with the Billikens.

In one game, as reported in *Time* magazine, Ed Macauley might have invented trash talk of a sort: after an opposing player tried to divert his attention by misinforming Macauley that his shoe was untied, Easy Ed rejoined, "You tie it for me, junior, while I make this point." Other than that, he quietly starred as a very tall (6'8") and very skinny (even as a pro he played at about 185 pounds) center, until he was drafted by the NBA's St. Louis Bombers.

The Bombers imploded after Macauley's first season in 1949–1950, so the Celtics picked him up in the dispersal draft, a fairly common occurrence for the league at that time, as franchises kept folding.

The start of Macauley's career in Boston coincided with the first year of Bob Cousy, which assured Red Auerbach a winning inaugural season as a coach. The two young stars did most of the scoring for a still fairly undistinguished cast, but neither of them provided what the team needed to become championship caliber, a dominating rebounding and defensive center. The thin Macauley too often got pushed around in the paint by stronger players.

A seven-time All-Star, he habitually ended up each year in the top 10 in scoring and even won the MVP award at the All-Star Game for the 1950–1951 season, although he did not actually receive a trophy for this feat until years later.

After the trade for Russell, Macauley's St. Louis story continued, and he even helped his new team to a title in 1957–1958, with
the help of a strong team led by Bob Pettit. But it was the Celtics'
turn the next year and for many years after that as Easy Ed retired
in 1959, maintaining ties to basketball as the Hawks' coach and as
a broadcaster. He was elected to the Basketball Hall of Fame in
1960. In addition to his post-career work in basketball, Ed
Macauley became a Catholic deacon in 1989 and has coauthored a
book about giving good church homilies.

98 Camp Milbrook

If you are unfamiliar with Massachusetts, there is Boston, with
everything north to the New Hampshire border termed the "North
Shore," and likewise all the ocean front from Boston down to Cape
Cod called the "South Shore." And in the early 1960s a man named
Jerry Volk ran a summer camp for adolescents in the South Shore
town of Marshfield known as Camp Milbrook.

Volk liked the Celtics, and undoubtedly so did some of his staff
members and eager campers, but otherwise the bucolic grounds had
no relation to the professional basketball team until Volk
approached Red Auerbach with an offer to let the team use the
camp in mid-August. Usually Auerbach rolled his eyes at such sug-
gestions, but even though the team had survived near bankruptcy
in its first 10 years of existence, it still did not have a surfeit of spare
cash, so he accepted the offer on behalf of the team.

So, before Labor Day from the early 1960s to the 1980s, the
Celtics staged a rookie camp there, allowing Auerbach to survey
the then-numerous rookies and free agents (particularly back when
the NBA Draft consisted of more than two rounds), and also work

in some conditioning for these newcomers and perhaps some veterans who drove down to look at the new crop.

The participants seemed to have fun, this in an era before every five-year-old ballplayer with talent got shunted into a travel program. The players slept in bunk beds and ate their meals with the other campers. They played on an indoor court when it rained but spent most of their time on an outdoor court, surveyed by Red and the coaches and the other campers. During their free time, the Celtics' rookies often watched some of the high school players train and play their camp-sponsored games.

Inconceivable today, the players came into camp and enjoyed the experience, away from weight rooms and five-star hotel accommodations. The distance between players and the public literally did not exist, and young people of all ability levels enjoyed playing ball and relaxing in a camp environment.

Eventually, the Celtics became a cash cow, and Camp Milbrook became nothing more than a pleasant memory for its past players, sort of their last summer camp experience before becoming professionals or realizing they had no future in the NBA. The camp itself closed, but Jerry Volk's son, Jan, later succeeded Red Auerbach as the general manager of the Celtics.

99 Il Messaggero

For a very brief time in late 1980s and early '90s, the Italian basketball club Il Messaggero drove the Celtics' front office nearly crazy. By this time pretty much everyone knew that the great Celtics run, which began with the drafting of Larry Bird, stood imperiled, and with little wiggle room left, the Italian franchise began to woo young Celtics away.

It all began after the 1988–1989 season, when the Italian basketball powerhouse approached Brian Shaw, the Celtics' talented rookie point guard, with an offer to play for them. The Celtics certainly had set what they felt constituted the proper price for Shaw's services, and now with another bidder involved, miscommunication occurred. Perhaps the Celtics believed that Shaw would never go to Italy, and to a certain extent Shaw might have even felt the same way.

Exacerbating the situation was the disconnect between the Celtics' front office and Shaw's agent, Jerome Stanley. In addition, the Celtics' front office itself had a number of big personalities involved in negotiations, with Red Auerbach the president, Jan Volk the general manager, and David Gavitt the CEO all trying to fathom why any talented ballplayer wanted to go abroad. In the end Shaw and Stanley played the Italian card, sending Shaw to what he believed was a two-year commitment to the Il Messaggero club. Joining him was graduating Duke star Danny Ferry, indicating a possible league-wide challenge by young men who now had an option other than automatically signing with the NBA club that had their rights.

By way of a further disaster, the Celtics had drafted Croatian star center/forward Dino Radja in the NBA Draft in June 1989, and he too passed on the Celtics after signing elsewhere. His new club? None other than Il Messaggero. By this time Red Auerbach was seeing red, quite literally in fact, as the Italian club used that color for its jerseys.

Exploiting a contractual loophole, Jan Volk flew to Italy in the winter of 1990 and, during a brief window when the young point guard did not have representation, signed Shaw to a contract with Boston to begin the next season. Litigation followed in federal court, but ultimately Shaw had to play in Boston that season. The war was more than on.

Unfazed, Stanley signed up Reggie Lewis as a client, and now it appeared that the Celtics had to deal with the real possibility that

Stanley might entice other clients to Italy if the Celtics did not accede to contractual requests. Now Lewis made noises about possibly leaving Boston.

Ultimately, the threat receded because most NBA players did not want to play in Italy when they could star at home and most likely make considerably more money in doing so. While the level of international play had improved over time, the NBA was still where players wanted to go. Radja ended up playing in Boston years later, while the Celts quietly dealt Shaw on January 10, 1992, to Miami in exchange for Sherman Douglas. Although Shaw played in the NBA through the 2002–2003 season, his promise faded after he left Boston.

Il Messaggero has long since waned as an attractive alternative to service in the NBA, as foreign talent has flooded into the American market. For a brief time, though, the Italian club wreaked havoc on the Celtics' efforts to reload as the Bird era dissipated, contributing to the further decline of Boston's fortunes.

100 Gene Guarilia

In his four seasons in Boston, from 1959 to 1963, Celtics forward Gene Guarilia scored exactly 413 points, never starting one game or playing for any other franchise. For a few brief moments in the 1962 playoffs, Gene Guarilia saved his team and was remembered fondly for several years thereafter by his teammates and fans of the day.

Early in overtime in the seventh game of this championship series against the Lakers, Celts stars Tommy Heinsohn, Satch Sanders, Frank Ramsey, and Jim Loscutoff (all of whom have their numbers or nickname hanging from the Garden rafters) had all fouled out, and someone had to cover Lakers forward Elgin Baylor.

Into the fray, for the first time in the Finals, came Gene Guarilia off the bench to face this most daunting assignment.

Baylor, honored later as one of the 50 greatest NBA players ever, only had to run circles around the little-used Guarilia for his team to win.

Guarilia achieved greatness in the four minutes of overtime allotted to him in the series, grabbing a key rebound and shutting down Baylor, until the Lakers star himself fouled out. The Celtics held on and won 110–107, with Jungle Jim Loscutoff telling Guarilia, "You really earned your money." Bill Russell praised him more succinctly: "He was great, too." In fact, Russell did one better. As the newspaper writers circled him for an interview, Russ claimed they were "talking to the wrong guy" and pointed the scribes over to Guarilia.

Because of his surprising contribution, the Celtics won that particular championship. Of course, the press raved about the performance of the club's reserve forward, intimating that his efforts would live forever more, and yet within his lifetime fans either largely forgot him or never knew what he once accomplished. In 1962–1963 Guarilia injured the quadriceps in both his legs, restricting him to only 11 games that season. He never played again and lost a year in his pension because he failed to play in the requisite number of games.

When the Celtics fail to win, everyone suffers, and yet it is apt to remember that they rarely win championships without every player contributing at some key moment during the season. Bill Russell made the Celtics great, role players like Gene Guarilia sometimes accomplished that little bit that pushed them into immortality. He contributed to the perpetuation of the Celtic mystique and, most concretely, to one of their titles. Like so many of the other men who played for the team, his efforts deserve the appreciation of the fans.

Acknowledgments

I would like to extend special thanks to the staffs of the Basketball Hall of Fame and the New England Sports Museum. Again, special notice is due to the patient professionals at the microfiche department of the Boston Public Library. Former Celtics were very generous with their time and insights, as was former NBA referee extraordinaire Mark Schlafman. Jack Lee was terrific in filling me in on some of the special people who played important roles assisting his father Eddie at the Garden and in fostering the growth of the Celts. Mike Connelly at the *Herald* was a terrific sounding board. From being able to recite the Boston Trojans' starting five in 1935 to being able to recite from memory the lifetime rebounds-per-game percentage of the busboy at the Last Supper, Jack McCormick was a huge help in answering questions and condensing information. I can still remember telling Richard A. Johnson 15 years ago that I would like to write a book, and not only did he not laugh out loud, he was a huge help in this project and all my other efforts. Huge thanks to Lori Hubbard and Billy Hubbard for their editing.

Basketball-reference.com and NBA.com served as my statistical resource throughout.

Final and most heartfelt thanks and love go out to my Heavenly Triplets, Lori, Billy, and Caroline.

Sources

Araton, Harvey, and Filip Bondy. *The Selling of the Green: The Financial Rise and Moral Decline of the Boston Celtics*. New York: HarperCollins, 1992.

Auerbach, Red, and John Feinstein. *Let Me Tell You a Story*. New York: Little, Brown and Company, 2004.

Connelly, Michael. *Rebound: Basketball, Busing, Larry Bird, and the Rebirth of Boston*. Minneapolis: Voyageur Press, 2008.

Cousy, Bob, and Bob Ryan. *Cousy on the Celtic Mystique*. New York: McGraw-Hill, 1988.

Levine, Lee Daniel. *Bird: The Making of an American Sports Legend*. New York: McGraw-Hill, 1988.

May, Peter. *The Last Banner*. Holbrook, MA: Adams Media Corporation, 1996.

Reynolds, Bill. *Cousy*. New York: Simon and Schuster, 2005.

Russell, Bill, and Taylor Branch. *Second Wind: The Memoirs of an Opinionated Man*. New York: Simon and Schuster, 1979.

Shaughnessy, Dan. *Ever Green—The Boston Celtics: A History in the Words of Their Players, Coaches, Fans, and Foes, from 1946 to the Present*. New York: St. Martin's Press, 1990.

Simmons, Bill. *The Book of Basketball: The NBA According to the Sports Guy*. New York: Ballantine Books, 2009.

Sullivan, George. *The Picture History of the Boston Celtics*. New York: Bobbs-Merrill Company, 1982.

Whalen, Thomas J. *Dynasty's End: Bill Russell and the 1968–1969 World Champion Boston Celtics*. Boston: Northeastern University Press, 2004.